THE
CANADIAN
KINGDOM

THE CANADIAN KINGDOM

150 YEARS OF
CONSTITUTIONAL MONARCHY

edited by
D. Michael Jackson

DUNDURN
TORONTO

Cover image: istock.com/Koshenyamka
Printer: Webcom

Library and Archives Canada Cataloguing in Publication

The Canadian kingdom : 150 years of constitutional monarchy / edited by D. Michael Jackson.

Includes bibliographical references.
Issued in print and electronic formats.
ISBN 978-1-4597-4118-8 (softcover).--ISBN 978-1-4597-4119-5 (PDF).--
ISBN 978-1-4597-4120-1 (EPUB)

1. Monarchy--Canada. 2. Federal government--Canada. 3. Constitutional history--Canada. 4. Canada--Politics and government--1867-. I. Jackson, D. Michael, editor

JL15.C32 2018   320.471   C2017-907760-0
                                                          C2017-907761-9

1 2 3 4 5   22 21 20 19 18

We acknowledge the support of the **Canada Council for the Arts**, which last year invested $153 million to bring the arts to Canadians throughout the country, and the **Ontario Arts Council** for our publishing program. We also acknowledge the financial support of the **Government of Ontario**, through the **Ontario Book Publishing Tax Credit** and the **Ontario Media Development Corporation**, and the **Government of Canada**.

Nous remercions le **Conseil des arts du Canada** de son soutien. L'an dernier, le Conseil a investi 153 millions de dollars pour mettre de l'art dans la vie des Canadiennes et des Canadiens de tout le pays.

Care has been taken to trace the ownership of copyright material used in this book. The author and the publisher welcome any information enabling them to rectify any references or credits in subsequent editions.
— *J. Kirk Howard, President*

The publisher is not responsible for websites or their content unless they are owned by the publisher.

Printed and bound in Canada.

VISIT US AT

dundurn.com | @dundurnpress | dundurnpress | dundurnpress

Dundurn
3 Church Street, Suite 500
Toronto, Ontario, Canada
M5E 1M2

Dedicated to the Right Honourable David Johnston,
Governor General of Canada, 2010–2017
"A Model Governor General"

Contents

Part 1: The Crown in Canadian History

Part 2: The Crown and Indigenous Peoples

Part 3: The Crown and Contemporary Canada

Part 4: The Crown and the Realms

Preface

The Institute for the Study of the Crown in Canada at Massey College is pleased to sponsor this second book published by Dundurn Press. The first book, *The Queen at the Council Fire: The Treaty of Niagara, Reconciliation, and the Dignified Crown in Canada*, by Nathan Tidridge, appeared in 2015. It illuminated one of the most significant facets of the Canadian Crown and indeed one of the key issues facing Canada in the twenty-first century: its relationships with Indigenous Peoples, also a theme of the present volume. *The Canadian Kingdom: 150 Years of Constitutional Monarchy* marks the sesquicentennial of Canadian Confederation — an appropriate juncture to review the historical and present role of the Crown in Canada.

About the Institute and Massey College

The Institute for the Study of the Crown in Canada at Massey College / *L'Institut d'études sur la Couronne au Canada à Massey College* originated in the "Friends of the Canadian Crown." Formed in 2005, this was an informal network of people from a variety of backgrounds interested in promoting knowledge and understanding of the institution of constitutional monarchy in Canada.

The Institute is based at the graduate college founded at the University of Toronto in 1963 by the first Canadian-born governor general, the Right Honourable Vincent Massey. In 2017, Massey College strengthened its links with the Crown when Her Majesty Queen Elizabeth II approved the designation of its St. Catherine's Chapel as the third Chapel Royal in the country and the first-ever interdenominational one. This chapel, symbolizing reconciliation, is allied to the Mississaugas of the New Credit First Nation.

The Institute commissions studies and papers dealing with the constitutional, historical, and institutional reality of the Crown in Canada. It seeks alliances, associations, or liaison status with vice-regal offices, appropriate public policy and governance institutes, Indigenous organizations, academic and general publishers, and parallel institutions in other countries with similar constitutional arrangements. The Institute is a resource for further studies in this area; as well, it helps to make available recognized scholars and other spokespeople in the field of the constitutional Crown.

Conferences and Publications

The Friends of the Canadian Crown convened a first conference at the Senate in Ottawa in June 2010, "The Crown in Canada: Present Realities and Future Options," with the support of the Institute of Intergovernmental Relations at Queen's University. An outcome of this conference was *The Evolving Canadian Crown*, a book of essays edited by Jennifer Smith and D. Michael Jackson and published by McGill-Queen's University Press in 2012. That same year, marking the Diamond Jubilee of Queen Elizabeth II, the Friends convened a second conference, "The Crown in Canada: A Diamond Jubilee Assessment." Held at Government House, Regina, in October 2012, this initiative was supported by the Government of Saskatchewan and the Johnson-Shoyama Graduate School of Public Policy in the University of Regina. Another book resulted, *Canada and the Crown: Essays on Constitutional Monarchy*, edited by D. Michael Jackson and Philippe Lagassé and published in 2013, again by McGill-Queen's University Press.

By then, the Friends of the Canadian Crown were transmuting into the present Institute, which was inaugurated in 2014 on the occasion of book launches of *Canada and the Crown* at Government House in Victoria, the

PREFACE

House of Commons in Ottawa, Queen's Park in Toronto, and Government House in Regina. The Institute arranged a third conference in January 2016 at Government House, Victoria, supported by the Government House Foundation of British Columbia and the Weston Foundation. Entitled "The Crown in the 21st Century: Deference or Drift?" this conference extended its scope to some of the Queen's other realms: Australia, New Zealand, and the United Kingdom. A special issue of the University of Alberta's *Review of Constitutional Studies* in 2017, edited by Philippe Lagassé and Nicholas A. MacDonald, featured the constitutional issues raised at this conference.

We thank Dundurn Press and its president and publisher, Kirk Howard, for making this book possible and for their consistent support of Canadian authors and publications in so many fields, including the Crown. We also thank Massey College for providing a congenial home for the Institute, and the Weston Foundation for its financial assistance to the Institute's publications.

John Fraser, Founding President
D. Michael Jackson, President
Institute for the Study of the Crown in Canada at Massey College
L'Institut d'études sur la Couronne au Canada à Massey College

Introduction: The Canadian Crown at 150 Years

D. Michael Jackson

"One hundred and fifty years of constitutional monarchy" in Canada. The secondary title of this book is a neat turn of phrase, but it is not quite the full story. As Barbara J. Messamore points out in the first chapter, *constitutional* monarchy predated the Confederation of 1867 by some two decades: responsible government was achieved first in Nova Scotia in 1848 and then in the United Province of Canada in 1849 (one might add Prince Edward Island in 1851, New Brunswick in 1854, and Newfoundland in 1855). *Monarchy* in what is now Canada goes back half a millennium, to King Henry VII of England in 1497 and King Francis I of France in 1534. And of course, the history of "Canada" can be traced for millennia, to the ancient origins of the Indigenous Peoples.

Still, the sesquicentennial of Confederation in 2017 provided a timely opportunity to review and reconsider the Crown as a seminal institution of the federal, monarchical, parliamentary Canadian state launched one hundred and fifty years earlier. And it *is* a seminal institution. The Crown is far more than symbolic: it penetrates, permeates, colours, and enables all aspects of the Canadian constitutional arrangement — among them Parliament and legislatures, the executive, the Indigenous Peoples, the courts, honours, and the armed forces. David E. Smith, Canada's pre-eminent scholar of the Crown and Parliament, makes this abundantly clear in his 2017 book *The Constitution in a Hall of Mirrors: Canada at 150*. "Keystone of the constitutional architecture" of Canada, he says, the Crown is "an index both of the history of

Canadian development as a federation and as an autonomous member of the Commonwealth."[1]

The Canadian manifestation of the monarchy is not only historical and constitutional: it is political, cultural, and social, reflecting, and contributing to, change and evolution in Canada's governance, autonomy, and identity. Moreover, the Crown is an extraordinarily subtle, fluid, and malleable institution. The distinguished Australian scholar Anne Twomey coined the memorable phrase "Chameleon Crown" to describe its equivalent in her country.[2] This underscores a distinct feature of the monarchy in Canada: it is inherited (literally) from the United Kingdom and, in the person of the reigning monarch, is shared with that country and fourteen other Commonwealth realms, giving it a unique international dimension. Yet Canada has put its own stamp on the institution: over the past century and a half a recognizably Canadian brand of monarchy has evolved, which has had an effect on its counterparts in "the Queen's other realms" — the title of a book by a contributor to this volume.[3]

The continuing relevance and profile of the Crown in Canada may surprise those who view it as picturesque but *passé*, a holdover from colonial times. Yet the Constitution Act, 1982 entrenched the monarchy by requiring unanimity between Parliament and the provincial legislatures to change it.[4] Recent court rulings dealing with the oath to the sovereign and the succession to the throne have confirmed the centrality of the Crown in the Canadian political order. This continues a historic pattern of judicial interpretation dating back to the Maritime Bank case of 1892 and the Manitoba Initiative and Referendum Act of 1919, which affirmed the autonomy of the provincial Crown through the office of lieutenant governor. Furthermore, a series of court decisions since *Guerin v. The Queen* in 1984 has clearly established the obligations of the Crown toward Indigenous people.[5]

Events, too, have underscored the constitutional function of monarchy in Canada. In the much-discussed dissolution and prorogation of Parliament by the governor general in 2003, 2008, and 2009, the national vice-regal role showed itself to be far more than a cipher. The provincial dimension of vice-regal discretion came to the fore in 2017 when British Columbia's lieutenant governor exercised her prerogative power to decline the advice of a premier, just defeated in the assembly, to dissolve the legislature, and instead invited the leader of the opposition to form a government. In constitutional and administrative terms, the Crown is arguably, and ironically, more potent now in Canada than it is in the United Kingdom, where the monarch's powers have virtually evaporated.[6]

The Canadian Crown has not remained a static institution. Its hallmarks are flexibility and adaptability. A case in point is the evolution from a focus on the person of the monarch to an emphasis on "the Crown" as a legal and constitutional entity. This is not a new concept: it was articulated by Frank MacKinnon and Jacques Monet in the 1970s.[7] But the process of "Canadianization" of the Crown picked up momentum in the twenty-first century. Once again, David E. Smith puts his finger on it: "The abstraction of the Crown has increasingly come to replace the matrix of the monarchy as an object of loyalty."[8] *Globe and Mail* editorial writers expressed a similar view: "The Canadian innovation has been to keep monarchy, while turning a non-resident monarch into less of a physical presence and more of an abstraction. And abstract ideas can be more powerful, durable and flexible than physical things."[9]

At the same time, the importance of the Crown to Indigenous people, featuring their personal link to the sovereign, has been undiminished: current efforts at reconciliation are imbued with the monarchical ethos. And there is a risk in depersonalizing the real-life, flesh-and-blood monarchy to which people can relate. One commentator has pointed out that "it is the Queen herself — an actual person, a living human being and, in the ancient terms of fealty, our Sovereign Liege Lady — who may be said to symbolize the Crown at least as much as the Crown may be said to symbolize the Monarch."[10] The symbolic side of monarchy was considerably enhanced by the Conservative government that held office from 2006 to 2015, with a number of successful tours by the Queen and members of the royal family, restoration of the "royal" designation to the navy and air force, and a major celebration of the Queen's Diamond Jubilee in 2012.

As Canada approached the 150th anniversary of Confederation, there was an upsurge in the attention paid to this "evolving Canadian Crown," to cite a pertinent book title.[11] We have mentioned in the preface the conferences and publications associated with the Institute for the Study of the Crown in Canada, whose creation was a sign of the times. Other publications and conferences have demonstrated the revival of interest in the Crown.[12] The essays in the present volume, the second book published by Dundurn Press with the Institute, continue the momentum. This is an eclectic book, featuring a variety of topics and approaches — some academic, others more personal. Among the authors are scholars, practitioners, a former lieutenant governor, a teacher, and a journalist. All share a common interest in and experience of the Crown, not only in Canada but in the Queen's other realms.

The first section is entitled "The Crown in Canadian History." Barbara J. Messamore begins in "Confederation, Continuity, and the Crown: Some Reflections on Canada 150" by challenging some misconceptions about Confederation. It was not, she says, Canada "coming into being" in 1867, or achieving independence, or even a union of English and French Canadians; these all developed incrementally over decades. Messamore emphasizes "just how central the representatives of the Crown were to the process" of forming the new country and observes "the striking degree of continuity in the institution of the Crown before and after Confederation." The royal governors played a key role even before 1867: Lord Elgin implemented responsible government in the United Province of Canada in 1849; Lord Monck, occupying the same position from 1861, deployed his considerable diplomatic skills to persuade and cajole the colonial politicians to accept Confederation. After 1867, Monck and his successors influenced the course of events in a generally positive way as Canada carved out its autonomy within the British Empire and asserted its control over international relations.

In "Royalty and the Arts in Canada," Carolyn Harris examines royal interest in Canadian culture over the three centuries since Queen Anne. Members of the royal family have paid particular attention to the artistic heritage of Indigenous Peoples, paralleling the intimate link between the Crown and the Indigenous Peoples in Canada. A daughter of Queen Victoria, the accomplished artist Princess Louise, gave a big boost to Canadian culture when she was chatelaine of Rideau Hall while her husband, Lord Lorne, was governor general from 1878 to 1883. Vigorous royal support resumed when the artistic Princess Patricia, daughter of Louise's brother the Duke of Connaught, accompanied her father during his term as governor general from 1911 to 1916. Harris points out that the present Queen and her family are very much involved as patrons and collectors of the arts in contemporary Canada. Indeed, she refers to Elizabeth II as the "curator monarch," and believes that "the continued close ties between the royal family, the creation of fine art, and the Royal Collection suggest a dynamic future for royal involvement in the arts in Canada."

The third chapter takes us into a very different area of royal involvement in Canada. In "Vimy and the Role of Canada's Monarchy," Robert E. Hawkins focuses on a defining moment in Canadian military history, the 1917 Battle of Vimy Ridge, which marked its centennial in the same year as Canada 150. King George V visited Canadians in the field in France and in hospitals in Britain, and knighted General Arthur Currie on the battle-field. The towering monument at Vimy Ridge to the Canadian fallen was inaugurated in July 1936 in a spectacular ceremony by King Edward VIII — one of very few official engagements during his eleven-month reign. In 2007, his niece, Queen Elizabeth II, dedicated the restored monument on the ninetieth anniversary of the battle. And in 2017, her son, Charles, Prince of Wales, spoke eloquently at the commemoration of the centennial. Hawkins concludes that "the story of Vimy, the battle and the monument, illustrates perfectly the role, and the dedication, of Canada's monarchy. It shows the Crown as Canada's willing partner, there to assist, in good times and bad, as the country develops its distinct national identity."

The second section of the book is devoted to "The Crown and Indigenous Peoples" — a key dimension of the Crown in Canada since the eighteenth century and a major contemporary issue, as Canadians seek to reconcile, and redefine their relationship, with First Nations, Métis, and Inuit. Two contributors look at the historical and current perspectives from very different but complementary points of view.

The Honourable Steven Point experienced the Crown-Indigenous connection from both sides of the fence, so to speak, as a First Nations youth growing up in modest conditions on a reserve, then as an activist for Indigenous rights, and finally as the representative of the Crown in British

Columbia. Point does not mince words as he describes how the nineteenth-century colonial governors dealt with the "Indians" in British Columbia, or the straitened circumstances faced by most Indigenous people until the present time. As the province's first Indigenous lieutenant governor, he was apprehensive about his role, but discovered that his people took pride in it and that he was able to have a positive impact on their relationship with other Canadians. "A new relationship," he says, "begins with reconciliation — that is, to acknowledge the past, *then* apologize and start anew."

Nathan Tidridge approaches the question from the perspective of an engaged non-Indigenous person living in Ontario. He emphasizes the importance of the relationship between the First Peoples and the Crown since the Royal Proclamation of 1763 and the landmark Treaty of Niagara in 1764: "The Treaty relationship was a personal one — a kinship — with the King regardless of the government or political developments of the day." Tidridge goes on to apply this principle to the contemporary vocation of what he calls the "Dignified Crown," citing the active roles of lieutenant governors in Ontario, Nova Scotia, New Brunswick, and Saskatchewan, and members of the royal family such as the Duke and Duchess of Cambridge and the Countess of Wessex, in furthering reconciliation. "With their unique ability to create community, connect with government, and be seen as above the political fray, the Queen and her representatives are as relevant today as they were when Treaty relationships were first established."

The third section deals with "The Crown and Contemporary Canada." The first two contributors address the question mentioned earlier, of an evolution from "monarchy" to "Crown."

Andrew Heard leads off in "The Crown in Canada: Is There a Canadian Monarchy?" Attitudes to the monarchy changed profoundly as Canada achieved full autonomy from Britain in the twentieth century. This was reflected in a deliberate government policy to rebrand the monarchy as Canadian rather than British — the sovereign was now "Queen of Canada." To what extent was this successful and realistic? The legal challenge to the Canadian succession to the throne legislation of 2013 demonstrates a conundrum: either Canada and the other realms simply recognize the

British monarch as their sovereign, or the sovereign is a separate office for each realm and "the entire legal edifice of the monarchy must now be viewed as being transplanted into each country." Heard opts for the former: the "Canadian" monarchy is largely "a cultural and political construction," even a "legal fiction." But, he says, this does not detract from "a real and positive relationship between Canada and the Queen." Canada is one of the realms "which are proudly independent nations and yet accept that the Queen of the United Kingdom acts as their sovereign."[13]

Senator Serge Joyal delves into a related issue in "The Oath of Allegiance: A New Perspective." Like Heard, Joyal notes the progressive substitution of the notion of the "Queen of Canada" for that of the British monarch. While the oath of allegiance to the Queen continued unchanged, it was eventually challenged, first on political grounds by the Parti Québécois and the Bloc Québécois, then in a series of court actions in Ontario between 1992 and 2015, stemming from the adoption of the Charter of Rights and Freedoms in 1982. The courts have upheld the validity of the oath to the Queen for new citizens, parliamentarians, and armed forces personnel on the grounds that "the oath to the Queen of Canada is an oath to our form of government, as symbolized by the Queen as the apex of our Canadian parliamentary system of constitutional monarchy." This, says Joyal, "has removed any personal association with Her Majesty. It is essentially an oath to our parliamentary system of democratic constitutional monarchy."

In "The Vulnerability of Vice-Regal Offices in Canada," Christopher McCreery turns his attention to the representatives of the sovereign, the governor general and the lieutenant governors, who incarnate the national and provincial manifestations of the Crown and carry out its day-to-day functions. Tracing a history of their relationship with ministers and legislators, he finds that it has often depended on personality and not best practices, and has sometimes resulted in conflict with the heads of government. While governors normally act "on advice" of their ministers, they retain the right to evaluate this advice and they require the institutional means and resources to fulfil their constitutional role. McCreery notes occasions where the administrative independence of the vice-regal representatives has been jeopardized. He calls for stronger recognition and support for their offices, analogous to that enjoyed by officers of Parliament.

* * *

The fourth and last section of *The Canadian Kingdom*, "The Crown and the Realms," looks at the phenomenon of the shared monarch. Australian Peter Boyce compares his own country's Crown with Canada's; Sean Palmer, a Canadian living in New Zealand, considers the symbols of monarchy across the Commonwealth realms; and John Fraser suggests how the Canadian experience with the Crown should be of interest for its source, the United Kingdom.

In "Australian Perspectives on a Shared Monarchy," Peter Boyce notes that the Canadian Confederation of 1867 did influence the Australian federation created in 1901 — but only to a point. The Crown in the Australian states retained its autonomy: the state "governors," unlike Canadian "lieutenant governors," were (and are) not subordinate to the central government. Their prestige challenged that of the governor general, and they still enjoy far more profile and resources than their Canadian provincial counterparts. Boyce provides intriguing comparisons between the vice-regal offices, national and sub-national, in the two realms. The Australian governors, for example, have exercised reserve powers more frequently than their Canadian equivalents, largely due to deadlocks between the upper and lower chambers (all states but one are bicameral). Boyce recounts the current debate over a republican form of government, much more acute in Australia than in Canada. Here again, the two sister realms differ markedly in their approaches to their shared monarchy.

Sean Palmer considers symbols of the Crown in "The Path to Nationalization: How the Realms Have Made the Monarchy Their Own." The realms, he believes, have succeeded in adapting the Crowns to their own cultures, while retaining the British monarch as their sovereign. Canada led the way in "nationalizing" heraldry, starting with a personal standard or flag for the Queen in Canada — a practice recently extended only in Canada to other members of the royal family. Palmer also examines the different flags for the governors general and, in Canada, for the lieutenant governors. He describes the evolution of the Queen's effigy on the coinage of her various realms (it would have been interesting to look at postage stamps, too). National portraits of the Queen and the insignia of honours serve to differentiate the sovereign in each of her realms. "The divisibility of the Crown is made tangible" by the adoption of distinctive national royal symbols, Palmer says, thus "bolstering the relevance of the monarchy in each nation."

The final chapter is whimsically entitled "A Tale of Two Sovereigns; or, How the Queen of Canada Helps the Queen of the United Kingdom." Here, John Fraser colourfully and wittily encapsulates the history and experience of the Canadian Crown, not glossing over its shortcomings but pointing out how well it works in practice. The vice-regal representatives reflect cultural and racial diversity, "a hugely effective way to localize the Crown and give it a distinctive national or regional face." Indeed, the Crown in Canada does this better than its British equivalent. The Canadian federal monarchy could also provide some pointers to the "United" Kingdom in handling devolution and possible division. "The United Kingdom may yet become a pair of federated kingdoms, if not a trio"; the Queen of England may conceivably have to negotiate with the Queen of Scotland and "reconcile the seemingly irreconcilable." Echoing Steven Point and Nathan Tidridge, Fraser ends by lauding the Crown's role in seeking sorely needed reconciliation with Indigenous Peoples. It is a fitting conclusion to the book.

Where does the Canadian Crown stand at "Canada 150" and what are its prospects? Our eleven contributors approach these questions from very diverse perspectives. However, their viewpoints converge on the continued relevance of the monarchy to Canada in the twenty-first century, whether constitutionally or culturally. The Crown is inextricably intertwined with Canada's historical evolution and its current system of governance. Loyalty to the person of the monarch may indeed have receded in the public consciousness, but the institution of the Crown has acquired an increased profile through its ongoing constitutional role, court rulings, and especially the relationship with Indigenous Peoples.

Through the past 150 years, Canada has demonstrated originality in adapting the ancient monarchical institution inherited from Britain. The other Commonwealth realms have followed its lead. Using the instrument of the Crown, Canada formed the first federal parliamentary monarchy, emulated by Australia. It attained autonomy within the British Empire, notably in the First World War, symbolized by Vimy Ridge, then complete independence through the development of the divisible Crown, culminating in the Statute of Westminster in 1931. Since then, Canada has thoroughly "nationalized" the monarchy, as shown by the evolution of symbols and practices and the concept of the "Queen of Canada." Again, the other realms have benefited from Canadian precedents and adapted them to their own needs.

Unlike Australia, the "republican option" has made little headway in Canada.[14] Andrew Heard concedes that "the Queen and the royal family are British and not Canadian," yet "in the modern era, a majority of Canadians have supported continued links to the monarchy, with only fleeting swings toward republicanism." John Fraser adds that while Canada is "a constitutional monarchy not exactly seething with royalist fervour," most Canadians "understand how the Crown represents a certain stability but, equally importantly — if not more importantly — is infinitely less scary than all the posited alternatives." In that sense, the Crown is a pragmatic accommodation by a pragmatic people, a tacit recognition by Canadians that their success as a nation owes much to the institutions of governance that have endured since 1867. Or, to again quote an editorialist, "Our unique constitutional monarchy, the product of 150 years of thought, compromise and accident, is a fluke work of genius."[15]

These sentiments are encouraging for those who see the monarchy as an intrinsic, positive, humanizing, and colourful part of Canada's national polity and its unique identity as a sovereign kingdom in the Americas, and as a key to reconciliation and relationships with Indigenous Peoples. Yet, like democracy itself, the Crown can be fragile. It needs to be nurtured, supported, and never taken for granted. The vice-regal offices in particular are vulnerable and require "tender, loving care," adequate resources, and wise appointments.

In 2017, Canada's revered and beloved monarch Queen Elizabeth II turned ninety-one. Her son and heir, Charles, Prince of Wales, represented her at the 150th Canada Day celebrations in Ottawa, raising the usual questions about whether he would eventually become King of Canada.

There were also questions about the durability of the monarchical revival that occurred under Stephen Harper's Conservative government between 2006 and 2015. Yet Justin Trudeau's Liberal administration did little to turn the clock back, apart from discontinuing the advisory committee on vice-regal appointments instituted by Harper in 2010.

The first beneficiary of that process, David Johnston, served seven years as governor general, stepping down late in 2017. The Canadian Crown flowered and flourished during his tenure at Rideau Hall. In an opinion piece entitled "A Model Governor General," three of the contributors to this book paid tribute to Johnston: "He brilliantly incarnated the vice-regal constitutional and socio-cultural roles. He struck the perfect balance of loyalty to the Sovereign he represented and the national expression of the Canadian Crown. David Johnston has been the ideal governor general to preside over the 150th anniversary of Confederation."[16] We are privileged to dedicate *The Canadian Kingdom* to him.

Notes

1. David E. Smith, *The Constitution in a Hall of Mirrors: Canada at 150* (Toronto: University of Toronto Press, 2017), xiii, 135.
2. Anne Twomey, *The Chameleon Crown: The Queen and Her Australian Governors* (Sydney: Federation Press, 2006).
3. Peter Boyce, *The Queen's Other Realms: The Crown and Its Legacy in Australia, Canada and New Zealand* (Sydney: Federation Press, 2008).
4. Section 41 (a) of the Constitution Act, 1982 specifies that an amendment to the Constitution of Canada with respect to "the office of the Queen, the Governor General and the Lieutenant Governor of a province" requires "resolutions of the Senate and House of Commons and the legislative assembly of each province."
5. See "Court Rulings" in *Canada and the Crown: Essays on Constitutional Monarchy*, D. Michael Jackson and Philippe Lagassé, eds. (Montreal and Kingston: McGill-Queen's University Press, 2014), 305–12.
6. See Robert Hazell and Bob Morris, "If the Queen Has No Reserve Powers Left, What Is the Modern Monarchy For?" in "The Crown in the 21st Century," eds. Philippe Lagassé and Nicholas A. MacDonald, special issue, *Review of Constitutional Studies* 22, no. 1 (2017).
7. Frank MacKinnon, *The Crown in Canada* (Calgary: Glenbow-Alberta Institute / McClelland & Stewart West, 1976); Jacques Monet, *The Canadian Crown* (Toronto: Clarke Irwin, 1979).
8. David E. Smith, *The Constitution in a Hall of Mirrors*, 45.
9. "Canada 150: Monarchy. A Strange Accident That Actually Works," *Globe and Mail*, July 20, 2017, A10.
10. Warren J. Newman, "Some Observations on the Queen, the Crown, the Constitution, and the Courts," *Review of Constitutional Studies* 22, no. 1 (2017), 63.
11. See Jennifer Smith and D. Michael Jackson, eds., *The Evolving Canadian Crown* (Montreal and Kingston: McGill-Queen's University Press, 2012).
12. For example: Edward McWhinney, *The Governor General and the Prime Ministers: The Making and Unmaking of Governments* (Vancouver: Ronsdale Press, 2005); Barbara J. Messamore, *Canada's Governors*

General, 1847–1878: Biography and Constitutional Evolution (Toronto: University of Toronto Press, 2006); Colin M. Coates, ed., *Majesty in Canada: Essays on the Role of Royalty* (Toronto: Dundurn, 2006); Nathan Tidridge, *Canada's Constitutional Monarchy* (Toronto: Dundurn, 2011); John Fraser, *The Secret of the Crown: Canada's Affair with Royalty* (Toronto: House of Anansi Press, 2012); D. Michael Jackson, *The Crown and Canadian Federalism* (Toronto: Dundurn, 2013); Michel Bédard and Philippe Lagassé, eds., *La Couronne et le Parlement / The Crown and Parliament* (Montreal: Éditions Yvon Blais, 2015).

13. For differing points of view on the succession legislation, see Anne Twomey, "Royal Succession, Abdication, and Regency in the Realms," and Warren J. Newman, "Some Observations on the Queen, the Crown, the Constitution, and the Courts," in *Review of Constitutional Studies* 22, no. 1 (2017). See also Mark D. Walters, "Succession to the Throne and the Architecture of the Constitution of Canada"; Serge Joyal, "La monarchie constitutionnelle au Canada: une institution stable, complexe et souple"; and Anne Twomey, "Succession to the Crown in Canada," in Michel Bédard and Philippe Lagassé, eds., *La Couronne et le Parlement / The Crown and Parliament*.

14. See David E. Smith, *The Republican Option in Canada, Past and Present* (Toronto: University of Toronto Press, 1999).

15. *Globe and Mail*, "A Strange Accident That Actually Works."

16. John Fraser, Michael Jackson, and Christopher McCreery, "In David Johnston, Canada Had a Model Governor General," *National Post*, July 26, 2017, http://nationalpost.com/opinion/john-fraser-michael-jackson-and-christopher-mccreery-in-david-johnston-canada-had-a-model-governor-general.

PART 1
THE CROWN IN CANADIAN HISTORY

1|

Confederation, Continuity, and the Crown: Some Reflections on Canada 150

Barbara J. Messamore

On New Year's Eve 2016, Governor General David Johnston launched the Canada 150 celebrations: the 150th anniversary of Canada's Confederation in 1867. The date is often seen as the hinge of our history, a major turning point. Most Canadians will know that the British North America Act was passed in Britain's parliament in 1867. But what exactly that signifies is less clear. Canadians might see in 1867 the creation of Canada from what had been separate British North American colonies. Alternatively, they might see it as our more peaceful equivalent of the Americans' 1776; the idea that Confederation marked the beginning of self-government and independence in Canada is very pervasive. They might also see Confederation as the occasion on which French and English Canadians opted to come together, to work in a kind of unified government. But, in fact, all of these prevalent views are distortions in one sense or another, and the real nature of Confederation is harder to understand. Before and after Confederation, the Crown has been an important part of Canada's constitution. Through an examination of some of the activities and functions of the Crown's representatives in the Confederation era, it is possible to gain a fuller sense of the real hinges of change and the real meaning of Confederation. Such an examination reveals not a dramatic change that pivots on 1867, but continuity, the gradual evolution that has characterized Canada's constitutional history.

* * *

The first premise — the idea that Canada came into being in 1867 — is inaccurate in a very obvious way. Canada in 1867 encompassed only a small part of what the country would ultimately become — it included only Nova Scotia, New Brunswick, and parts of Quebec and Ontario. The geographical bulk of today's Canada was not included, but was part of later piecemeal growth. All of the Prairies — the provinces of Manitoba, Saskatchewan, and Alberta — were acquired afterward, carved out of what had been the Hudson's Bay Company territory of Rupert's Land. British Columbia was joined to Canada in 1871, so was not part of the 1867 story. Prince Edward Island joined soon after that, in 1873. Britain transferred the Arctic Islands to the Dominion of Canada in 1880, and Newfoundland joined Confederation in 1949.

Faithfulness to historical accuracy is seldom an essential feature of official commemorations; these tend to focus on a narrative that is useful, that fits with our present needs. For example, the city of Richmond, British Columbia, prepared material for the Canada 150 celebrations that focused on its present, rather than its past. As it scarcely existed as a newcomer settlement in 1867, this is hardly surprising. Richmond's Canada 150 poster featured a strange montage of images: a Chinese dragon, someone who appears to be doing tai chi, a canoe, a Mountie — the RCMP did not exist in 1867 — some tugboats and canoes, and the Skytrain.

Canada's federal government sought to make the Canada 150 commemorations as diverse as possible, to include all the important elements that make up Canadian society. However, some First Nations rejected the idea of celebrating Canada 150, and a movement called "#Resistance150" protested against a celebration of what some called a history of colonialism. The 150 celebrations proved to be a way to draw attention to, and engage with, the contested nature of history — in itself a valuable exercise.

The second premise, that Canada achieved independence in 1867, is harder to address. This is because the real hinge of change was not marked by any new statute. Instead, Canada became self-governing by convention — by practice — and recognizing the transition is more difficult. The shift to colonial self-government in internal matters came in 1848. The real change occurred in the function of the Crown. But there was no structural change, no new legislation. Instead, while the basic *form* of government remained the same, the *workings* of it underwent an important change. From 1848 on, it was understood that the governor, the representative of the Crown, would appoint an executive council that enjoyed the confidence of the elected assembly. In other words, it became more of a "Cabinet" as we would think of it today. So, if a party held a majority of seats in the assembly, they had the right to form the government. And, in internal matters not touching British imperial interests, the governor would give his assent to legislation even if he personally did not approve of it.

The practice was first put into place in January 1848 in Nova Scotia, the first colony in the British Empire to be self-governing. Nova Scotia reformer Joseph Howe called it "a Revolution without bloodshed."[1] Howe was proud of the fact that, unlike Canada, Nova Scotia experienced no rebellions in the 1830s. He later reflected that the Canadians were "always in trouble," with Louis-Joseph Papineau keeping Lower Canada "in trouble for twenty years, and [William Lyon] McKenzie [sic] disturb[ing] the Upper Province for about the same period."[2] Contrary to some prevailing narratives, the rebellions had not hastened the advent of colonial self-government.

Instead, the shift to responsible government in the colonies was driven by a general philosophical and economic shift in Britain in the 1840s. Old mercantilist tariffs that had extended protection to colonial produce were being dismantled in favour of free trade, and with this economic change came political change. British public opinion now insisted that British taxpayers should not be burdened with the expense of colonies, nor should mature colonies with elected assemblies be governed by Britain in matters that had no bearing on the larger empire. British Colonial Office official Herman Merivale archly summed up the situation: "We give them commercial advantages, and tax ourselves for their benefit, in order to give them interest in remaining under our supremacy, that we may have the pleasure of governing them."[3] Both Britain's Conservative administration under Sir Robert Peel and their Whig successors led by Lord John Russell, who took office in mid-1846, endorsed the new orthodoxy of free trade.

Russell's secretary of state for the colonies, the 3rd Earl Grey, was firmly committed both to free trade and to a loosening of Imperial control over colonies that possessed representative government. In a November 1846 dispatch to the British-appointed governor of Nova Scotia, Sir John Harvey, Grey explained that the government of the colony should be modelled on that of the mother country. As the representative of the Crown, the governor should follow the wishes of his executive council as long as they possessed the confidence of the legislative assembly. If the council lost the support of the assembly, they would either resign, with the governor allowing their opponents to form a government, or there would be an election. "It cannot be too distinctly acknowledged that it is neither possible nor desirable to carry on the government of any of the British Provinces in North America in opposition to the opinion of the inhabitants."[4] While Harvey was loath to introduce partisanship into Nova Scotia politics, Grey insisted that "as every free government necessarily is a party government, I think it is better that Nova Scotia should submit to the evils of party government rather than be without the privileges of freedom."[5]

The advent of colonial self-government in Canada followed soon afterward in March 1848, although the transition would be less peaceful. James Bruce, the 8th Earl of Elgin, who came to Canada as governor in 1847, had been supplied with a copy of Grey's dispatch to Harvey as a guideline and he himself strongly believed in the principle of responsible government. Elgin avoided dissolving the legislature immediately — he was reluctant "to jump down every body's throat the moment I touch the soil of Canada," he explained to Grey.[6] But after elections had been held early in 1848, Elgin called upon reformers Robert Baldwin and Louis-Hippolyte LaFontaine to form a government on March 7; their supporters had won a majority of the seats in the legislature. Grey followed with interest Elgin's "great experiment."[7]

Early in the legislative session of 1849, the Baldwin-LaFontaine administration introduced the controversial Rebellion Losses Bill, a measure that would grant compensation to Lower Canadians whose property had been destroyed during the suppression of the insurrections in 1837–38. Conservatives protested that many who would be compensated had been treasonous and they demanded that Elgin refuse his assent. The legislative debate over the measure was divisive and bitter; the young member for Kingston, John A. Macdonald, accused Reformer William Hume Blake of deceitfulness and heatedly challenged him to a duel.[8] But the Reform-dominated legislative assembly supported the measure. Despite the deluge of Tory demands, Elgin recognized that responsible government required that he acquiesce in the advice of his advisors; this was an internal, not Imperial, matter.

On April 25, 1849, the governor general pronounced royal assent to the bill in Montreal's parliament buildings. Protesters, many of them drawn from the ranks of Montreal's commercial elite who had been hurt by the withdrawal of Britain's protective tariffs, turned angrily on the Crown's representative. Elgin was pelted with rotten eggs and paving stones pried up from the street. That evening's legislative sitting was disrupted by the crash of stones through the windows. The gas lamps were shattered, and Montreal's parliament was devoured by flames.

Lady Elgin kept a stone that had struck her husband as a souvenir, its significance neatly lettered on the side. In recent years, the Bruce family returned it for display in Canada. Elgin's great-grandson, the 11th Earl, considering the stone while visiting Canada, remarked that this was the rock upon which the Commonwealth was founded, that here was the beginning of the idea that a colony could be part of the Empire but permitted to govern itself.[9]

This important change in how the representative of the Crown would carry out his role, while not accompanied by any legislative change,

"The Rock upon Which Canada Was Founded."

signalled the beginning of self-government in internal matters — decades before Confederation.

Nor did Confederation herald the beginnings of autonomy in external affairs. Far from the Confederation scheme's being enacted in the teeth of British opposition, British policy-makers endorsed it, and even exerted pressure to bring it about. The British North America Act declared that Confederation would "promote the interests of the British Empire."[10] Shortly after the Quebec resolutions had been drafted, Edward Cardwell, Britain's secretary of state for the colonies, wrote privately to Lord Monck, Canada's governor general: "I need scarcely assure you that here there is but one desire — which is to promote to the utmost the work in which you are engaged."[11] Lord Stanley, Britain's foreign secretary, summed up his conception of Confederation in a private letter: "The Colonies will remain Colonies, only confederated for the sake of convenience."[12]

In common with the process by which Canada gained autonomy in internal matters, the incremental process by which Canada gained foreign policy autonomy can be better understood with an examination of the function of the Crown. Although the Statute of Westminster ultimately recognized formally the state of autonomy that had been achieved — that by 1931 the governor general was no longer answerable to Britain's Cabinet — the small steps by which this condition was reached were not usually marked by any legislative change.

A few examples will suffice. During the 1871 Treaty of Washington negotiations, it was deemed advisable to have a Canadian diplomatic presence at the table in addition to British and American delegates, and John A. Macdonald took part to represent Canada. The British-appointed governor general, Lord Lisgar, pressed Britain's government to provide compensation in exchange for Canada's acceptance of some less-than-satisfactory terms, but was not himself part of the negotiations.[13] A generation earlier, his counterpart Lord Elgin had directly concluded the 1854 Reciprocity Treaty with the Americans, which addressed some of the same issues.

The gradual obsolescence of the power to reserve or disallow Canadian legislation that exceeded the powers of the Dominion is another example of this incremental change. Even after Confederation, the governor general could withhold royal assent from a bill or reserve it for the consideration of the Imperial parliament; beyond this, an act to which he assented could be overturned by Britain within two years. In practice, the last act to be disallowed by the Imperial parliament was the Oaths Act in 1873, passed to allow evidence to be taken under oath concerning the Pacific Railway Scandal that had embroiled John A. Macdonald's administration. Lord Dufferin chose not to withhold assent despite concerns about the bill's legality, since he did not want to be seen to be standing in the way of the investigation of the scandal.[14] The act was disallowed by Britain's Law Officers of the Crown on technical grounds.[15]

Macdonald, once he had returned to power in 1878, was not above manipulating the governor general to push the boundaries of Canadian autonomy. Macdonald's high-tariff National Policy extended into an area of British Imperial jurisdiction. Based upon the prime minister's assurances, the governor general, Lord Lorne, reported to the secretary of state for the colonies in December 1878 that the "English papers were entirely mistaken" in reporting that Canada planned to implement a protective tariff. "It would be a Revenue Tariff."[16] Sir Michael Hicks-Beach reminded Lorne that any differential duties act affecting Britain would be subject to disallowance if it had not been previously sanctioned by the British government and noted that Macdonald had promised to submit any financial proposals to them first.[17] But only in the very week that the budget was to go before Canada's Parliament was Lorne able to hurriedly and apologetically telegraph the proposed budget to Britain. He urged that the "proposals be left alone as far as possible."[18] Hicks-Beach had already arrived at the same conclusion: the British government "should not think of refusing our consent (it would be useless for us to try)."[19]

Lorne's successor, Lord Lansdowne, reserved a bill for Her Majesty's pleasure in 1886 — the last such instance in Canada — but, contrary to appearances, this was not a case of heavy-handed Imperial interference in Dominion legislation.[20] Rather, Prime Minister John A. Macdonald used the convenient loophole of reservation to dodge unpleasant political consequences. The governor general acted on Macdonald's advice in reserving Fisheries Minister George Eulas Foster's "foolish little bill" that was hostile to American fishermen. Macdonald, fearing a backlash in Nova Scotia with an election looming, did not "venture to squash" the bill himself,

Lansdowne explained to a friend, "and I had to stop it, 'for the signification of H. Majesty's pleasure thereon.'"[21]

Another change in the function of the Crown that had significance for Canada's gradually evolving autonomy concerns the mechanisms for the conduct of foreign policy. Even before the official advent of autonomous foreign relations in 1931, incremental steps had stretched the boundaries of Canada's freedom of action. The governor general had traditionally been the conduit of all correspondence between Canada and any foreign power, with this communication travelling through Britain's Colonial Office. Since 1880, and unofficially even earlier, Canada kept a quasi-diplomatic presence in Britain, the Canadian High Commission. (Members of the Empire — later, the Commonwealth — were not strictly foreign nations, and so this was not an embassy.) And, perhaps surprisingly, a distinct Department of External Affairs, established in Canada in 1909, was a very direct, but unwitting, result of an initiative by the governor general, the 4th Earl Grey. He had been frustrated by Prime Minister Sir Wilfrid Laurier's procrastination and apparent forgetfulness in communicating matters of foreign affairs, and by a lack of system in the management of important background documents. Along with the British ambassador to the United States, James Bryce, Grey pushed for the establishment of a government department devoted to external affairs. Grey was alarmed to see that Laurier's bill to put this into effect said that the department would "have the conduct of all official communications between the Government of Canada and the government of any other country in connection with the external affairs of Canada." Grey disliked the phrase "have the conduct" and protested to Laurier that this would bypass the governor general. Laurier promised to amend the bill but neglected to do so, and Grey did not want to take the dramatic step of refusing assent to it. Grey at least hoped that the department would be situated in Parliament's East Block, near his own office, but was dismayed to return from a trip to discover that it had been located over a barber shop on Bank Street. He lamented that it might as well be in Calcutta![22]

These few examples demonstrate the extent to which changes in the function of the governor general provide insight into the evolving relationship between Canada and the Empire. They also illustrate that the real hinge of change in Canada's colonial status is not to be found in Confederation in 1867.

The third basic premise, the idea that Confederation represented a decision by French and English Canadians to come together, is also flawed. It is, however, one of our most-cherished notions about Confederation. It also renders inexplicable the apparently sudden flowering of Quebec nationalism in the 1960s and 1970s. F.R. Scott reflected a pervasive misunderstanding when he wrote, in reference to a 1937 Judicial Committee of the Privy Council decision, that "if the provinces had wished to 'preserve their autonomy,' they would never have entered Confederation."[23] The main problem with this paradigm is that it fails to recognize that French and English Canada were *already* united at the time Confederation talks began. The perhaps less romantic truth is that Confederation promised the Province of Canada a way out of the bad marriage that it had been locked into with the 1840 Act of Union.

Upper and Lower Canada had been created in 1791, shortly after the arrival of Loyalist newcomers into what was then Quebec. British policy-makers knew that these mostly English-speaking Protestants would expect representative political institutions and would not coexist on happy terms with a French Roman Catholic majority, and so divided the colony of Quebec into two. But in 1840, with the Act of Union, Britain reversed policy and recombined these two colonies, creating the Province of Canada. This forced union — in part a response to the rebellions of 1837–38 — was part of a plan to assimilate the French Canadians.

Even though Canada was a single colony after 1840, it was divided into two districts: Canada East, which was largely French, and Canada West, which was largely English. This new united colony had one legislative assembly, with an equal number of seats allocated for each district, something that was plainly an injustice to the more populated Canada East.

Equal does not always mean fair. Lord Durham, the governor and commissioner whose 1839 *Report on the Affairs of British North America* recommended union of Upper and Lower Canada as a way to speed up the assimilation of the French, is usually seen as the villain behind this manoeuvre. But in fact Durham specifically warned against any attempt to manipulate representation: "If the Canadians are to be deprived of representative government, it would be better to do it in a straightforward way than to attempt to establish a ... system [of] electoral frauds. It is not in North America that men can be cheated by an unreal semblance of representative government, or persuaded that they are out-voted, when, in fact, they are disfranchised."[24] What is more, as an assimilationist scheme, the measure proved short-sighted: by 1851, Canada West's population had exceeded that of Canada East. The Clear Grit reformers, led by George Brown, then demanded "rep by pop" — representation by population.

Despite a political alliance between Canada East's Parti bleu, led by George-Étienne Cartier, and Canada West's Liberal-Conservatives, led by John A. Macdonald after 1856, no one party could command a majority in the legislature of the colony on any sustained basis. By June 1864, when a three-month-old administration led by Étienne-Paschal Taché appealed to the governor general, Lord Monck, for a dissolution, there had been nine ministries in office in just ten years. Some sort of structural change seemed the only way to break the impasse.

The idea of a wider British North American union was not new. Even before the American Revolution, the 1754 Albany conference organized by statesman, inventor, and polymath Benjamin Franklin considered the idea. In 1850, former attorney general of Canada West Henry Sherwood published a plan for a "Federative Union of the British North American Provinces" and even drafted up legislation. Nova Scotia's J.W. Johnston argued the case for union in 1854, and Canada East politician Joseph-Charles Taché in 1858 published *Des provinces de l'Amérique du Nord et d'une union fédérale*, recommending confederation.[25]

Representatives of the Crown were among those who endorsed union or federation schemes. Sir Edmund Head, while serving as governor of New Brunswick in 1853, had drafted a memorandum on British North American colonial union for the then secretary of state for the colonies, the Duke of Newcastle.[26] While serving as Canada's governor general in 1857, he again raised the topic with one of Newcastle's successors, Henry Labouchere, and was instructed to "take it in hand."[27]

A series of acrimonious ministerial crises in the Province of Canada in 1858 lent urgency to the plan, and Head drew up a series of resolutions.[28] At the closing of the legislative session, Head announced that he proposed to "communicate with Her Majesty's Government and with the Governments of our sister Colonies ... [about] the principles on which a bond of a federal character uniting the Provinces of British North America may hereafter be practicable."[29]

Unfortunately for Head and the Confederation scheme there was a virtual revolving door to the Colonial Office; during Head's seven-year tenure in Canada, some eight successive secretaries of state for the colonies held office. Incumbents were more apt to be putting out immediate fires than planning long-range policy. Sir Edward Bulwer-Lytton was evidently unaware of the objectives his predecessors had encouraged and privately minuted that Head's speech had caused the "gravest displeasure."[30] In his mild official rebuke to Head, Bulwer-Lytton opined that any federation scheme properly belonged to the "executive authority of the Empire, and not that of any separate province, to initiate."[31]

The same condition of chronic political instability that caused Head such difficulty had not abated by the mid-1860s and his successor, Lord Monck, was likewise plagued by an inability to keep an administration in office. Monck was an affable pragmatist who had had some personal experience with political coalitions while serving as a parliamentary back-bencher in Britain; Prime Minister Lord Aberdeen had in 1852 brought together Peelite Conservatives and Whigs. Monck recognized that George Brown commanded considerable support in Canada West and was an essential ingredient in any lasting administration. In the spring of 1863, Monck began a charm offensive to win Brown over. He met with him privately, expressed support for some of Brown's ideas, and encouraged him to embrace co-operation with political rivals.[32] Social invitations to Government House followed, some of which featured lively sing-alongs and even melodious solos by Cartier. While the time was not yet ripe, important groundwork had been laid. Some have speculated that Brown's late-in-life marriage to Anne Nelson, the sister of one of his Edinburgh school friends, may have softened the crusty reformer and made him more amenable to compromise.

Monck played for time when Étienne-Paschal Taché sought dissolution in June 1864, neither consenting nor refusing. Instead, he took steps to avoid another inconclusive election and to bring about the so-called Great Coalition that negotiated Confederation.[33] Monck wrote to Brown to plead that "the success or failure of the negotiations … depends very much on your consenting to come into the Cabinet." He reminded Brown of "the grave responsibility which you will take upon yourself if you should refuse to do so."[34] Brown, seeing a route to putting into effect the federal scheme he favoured and achieving rep by pop, consented to join the coalition and become part of a Cabinet that would include John A. Macdonald, George-Étienne Cartier, Étienne-Paschal Taché, Hector-Louis Langevin, and other leading Canadian politicians.[35] Monck later acknowledged that he was "in some measure overstepping the strict line of his constitutional duties,"[36] but reflected with satisfaction on the success of his gamble. He concluded that "when I formed the present Administration … my last card in that suit had been played."[37] W.L. Morton described Monck as the "advocate as well as inspirer of the idea of [the Great] coalition."[38]

Monck's Maritime counterparts were likewise instrumental in promoting Confederation. In fact, Britain reassigned Nova Scotia's representative of

Charles Stanley Monck, Lord Monck, governor general of Canada.

Sir Arthur Hamilton Gordon, governor of New Brunswick.

the Crown, Sir Richard Macdonell, to Hong Kong in 1865, since he seemed resistant to the idea of Confederation. His replacement, Sir William Fenwick Williams, was a more active force in promoting it. British policy favoured some type of amalgamation, insofar as it would make colonial administration more cost-effective and presumably enhance defence. In New Brunswick, Governor Arthur Hamilton Gordon actively promoted the scheme of Maritime union. When Prince Edward Island Liberal leader George Coles expressed support for Confederation in the summer of 1863, and a new pro-union Conservative government under Charles Tupper took office in Nova Scotia, Gordon pressed New Brunswick premier Samuel Leonard Tilley to take advantage of the favourable climate. Gordon has been widely credited as the initiator of the 1864 Charlottetown conference that culminated in the Confederation proposals.[39]

Canadian delegates, having wangled invitations to a conference that had been intended to discuss only Maritime union, won over most of the Maritime delegates and secured acceptance of a plan for a wider federation. For the Maritime delegates, the proposal of a wider federation was actually a less bold change; it offered the security of retention of their own local legislatures, which would have been lost in any scheme for Maritime legislative union. A follow-up conference at Quebec just a month after the Charlottetown meeting produced the Quebec Resolutions, the agreements that would form the basis of the British North America Act.

Both Gordon and Monck favoured an arrangement in which the power of the central government was unquestionably paramount. In fact, Gordon preferred a simple union and offered his resignation to Newcastle when it became clear a federation was to be enacted: "I can do what I am bid, but you may wish it done more heartily.... I think you will be better served by someone who agrees with you."[40] Edward Cardwell, Newcastle's successor at the Colonial Office, reassured Gordon that "we all agree in favouring a complete fusion not a federation."[41]

Even after the terms had been agreed upon, Monck wrote privately in September 1866 to the Colonial Office (the Earl of Carnarvon was now secretary of state) to make a case for why it would be unwise to call the new arrangement a "federation." "I fear that the use of this word as descriptive of the intended Union is calculated to direct into a wrong channel the minds of persons who have not very carefully considered the terms," he explained, alluding to the American example. Monck pointed to the fact that no powers were listed as belonging "exclusively" to the provincial governments, that the lieutenant governors were Dominion appointees, and that the Dominion government had power of disallowance over provincial legislation. The provinces, he maintained, had a "completely subordinate & municipal character for the administration of purely local affairs."[42]

That said, it is instructive to note that different observers regarded the same Quebec Resolutions in very different ways — a point that must be remembered when there is any discussion of the intentions of the "Fathers of Confederation." It brings to mind the parable of the blind men and the elephant. John A. Macdonald shared Monck's centralizing view of the terms that had been reached. He privately acknowledged that it was, if not the best plan, "the only practicable plan." He was confident that, over time, the provincial level of government would organically wither away, that they would "see both local Parliaments and Governments absorbed in the General power. This is as plain to me as if I saw it accomplished but of course it does not do to adopt that point of view in discussing the subject in Lower Canada."[43] Perhaps surprisingly, Antoine-Aimé Dorion, leader of the sovereigntist Parti rouge, had a similar view, and condemned the agreement as "union in disguise."[44]

George Brown, who had long railed against priestly encroachment in Canadian politics and sought to limit the pernicious influence of Roman Catholicism, wrote excitedly to his wife in the wake of the Quebec Conference: "All right!!! Conference through at six o'clock this evening — constitution adopted — a most creditable document — a complete reform of all the abuses and injustice we have complained of! Is it not wonderful? French Canadianism entirely extinguished!"[45]

By contrast, Quebec advocates of the scheme — who formed the majority in the eastern half of the colonial legislature[46] — saw in Confederation a "formal recognition of our national independence," as the Bleu newspaper *La Minerve* put it. "As a distinct and separate nationality, we form a state within the state."[47] Étienne-Paschal Taché applauded the restoration of "our complete autonomy." "We've been separated from Upper Canada," he said. "We're going to have our own legislature, where everything will be done by and for French Canadians, and in French. You'd have to be a renegade … not to be moved to tears, not to feel your heart pound with an indescribable joy.…"[48] Those French Canadian politicians who supported Confederation saw in it, not a marriage, but a divorce. It promised a way out of the unhappy forced union of 1840. The agreement promised a way to preserve their distinctiveness; it was not a repudiation of it.

An examination of the events surrounding Confederation reveals just how central the representatives of the Crown were to the process. It is useful also to reflect on the striking degree of continuity in the institution of the Crown before and after Confederation. The British North America Act declared that "the Executive Government and Authority of and over Canada is hereby declared to continue and be vested in the Queen."[49] In fact, continuity was an overwhelming theme of the immediate post-Confederation era. Paul Cornell has remarked of the first session of the Dominion Parliament that "the situation was not really new." Some 48 percent of the members had been present in the pre-Confederation legislative chamber.[50] A modest British garrison remained in Canada until 1871; most troops had been recalled in the 1850s, for reasons that had nothing to do with Confederation. Command of Canada's own forces remained with a British-appointed officer, the General Officer Commanding the Canadian Militia (GOC). Lord Monck, who had been serving since 1861, continued on as governor general after Confederation. There was no official change to the description of his duties; only in 1878 were the documents defining the role revised, and even then only to remove long-obsolete clauses, none of which had been affected by Confederation itself.[51]

Monck's down-to-earth and easy going nature undoubtedly helped him to fulfil his important function in facilitating the coalition-building that led to Confederation. But he might have taken too casual an approach to the occasion that some Canadians thought warranted a little bit of ceremony. Instead of presiding over the festivities to proclaim Confederation in his cocked hat and ceremonial uniform trimmed with gold braid, Monck simply turned up in his ordinary street clothes. His letter to his son described his plans for the momentous occasion of July 1, 1867: he blandly noted that he would be "obliged to go to Ottawa for a few days for some business."[52]

Notes

1. Joseph Howe to Charles Buller, 12 February 1848, in Chester Martin, "The Correspondence Between Joseph Howe and Charles Buller, 1845–1848," *Canadian Historical Review* 6, no. 4 (1925): 324.
2. "The Botheration Scheme," *Halifax Morning Chronicle,* January 11, 1865, Library and Archives Canada, www.collectionscanada.gc.ca/confederation/023001-7135-e.html.
3. As quoted in Klaus E. Knorr, *British Colonial Theories 1570–1850* (Toronto: University of Toronto Press, 1944), 340.
4. Grey to Sir John Harvey, dispatch, 3 November 1846, in W.P.M. Kennedy, ed., *Statutes, Treaties and Document of the Canadian Constitution, 1713–1929,* 2nd ed. (Toronto: Oxford University Press, 1930), 494–96.
5. Grey to Harvey, draft dispatch on responsible government, in James Bruce Elgin, *The Elgin-Grey Papers, 1846–1852; Edited with Notes and Appendices by Sir Arthur G. Doughty* (Ottawa: J.O. Patenaude, 1937), 3:1151–55.
6. Elgin to Grey, secret, 24 February 1847, in Elgin, *Elgin-Grey Papers,* 1:13.
7. Grey to Elgin, private, 22 March 1848, in Elgin, *Elgin-Grey Papers,* 1:125–27.
8. Donald Creighton, *John A. Macdonald: The Young Politician* (Toronto: Macmillan, 1952),136–38; John Charles Dent, *The Last Forty Years: Canada Since the Union of 1841* (Toronto: George Virtue, 1881), 2:149–55.
9. Speech by Lord Elgin, 16 October 2003, University of the Fraser Valley, Abbotsford, British Columbia.
10. Government of Canada Department of Justice, British North America Act, 1867, 30–31 Vict. c. 3 (U.K.), http://canada.justice.gc.ca/eng/rp-pr/csj-sjc/constitution/lawreg-loireg/p1t11.html.
11. Cardwell to Monck, personal communication, 26 November 1864, Monck Papers, microfilm A 755, Library and Archives Canada.
12. Lord Stanley to Frederick Bruce, 23 March 1867, as quoted in C.P. Stacey, "Britain's Withdrawal from North America, 1864–1871," *Canadian Historical Review* 36, no. 3 (1955): 191.

13. Barbara J. Messamore, "Diplomacy or Duplicity? Lord Lisgar, John A. Macdonald, and the Treaty of Washington, 1871," *Journal of Imperial and Commonwealth History* 32, no. 2 (2004): 29–53.

14. Dufferin to Kimberley, personal communication, 25 April 1873 and 2 May 1873, Dufferin Papers, A 407, Library and Archives Canada.

15. Dufferin to Kimberley, personal communication, 15 May 1873, Dufferin Papers, A 407, Library and Archives Canada.

16. Lorne to Hicks-Beach, 3 December 1878, Lorne MS, A 717 Library and Archives Canada.

17. Hicks-Beach to Lorne, 31 December 1878, Lorne MS, A 717.

18. Lorne to Hicks-Beach, March 1879, Lorne MS, A 717.

19. Hicks-Beach to Lorne, 11 February 1879, Lorne MS, A 717.

20. Assent was withheld from two New Zealand bills after this period: the Asiatic Restriction Bill of 1896 and the 1910 Shipping and Seamen Amendment Bill. See John E. Martin, "Refusal of Assent — A Hidden Element of Constitutional History in New Zealand," *Victoria University of Wellington Law Review* 41, no. 1 (2010): 55.

21. Lansdowne to Lord Melgund, 4 July 1886, Canadian Papers of the 4th Earl of Minto, MS 12378, British Records Relating to America in Microform (BRRAM) series.

22. Mary Elizabeth Hallett, "The Fourth Earl Grey as Governor General of Canada, 1904–1911" (Ph.D. dissertation, University of London, 1970), 252–54.

23. As quoted by Paul Romney, *Getting It Wrong: How Canadians Forgot Their Past and Imperilled Confederation* (Toronto: University of Toronto Press, 1999), 172.

24. Lord Durham, *Lord Durham's Report, New Edition*, Janet Ajzenstat and Gerald M. Craig, eds. (Montreal and Kingston: McGill-Queen's University Press, 2006), 153.

25. L.F.S. Upton, "The Idea of Confederation: 1754–1858," in *The Shield of Achilles: Aspects of Canada in the Victorian Age*, W.L. Morton, ed. (Toronto: McClelland & Stewart, 1968), 186–202.

26. Ged Martin, *Britain and the Origins of Canadian Confederation, 1837– 67* (Vancouver: UBC Press, 1995), 94–95.

27. Minute by Herman Merivale, 31 August 1858 on Head to E. Bulwer-

Lytton, dispatch 108, 26 August 1858, CO 42/614, B 230, Library and Archives Canada.

28. James A. Gibson, "The Life of Sir Edmund Walker Head, Baronet" (D.Phil. thesis, Oxford University, 1938), 181–82.

29. Governor General's Address to the Legislative Assembly and Legislative Council, enclosed in Head to Lieutenant Governors of Nova Scotia, New Brunswick, Prince Edward Island and Newfoundland, 10 September 1858, CO 42/615, B 230, Library and Archives Canada.

30. Minute by E. Bulwer-Lytton on Head to E. Bulwer-Lytton, dispatch 108, 26 August 1858, 42/614, B 230, Library and Archives Canada.

31. E. Bulwer-Lytton to Head, 55, 10 September 1858, CO 42/614, B 229, Library and Archives Canada.

32. George Brown to Gordon Brown, 11 May 1863, as quoted in J.M.S. Careless, *Brown of the Globe* (Toronto: Macmillan, 1959), 2:93; Bruce Willard Hodgins, "The Political Career of John Sandfield Macdonald to the Fall of His Administration in March 1864" (Ph.D. thesis, Duke University, 1965), 371.

33. A printed pamphlet, *Ministerial Explanations,* issued by Parliament on June 23, 1864, described the goal of a federal arrangement and also explained the negotiations that led to the construction of the coalition. Perhaps unsurprisingly, little mention was made of Monck's role. Enclosure D, "Ministerial Explanations," printed pamphlet, 23 June 1864, Parliament of Canada, in Monck to Cardwell, dispatch 97, 30 June 1864, CO 42/641, B 458, Library and Archives Canada. Historical accounts similarly downplay or ignore Monck's intervention. See, for example, John Boyd, *Sir George Etienne Cartier, Bart. His Life and Times: A Political History of Canada from 1814 until 1873* (Toronto: Macmillan, 1914), 186–89. Boyd provides a detailed account of the process of coalition-building, but fails to mention Monck at all. Chester Martin, however, acknowledged that "it is clear from the correspondence of both [Monck and Brown] … that no direct personal influence outweighed the governor general's in bringing Brown into the coalition of 1864." See Chester Martin, "British Policy in Canadian Confederation," *Canadian Historical Review* 13, no. 1 (1932): 16.

34. Monck to George Brown, 21 June 1864, Monck Papers, A 757, Library and Archives Canada. This is also printed in Alexander Mackenzie, *The Life and Speeches of Hon. George Brown* (Toronto: Globe Printing Company, 1882), 96.

35. James Young, *Public Men and Public Life in Canada*, 2nd ed. (Toronto: William Briggs, 1912), 1:217.

36. Lord Monck, 6 June 1866, "Memorandum" to Executive Council, printed in Joseph Pope, *Memoirs of the Right Honourable Sir John Alexander Macdonald* (Ottawa: J. Durie & Son, 1894), 1:373.

37. Monck to Macdonald, 21 June 1866, in Pope, *Memoirs of the Right Honourable Sir John Alexander Macdonald*, 1:299.

38. W.L. Morton, "Lord Monck, His Friends, and the Nationalizing of the British Empire," *Character and Circumstance: Essays in Honour of Donald Grant Creighton*, John S. Moir, ed. (Toronto: Macmillan, 1970), 52.

39. Numerous sources acknowledge Gordon's role in initiating the Charlottetown Conference. See, for example, Francis W.P. Bolger, "The Charlottetown Conference and its Significance in Canadian History," *Canadian Historical Association Report* 27 (1960): 11–23; Christopher Moore, *1867: How the Fathers Made a Deal* (Toronto: McClelland & Stewart, 1998), 37.

40. Arthur Hamilton Gordon to the Duke of Newcastle, 19 December 1864, as quoted in *Settler Self-Government, 1840–1900: The Development of Representative and Responsible Government. Select Documents on the Constitutional History of the British Empire and Commonwealth*, Frederick Madden with David Fieldhouse, eds. (Westport, CT: Greenwood Press, 1990), 4:720.

41. As quoted by J.K. Chapman, "Arthur Hamilton Gordon," in *Dictionary of Canadian Biography*, http://biographi.ca/en/bio/gordon_arthur_hamilton_14E.html.

42. Monck to the Earl of Carnarvon, confidential, 7 September 1866, W.M. Whitelaw, "Lord Monck and the Canadian Constitution," *Canadian Historical Review* 21 (1940): 300–01.

43. As quoted by Ged Martin, "Introduction to the 2006 Edition," *The Confederation Debates in the Province of Canada, 1865*, 2nd ed., P.B. Waite, ed. (Montreal and Kingston: McGill-Queen's University Press, 2006), xxv.

44. As quoted by W.L. Morton, *The Critical Years: The Union of British North America, 1857–1873* (Toronto: McClelland & Stewart, 1964), 165.

45. As quoted by J.M.S. Careless, *Brown of the Globe* (Toronto: Macmillan, 1959), 2:171.

46. The 1865 Confederation debates in the Province of Canada ended with a resolution in favour of acceptance. It passed with ninety-one members in favour and thirty-three opposed. In Canada West, the vote was fifty-four in favour and eight opposed; in Canada East the vote was thirty-seven in favour to twenty-five opposed.

47. As quoted by A.I. Silver, *The French Canadian Idea of Confederation, 1864–1900*, 2nd ed. (Toronto: University of Toronto Press, 1997), 41.

48. As quoted by Silver, *The French Canadian Idea of Confederation, 1864–1900*, 45.

49. British North America Act, 1867, 30–31 Vict. c. 3 (UK).

50. Paul Cornell, *The Great Coalition, June 1864* (Ottawa: Canadian Historical Association, 1966), 3.

51. Barbara J. Messamore, "'The Line Over Which He Must Not Pass': Defining the Office of Governor General, 1878," *Canadian Historical Review* 86, no. 3 (2005): 453–83.

52. As quoted by Ged Martin, *Britain and the Origins of Canadian Confederation, 1837–67* (Vancouver: UBC Press, 1995), 290.

2 |

Royalty and the Arts in Canada

Carolyn Harris

On February 6, 2017, Queen Elizabeth II reached her blue sapphire jubilee, having reigned for sixty-five years in the United Kingdom, Canada, and other Commonwealth realms. While the name of the Queen's great-great-grandmother, Queen Victoria, became synonymous with her era, the description of the current Queen's reign as a "new Elizabethan age" did not endure for more than a few years after her accession in 1952 and coronation in 1953.[1] Elizabeth II has reigned over a period of such profound social, political, and cultural change that the unifying themes that will determine her historical legacy remain a matter of debate. The Queen has been praised for her roles as Head of the Commonwealth, a politically impartial constitutional monarch, the leader of a "service monarchy" devoted to philanthropy, and matriarch of a multi-generational royal family that represents the future of the dynasty.

In a 2012 biography written on the occasion of the Queen's Diamond Jubilee, journalist Robert Hardman speculated that the Queen will have another lasting legacy: the "curator monarch."[2] Since the reign of King Henry VIII, the Queen and her predecessors have accumulated a vast collection of between seventy-five thousand and one million paintings, decorative objects, and sculptures.[3] For centuries, these cultural treasures were accessible to a privileged few and managed by a small curatorial staff, but the Queen has ensured that the Royal Collection has become accessible to a wide international audience.

In addition to displaying items from the collection at Buckingham Palace, Windsor Castle, and Holyroodhouse, the Queen has approved touring exhibitions that have showcased the Royal Collection to an international audience and loaned individual pieces to museums and galleries abroad. Richard Dorment, art critic for the *Daily Telegraph* newspaper in Britain, praised the Queen's expansion of public access to the Royal Collection, writing at the time of her Diamond Jubilee in 2012, "It is the Queen who set up specialist conservation studios for the care and preservation of paintings, furniture, frames, armour, textiles, ceramics, works on paper, and bookbinding. She is also renowned for her generosity in lending works of art from the Royal Collection to other institutions here and abroad."[4] Dorment observed that most major international exhibitions include pieces from the Royal Collection, as the Queen's policy is to agree to all requests from reputable cultural institutions for loans of art works that are in a suitable condition to travel.

The Queen's role as curator monarch has exerted a profound impact on Canadian art and culture, building upon centuries of patronage of Canadian artists, architects, and cultural institutions by past generations of royalty, most notably members of the royal family who resided in Canada for years at a time. A number of Canada's past royal residents, including Queen Victoria's daughter Princess Louise and granddaughter Princess Patricia, were accomplished artists in their own right who raised the profile of Canadian galleries by founding new cultural institutions, attending events, submitting their pieces for judgment in Canadian exhibitions, and donating their work. Over the course of her reign, Queen Elizabeth II has loaned or donated art to Canadian cultural institutions and acquired works by Canadian artists for the Royal Collection, expanding the scope of royal involvement in the arts in Canada and setting precedents for future generations in the royal family.

The patronage of art and culture was part of the identity of English and French monarchs from the time of their first engagement with the lands and peoples of North America. Medieval monarchs were valued for their ability to lead troops into battle and administer justice, but a sixteenth-century king or queen was also expected to preside over a cultured court frequented by artists and writers who helped shape the monarch's image. In England, King Henry VIII and members of his family were painted by Hans Holbein, while Henry's contemporary, King François I of France, provided Leonardo da Vinci with a residence in the Loire Valley, Clos Lucé, a short distance from the royal palace at Amboise.[5] The artistic output of the English and French royal courts was intended for an international audience. Diplomacy between monarchs included exchanges of portraits, and artists travelled widely to seek royal patronage.

European engagement with First Nations leaders prompted early examples of royal art patronage in a Canadian context. In 1710, Queen Anne invited "the four Kings of Canada" — three Mohawk chiefs from the Iroquois Confederacy, including Peter Brant (grandfather of Joseph Brant), and a Mahican leader of the Algonquin peoples — to Britain as part of diplomatic mission to negotiate a continued alliance against France. Anne commissioned four majestic portraits of her visitors by the Dutch artist Jan Verelst,[6] which were displayed at Kensington Palace in London until the current Queen's reign. In 1977, when Elizabeth II toured Canada on the occasion of her Silver Jubilee, she presented the paintings to the National Archives of Canada. In 2010, the images appeared on a Canadian postage stamp to commemorate the three-hundredth anniversary of the meeting between Queen Anne and the four kings.[7] In 2017, the paintings went on display in the new Canadian History Hall at the Canadian Museum of History in Gatineau.[8]

Early visits by members of the royal family to what is now Canada focused on military matters rather than cultural patronage. The only recorded interaction between the future King William IV and an artist on the voyage of the HMS *Pegasus*, which visited Newfoundland and Nova Scotia in 1787 as part of a larger voyage, was an altercation with a German landscape painter in the Caribbean who offended the prince.[9]

William's younger brother, Prince Edward, Duke of Kent and Strathearn (Queen Victoria's father), spent the 1790s in Canada, eventually becoming commander-in-chief of the British North American forces. Edward's time in Canada coincided with an expansion of European-inspired fine art and architecture in Lower Canada (now Quebec), as church-building and portrait-commissioning expanded.[10] Edward himself tried his hand at painting, enclosing a watercolour of members of the Mi'kmaq First Nation in one of his letters.[11] The lasting aesthetic impact of the Duke of Kent's time in Canada, however, was architecture. In Halifax, he commissioned improvements to Fort George, including the town clock, and the city saw an expansion of new building projects in the classical Palladian style of the period. Edward himself has been credited with designing the floor plan of

St. George's (Round) Church, which received a generous donation of £200 from Edward's father, King George III.[12] Royal patronage of St. George's Round Church continues to the present day, as Charles, Prince of Wales, who attended services there in 1983 with his first wife, Diana, Princess of Wales, contributed to fundraising efforts after the building was damaged by fire in 1994.

In Quebec City, the Duke of Kent ordered extensive renovations to his summer estate at Montmorency Manor, near Montmorency Falls. Following his return in the United Kingdom in 1799, Edward became a patron of Edward Angell, who would be the first architect in Canada to advertise himself as "a House Surveyor and Architect to lay out building estate, draw ground plans, sections and elevations to order"[13] after immigrating to York (Toronto) in 1820. Despite this royal patronage, Angell had difficulty securing commissions for building projects and instead became involved in civil engineering projects, before returning to London in 1824 to found the Canada Land Agency.[14] The current Queen is a patron of the Royal Architectural Institute of Canada, continuing a two-hundred-year-old tradition of royalty providing patronage for Canadian architects, and the Prince of Wales is well-known for his interest in architecture.

The arts first assumed a prominent role in a Canadian royal tour in 1860, when Queen Victoria's eldest son, Albert Edward, the future King Edward VII, toured British North America, then the United States. In common with his parents and eight siblings, Albert Edward was an amateur artist with a keen aesthetic sense. As a child, he attended the Great Exhibition of the Works of Industry of All Nations in London, which provided an introduction to Canadian material culture and manufacturing. The Canadian contributions to the Great Exhibition included an enormous canoe, hanging between two galleries, "calculated to hold a crew of twenty men, with their stock of provisions and necessaries. It was made from the bark of the white birch, and was so light that it could be carried with ease by its crew."[15] Attendees noted the blend of English and Indigenous influences in the Canadian display[16] and this aesthetic may well have shaped Albert Edward's perception of the arts in Canada.

Albert Edward stated in a speech delivered at the Montreal Exhibition in 1860, "I am not ignorant of the high position obtained by Canada in the

Great Exhibition of 1851 … and carrying out the design of the memorable undertaking this smaller … but to Canada most interesting collection, of the products of your land, and of works of art and industry, has my entire sympathy and claims my best wishes for its success."[17] The prince continued to engage with cultural institutions over the course of his tour, opening Canada's first public art gallery during his time in Hamilton.

Over the course of the 1860 tour, Albert Edward expressed a particular interest in First Nations art and material culture. The majority of the items that the Prince acquired on the tour were gifts, including baskets filled with "Indian work" from the Mississauga people, but he also purchased moccasins in Sydney, Nova Scotia, and beadwork in Saint John, New Brunswick.[18] In his book about the tour, historian Ian Radforth describes the prince's acquisitions in British North America as shopping for "souvenirs" in common with other British travellers to North America;[19] but Albert Edward's subsequent travels as Prince of Wales suggest a lasting interest in collecting local art from various regions of the British Empire and in comparative artistic traditions. During his tour of India in 1875–76, he visited the School of Art in Bombay (now Mumbai) and expressed delight at receiving two paintings by the artist Ravi Varna, who combined Indian and Western techniques in his work.[20] After succeeding to the throne as King Edward VII, Albert Edward displayed the First Nations art that he acquired on his 1860 tour at the Swiss Cottage museum at Osborne House on the Isle of Wight.[21]

The tradition of collecting and curating Indigenous art in the Royal Collection continues to the present day. In 2014, Holyroodhouse in Edinburgh hosted an exhibition, "The Commonwealth: Gifts from the Queen," in honour of the Commonwealth Games in Scotland. The display included Indigenous art and allowed visitors to the palace to see pieces presented to the Queen in Canada. Gifts on display included a carved and painted totem pole by Simon Charlie presented to the Queen on her 2002 Golden Jubilee tour of Canada and a felt and wool hanging by Jessie Oonark presented in 1973 by the Inuit people of the Northwest Territories.[22] Gifts from royal tours are displayed to the public on regular occasions, most recently in the summer of 2017, when Buckingham Palace exhibited gifts from over one hundred countries to commemorate the Queen's sixty-five years on the throne.[23]

Albert Edward's 1860 Canadian tour also provided opportunities for painters and photographers, as the Government of the United Province of Canada presented the prince with artwork as official gifts, a tradition that continues to the present day. The prince acquired at least two paintings in British North America, a watercolour by C.J. Way entitled *The Prince's Squadron Off Gaspé Basin*, a purchase from a display by the Art Association of Montreal, and a portrait of Mary Christianne Paul, a Mi'kmaq woman, by William Gush, a gift from the City of Halifax. Albert Edward also received a collection of landscape photographs from Montreal's most prominent photographer of the period, William Notman.[24] The royal tour was an occasion for an outpouring of commemorative paintings by Canadian artists, including *The Arrival of the Prince of Wales at Toronto, September 1860* by William Armstrong,[25] which is now in the collection of the National Gallery of Canada.

After the death of Queen Victoria's consort, Prince Albert of Saxe-Coburg and Gotha, in 1861, the Queen retreated into comparative seclusion for a number of years and her adult children assumed the role of cultural patron expected of the monarch.[26] All three of Albert Edward's younger brothers and one of his five sisters spent time in Canada over the course of the late nineteenth and early twentieth century. In 1878, Queen Victoria's son-in-law, John Campbell, Lord Lorne, the future Duke of Argyll, became the fourth governor general of Canada since Confederation, serving in that role from 1878 to 1883. He travelled to Canada with his wife, Princess Louise Caroline Alberta, the first female member of the royal family to cross the Atlantic. Louise's presence in Canada provided increased opportunities for patronage of female artists and philanthropic organizations, benefiting women's education and vocational training.[27]

Louise was the first member of the royal family to attend a public educational institution and receive formal training as an artist alongside her peers. In 1863, she studied sculpture at the National Art Training School (now the Royal College of Art) in London. She submitted her sculptures and paintings to art exhibitions and expressed concern that her rank prevented honest critical appraisals of her work.[28] Her marriage to Lorne in 1871 provided her with opportunities to engage with the wider artistic community in London. During her time in Canada, she encouraged the development of national institutions that would allow Canadian artists to exhibit their work and be recognized without leaving for the United States or United Kingdom. On Victoria Day 1879, Lorne and Louise opened a new gallery for the Art Association of Montreal, when Lorne called for "a general art union in the country."[29] During their time in Canada, Lorne and Louise were instrumental in the founding of the Royal Canadian Academy of Arts in 1880 and the National Gallery of Canada in 1882.

During their first year at Rideau Hall, where Louise set up a studio for her own painting, Lorne and Louise lobbied prominent Canadians, requesting donations of both money and paintings for the first exhibition by the new Academy of Arts. In June 1880, Queen Victoria granted permission for the organization to become the Royal Canadian Academy of Arts, and it was officially incorporated by an act of Parliament in 1882. The academy would bring together painters, sculptors, architects, engravers, and industrial designers, and provide them with a space to exhibit their work and receive feedback from their fellow artists. Louise planned to exhibit a variety of works in the academy's first exhibition, including flower studies and a drawing of her sister-in-law.[30] In addition to her own work as an artist, Louise's social circle included other female artists such as the sculptor Henrietta Montalba, who visited her in Canada.[31] The academy allowed female artists to be members, accepting the Toronto painter Charlotte Schreiber as a founding member and displaying one of her works, *The Croppy Boy*, in the new National Gallery.[32] When Louise and Lorne opened the first Canadian National Exhibition in Toronto, the princess visited a display of works by women artists and acquired pieces by female artists for her own personal collection.

The involvement of royalty in the development of national arts institutions helped bring together provincial art organizations with a history of professional rivalries. Although the royal couple persuaded members of the Art Association of Montreal and the Ontario Society of Artists to join this new national organization, they soon found themselves mediating disputes between the members. "There is a marvellous amount of bitterness and bad language," Lorne wrote. "Half the artists are ready just now to choke the other half with their paint brushes."[33]

While this process of bringing together regional artists into a national organization was underway, Louise suffered an accident that limited her involvement in the future development of the National Gallery. On February 14, 1880, Louise and Lorne were travelling from the Senate Chamber to Rideau Hall in Ottawa when their sleigh overturned and horses bolted, dragging the party along the roadway. Lorne reported that Louise "has been much hurt, and it is a wonder that her skull was not fractured."[34] She would spend long periods convalescing in Europe and Bermuda during the remainder of Lorne's term as governor general.

Louise was still recovering from her injuries when the Royal Canadian Academy of Arts opened its first exhibition at Ottawa's Clarendon Hotel on March 6, 1880, and she was unable to attend. Nevertheless, she continued to take an interest in the collection, insisting that Lorne bring the paintings to her bedside so that she could view them before the official event. The opening received strong reviews, with the *Ottawa Citizen* observing that the new Academy would "elevate incalculably the art of Canada."[35]

Lorne and Louise arranged for the gallery to find its first permanent home, in a remodelled builders' workshop on Parliament Hill, attached to the Supreme Court of Canada. Despite Louise's decreased visibility in Canadian society during the final years of Lorne's tenure as governor general, she remained a popular figure with Canadian artists for her support of the development of the arts in Canada. In 1930, the Royal Canadian Academy of Arts presented her with a silver scroll in honour of the organization's fiftieth anniversary.[36]

In addition to her role as a patron of the National Gallery and Royal Canadian Academy of Arts, Louise donated her own works to Canadian institutions. Her portrait of her friend Henrietta Montalba hangs in the National Gallery and her statue of her mother, Queen Victoria, stands on the McGill University campus. Louise was also interested in photography and her Canadian albums are part of the collection at Library and Archives Canada.

Louise's niece, Princess Patricia, shared both her artistic talent and her determination to submit her work for critical appraisal. She resided in Canada from 1911 to 1916 while her father, Queen Victoria's third son, Prince Arthur, Duke of Connaught, served as governor general. As Patricia's mother, Louise Margaret of Prussia, Duchess of Connaught, suffered from recurring ill health, the Princess often acted as her father's hostess at Rideau Hall and achieved a high public profile in Canada, even appearing on the one-dollar bill in 1917. Today, Patricia's best known cultural contribution in Canada is her design and creation of the regimental flag, or "Ric-A-Dam-Doo," for Princess Patricia's Canadian Light Infantry: a crimson background with a royal blue centre and the gold initials "V. P." for "Victoria Patricia."[37]

During her time in Canada, however, Patricia was just as well known as an artist and supporter of Canadian cultural institutions, following the precedents set by Princess Louise. Patricia's father, the Duke of Connaught, opened a new Museum of the Art Association of Montreal (now the Montreal Museum of Fine Arts) in 1912, and became a patron of the Royal Canadian Academy of Arts. A 1931 volume about Canada's governors general recalled, "Princess Patricia is a devotee of Art, and during her stay in Canada, some of her paintings were frequently shown and attracted attention at different Art Exhibitions held there."[38] Patricia's participation in art exhibitions provided opportunities to engage with other artists and obtain commissions for them. In 1913, Patricia exhibited her work alongside the artist Gertrude des Clayes in a Royal Canadian Academy of Arts exhibition.[39] Des Clayes later painted the princess's portrait. The work was acquired by a private collector, then donated to the Montreal Museum of Fine Arts in 1986.

One of Patricia's paintings, depicting ice breaking up on the Ottawa River, is part of the collection of the Art Gallery of Ontario. She presented two other paintings to the National Gallery of Canada, which her parents visited during the first months of their time in Canada. Patricia's paintings received critical praise during her time in Canada. The *Montreal Gazette's* coverage of the twenty-ninth Spring Exhibition of the Montreal Art Association in 1912 opened with the headline, "A Princess Exhibits," then stated in the first paragraph, "… this year there is added interest by reason of six canvases from the brush of H.R.H. Princess Patricia of Connaught. The paintings … are entirely meritorious, showing sound drawing and good color. Their merit, apart from all other considerations, wins them the place which they occupy."[40]

Patricia's artistic output continues to appear as the centrepiece of Canadian art exhibitions to the present day. In 2014, eight of Patricia's paintings were displayed at the Bank of Montreal Centre in Calgary as part of the largest annual exhibition of western Canadian art. Cheyne Parkinson, chair of the Western Showcase Committee, explained, "The exhibit comes at a fitting time, as the Princess Patricia's Canadian Light Infantry celebrates their 100th Anniversary."[41] More than one hundred years after she appeared on the Canadian one-dollar bill, Princess Patricia's work continues to inform the arts in Canada.

The most recent royal couple to reside in Rideau Hall, the Earl and Countess of Athlone, governor general and vice-regal consort from 1940 until 1946, continued the commitment to the arts in Canada displayed by Princess Louise and Lord Lorne, the Duke and Duchess of Connaught, and Princess Patricia. Princess Alice, Countess of Athlone, a granddaughter of Queen Victoria through her father, Prince Leopold, Duke of Albany, described the royal portraits in Halifax's Province House in her memoirs, including a painting of her great-grandfather, the Duke of Kent, writing, "There was also a small full-length portrait of the Duke of Kent as slim, elegant young man in the 7th Fusiliers."[42] While Louise and Patricia devoted their efforts to painting and sculpture, Alice supported the theatre and classical music and frequently sponsored and attended performances in Ottawa.

On October 29, 1940, the *Ottawa Journal* announced the "12th Tremblay [concert] series under the Distinguished Patronage and in the Immediate Presence of His Excellency the Governor General and H.R.H. the Princess Alice, Countess of Athlone."[43] The actress Amelia Hall, who directed plays at the Ottawa Drama League (now the Ottawa Little Theatre) during the Second World War, recalled Alice taking a close interest in the costumes, including hats for a 1944 staging of J.B. Priestley's *When We Are Married* that "were very much admired by Princess Alice, Countess of Athlone, wife of Canada's wartime Governor General, when she came backstage. (It had been a benefit for the Women's Naval Auxiliary)."[44] The blend of the performing arts and fundraising for wartime relief continued throughout the Earl and Countess of Athlone's time in Canada, providing opportunities for theatrical companies and musicians.

Members of the royal family continue to be patrons of theatre and classical music in Canada to the present day and attend performances during royal tours. The Queen is patron of the Manitoba Theatre and the Royal Winnipeg Ballet. Charles, Prince of Wales, became patron of the Regina Symphony Orchestra in 2008 and has attended performances during his Canadian tours, most recently in 2012, when he represented the Queen in Canada for her Diamond Jubilee. Charles's youngest brother, Prince Edward, Earl of Wessex, is patron of the Globe Theatre in Regina and often incorporates the arts into his frequent working visits to Canada. In 2012, Sophie, Countess of Wessex, attended the Toronto International Film Festival and a reception at the lieutenant governor of Ontario's suite honouring the Canadian film industry.

During the current Queen's reign, Canadian artists have ensured that there is a lasting Canadian presence in the Royal Collection. In 1985, the Canadian Society of Painters in Watercolour celebrated its sixtieth anniversary. When plans to place a juried collection of sixty watercolours in a Canadian cultural institution proved unworkable for financial reasons, the Queen was approached through the Keeper of the Queen's Pictures with a proposal to expand the Royal Collection's Canadian holdings through the acquisition of these watercolours. The Queen accepted the portfolio at Ontario House in London in 1985. The Prince of Wales has taken a particular interest in the collection and attended an exhibition of the now seventy-five paintings at Canada House in London in 2001.[45]

Future reigns may see expanded royal art patronage in Canada, as the younger members of the royal family are closely engaged with the arts and philanthropy. The Prince of Wales is an amateur watercolourist, with a great enthusiasm for Canada's landscapes. He is an honorary member of the Canadian Society of Landscape Artists and of the Canadian Society of Painters in Watercolour.[46] His cousin, Lady Sarah Chatto (daughter of the Queen's late sister, Princess Margaret), is a professional painter who has donated works to charitable fundraisers.[47] In the next generation, Catherine, Duchess of Cambridge, holds an art history degree from the University of St. Andrews and is a member of the Royal Photographic Society, which she joined in 2017. She often takes the official photographs of her children for the media.[48] One of Catherine's major philanthropic interests is children's mental health and she has promoted initiatives that utilize art therapy in the treatment of mental illness.[49]

The arts, especially works by Indigenous artists, have been integrated into the Duke and Duchess of Cambridge's Canadian tours. During their 2016 tour of British Columbia, William and Catherine dedicated a new Indigenous art exhibition commemorating the University of British Columbia's centennial and viewed the witness blanket made by Kwakiutl artist Carey Newman to narrate the trauma of residential school survivors.[50] The royal family also maintains a close personal connection to the Royal Collection. The Queen's granddaughter Princess Eugenie completed an internship there in 2013 after earning a degree in English and the history of art from Newcastle University.[51]

Among the celebrations for the 150th anniversary of Confederation was an exhibition of Canadian pieces from the Royal Collection at Canada House in London, which had been opened by King George V and Queen Mary in 1925. The exhibition, inaugurated in July 2017 by Queen Elizabeth, included photographs of the Queen presiding over key events in Canada over the past sixty-five years. Oliver Urquhart-Irvine, royal librarian and assistant keeper of the Royal Archives, explained, "She was there. She knows the material better than I do."[52] There were also works from Canadian artists that had been presented as gifts to members of the royal family, including *Klee Wyck* by Emily Carr, which the artist gave to Princess Elizabeth and Princess Margaret in 1941. The Queen's presence at Canada House to view the exhibition demonstrates her long commitment to making the Royal Collection more accessible and showcasing the work of Canadian artists.

While the Prince of Wales and the Duchess of Cornwall toured Iqaluit, Ontario, and the National Capital region for the 150th anniversary of Confederation, the Queen, who has scaled back her overseas travel in recent years, chose to mark this milestone in Canada's history by meeting with Governor General David Johnston and other Canadians at Canada House and immersing herself in Canadian history and culture. One hundred and fifty years since Canada's Confederation and sixty-five years since she succeeded to the throne, Queen Elizabeth II continues to be the curator monarch, building on a long history of involvement in the arts in the Canada by past generations of the royal family. The continued close ties between the royal family, the creation of fine art, and the Royal Collection suggest a dynamic future for royal involvement in the arts in Canada.

Notes

1. Elizabeth Longford, *The Queen: The Life of Elizabeth II* (New York: Ballantine Books, 1984), 198.
2. Robert Hardman, *Our Queen* (London: Hutchison, 2011), 260.
3. Ibid., 261. The stated number of objects varies widely because of the different definitions of what constitutes a single piece in the collection. As Jonathan Marsden, director of the Royal Collection, explained to Robert Hardman, "It depends on whether you count the cup and saucer separately."
4. Richard Dorment, "The Royal Collection: Not Only for Queen but Also for Country," *Telegraph*, May 28, 2012.
5. See David Howarth, *Images of Rule: Art and Politics in the English Renaissance, 1485–1649* (Berkeley: University of California Press, 1997), passim, and Robert Jean Knecht, *Francis I* (Cambridge: Cambridge University Press, 1984), 264–65.
6. James Anderson Winn, *Queen Anne: Patroness of Arts* (Oxford: Oxford University Press, 2014), 525.
7. Nathan Tidridge, *Canada's Constitutional Monarchy* (Toronto: Dundurn, 2011), 132.
8. John Geddes, "How Indigenous Stories Are Taking Centre Stage in Ottawa," *Maclean's*, June 30, 2017.
9. Hans Rollman, "Prince William Henry in Newfoundland," Memorial University, www.mun.ca/rels/ang/texts/pwh.htm.
10. Russell Harper, *Painting in Canada: A History*, 2nd ed. (Toronto: University of Toronto Press, 1981), 67.
11. Nathan Tidridge, *Prince Edward, Duke of Kent: Father of the Canadian Crown* (Toronto: Dundurn, 2013).
12. Robert Tuck, *Churches of Nova Scotia* (Toronto: Dundurn, 2003), 43.
13. Eric Arthur, *Toronto: No Mean City*, 3rd ed., revised (Toronto: University of Toronto Press, 2003), 75.
14. Ibid., 241.
15. Joseph Nash, Louis Haghe, and David Roberts, *Dickinsons' Comprehensive Pictures of the Great Exhibition of 1851, from the Originals Painted for*

H.R.H. Prince Albert (London: Dickinson, Brothers, 1854).

16. The Committee of General Literature and Education, *Notes and Sketches of Lessons on Subjects Connected with the Great Exhibition* (London: 1852), 149.

17. Robert Cellem, *Visit of His Royal Highness The Prince of Wales to the British North American Provinces and United States in the Year 1860* (Toronto: Henry Rowsell, 1861), 162.

18. Ian Radforth, *Royal Spectacle: The 1860 Visit of the Prince of Wales to Canada and the United States* (Toronto: University of Toronto Press, 2004, 2012), 306–12.

19. Ibid.

20. Partha Mitter, *Art and Nationalism in Colonial India, 1850–1922: Occidental Orientations* (Cambridge: Cambridge University Press, 1995), 180.

21. Radforth, *Royal Spectacle*, 309.

22. The Royal Collection Trust, "Gifts to the Queen," 2014, www.royalcollection.org.uk/collection/themes/exhibitions/commonwealth-display/palace-of-holyroodhouse/gifts-to-the-queen#/.

23. Sophie Hirsh, "Buckingham Palace to Display the Extravagant Gifts Queen Elizabeth Has Received," *Condé Nast Traveler*, April 3, 2017.

24. Radforth, *Royal Spectacle*, 307–08.

25. Dennis Reid, *A Concise History of Canadian Painting* (Oxford: Oxford University Press, 1989), 71.

26. See Désirée de Chair, "Queen Victoria's Children and Sculpture (c. 1860–1900): Collectors, Makers, Patrons" (Ph.D. thesis, University of Warwick, 2015).

27. See Carolyn Harris, "Royalty at Rideau Hall: Lord Lorne, Princess Louise and the Emergence of the Canadian Crown," in D. Michael Jackson and Philippe Lagassé, eds., *Canada and the Crown: Essays on Constitutional Monarchy* (Montreal and Kingston: McGill-Queen's University Press, 2014).

28. Robert M. Stamp, *Royal Rebels: Princess Louise and the Marquis of Lorne* (Toronto: Dundurn Press, 1988), 70–71.

29. Stamp, *Royal Rebels*, 142.

30. Elizabeth Longford, *Darling Loosy: Letters to Princess Louise, 1856–1939* (London: Wiedenfeld and Nicholson, 1991), 47.

31. Jehanne Wake, *Princess Louise: Queen Victoria's Unconventional Daughter* (London: Collins, 1988), 229.

32. Sandra Gwyn, *The Private Capital: Ambition and Love in the Age of Macdonald and Laurier* (Toronto: McClelland & Stewart, 1984), 212.

33. Stamp, *Royal Rebels*, 158.

34. R.H. Hubbard, *Rideau Hall: An Illustrated History of Government House from Victorian Times Until the Present Day* (Montreal and Kingston: McGill-Queen's University Press, 1977), 57.

35. Stamp, *Royal Rebels*, 158.

36. Ibid., 159.

37. Edward C. Russell, *Customs and Traditions of the Canadian Armed Forces* (Ottawa: Deneau and Greenberg, 1980), 172.

38. L.J. Lemieux, *The Governors-General of Canada, 1608–1931* (London: Lake and Bell, 1931), 297.

39. Various Authors, *Catalogue of the Thirty-Fifth Annual Exhibition of the Royal Canadian Academy of Arts in the Art Association Galleries, 679 Sherbrooke St. West, Montreal, November the Twentieth, 1913*, https://archive.org/details/catalogueofexhib13nati.

40. "Art Opening, a Social Event: A Princess Exhibits," *Montreal Gazette*, March 15, 1912, 4.

41. Canadian Army, "Calgary Stampede Showcases Military Artwork," July 22, 2014, www.army-armee.forces.gc.ca/en/news-publications/national-news-details-no-menu.page?doc=calgary-stampede-showcases-military-artwork/hxukur8f.

42. Princess Alice, Countess of Athlone, *For My Grandchildren* (Chatham, Kent: W. and J. Mackay, 1966), 260.

43. *Ottawa Journal*, October 29, 1940, 12.

44. Amelia Hall, *Life Before Stratford: The Memoirs of Amelia Hall* (Toronto: Dundurn, 1990), 47–48.

45. *The Canadian Society of Painters in Watercolour*, "Royal Collection," http://198.96.117.138/index.php/royal-collection/.

46. "The Prince of Wales's Relationship with Canada," *The Prince of Wales and the Duchess of Cornwall*, www.princeofwales.gov.uk/features/canada.

47. Emily Banks, "Actress Sophie Thompson Donates Artwork to National Brain Appeal Exhibition," *Ham&High*, October 25, 2016, www.

hamhigh.co.uk/news/actress-sophie-thompson-donates-artwork-to-national-brain-appeal-exhibition-1-4749146.

48. Gordon Rayner, "Duchess of Cambridge's Family Portraits Earn Her Membership of Royal Photographic Society," *Telegraph*, January 3, 2017.

49. Natalie Evans, "Kate Middleton to Meet Young People Helped by Art Therapy Charity at National Portrait Gallery," *Mirror*, April 24, 2013.

50. Liam Britten, "Reconciliation and the Royals: William and Kate to View Witness Blanket," *CBC News*, September 18, 2016.

51. Camilla Tominey, "Hard-Working Princess Eugenie Goes to Derby with Her New Boss (The Queen!)," *Express*, June 2, 2013.

52. Gregory Katz, "Queen Visits Canada House to Mark Confederation," *Globe and Mail*, July 19, 2017.

3 |

Vimy and the Role of Canada's Monarchy[1]

Robert E. Hawkins

In 2017 Canadians marked the 150th anniversary of Canada's Confederation and the 100th anniversary of the Battle of Vimy Ridge. It is an ideal time, therefore, to reflect upon the part that the monarchy played at the time of that battle and continues to play in its commemoration, and to consider what this indicates about the future role of Canada's Crown.

Easter Sunday, April 8, 1917, was a beautiful spring day in northern France.[2] The good weather was especially welcome after the coldest winter in forty years. That evening, nearly a hundred thousand soldiers, from four divisions of the Canadian Expeditionary Force, scrambled down into the trenches below Vimy Ridge to await the dawn. The weather quickly turned cold and drizzly as wind and rain blew in. Snow accumulated along the ridge. The men were chilled to the bone.

Three months earlier, the commander of the four Canadian divisions, Lieutenant-General Sir Julian Byng, of the British Army, had sent Major-General Arthur Currie, of the First Canadian Division, to a series of lectures given by the French army on tactics that the French had developed for the Battle of Verdun. Currie reported back on the importance of aerial reconnaissance, the use of artillery, and the need for extensive troop training. The Canadian soldiers were then drilled in French farm fields set up to resemble the Vimy terrain so that they would be ready to execute the minute-by-minute plans for taking the ridge. They were meticulously prepared for the momentous events that they knew daybreak would bring.

At precisely 5:30 a.m. on Easter Monday, April 9, more than three thousand pieces of Canadian artillery roared to mark the start of the battle. One Canadian infantryman later said that he felt that if he had put his finger up he would have "touched a ceiling of sound."[3] On cue, the Canadian soldiers moved from their trenches. They stayed close behind a "creeping barrage" of field-gun fire that provided cover for them. The platoons advanced at a rate of one hundred yards every three minutes. They moved forward, not in a single line, but rather leapfrogging beside each other, doing the "Vimy Glide" through the muck, the barbed wire, the pock-marked fields, and the enemy machine-gun nests. By noon on April 9, the ridge was in the hands of the Canadians, except for its highest point, Hill 145, where the Vimy Memorial now stands. That hill was captured the next day and the entire operation was completed by April 12.

The Battle of Vimy Ridge was a great victory for the Canadian army. Its soldiers earned a reputation as an elite fighting force. They succeeded where the French twice, and the British once, had failed to capture the ridge.[4] Vimy was the first time all four Canadian divisions, with soldiers from every part of the country, fought as a cohesive formation on the same battlefield. Even though 60 percent of the soldiers were recent immigrants to Canada from Britain, they fought, and won, as Canadians.[5] Brigadier-General Alexander Ross, who was six years old when he emigrated from Scotland to Silton, Saskatchewan, and who commanded the 28th Battalion at Vimy, made the following observation on the fiftieth anniversary of the battle: "It was Canada from the Atlantic to the Pacific on parade. I thought then, and I think today, that in those few minutes I witnessed the birth of the nation."[6]

The exact moment of the birth of a nation is something for historians to debate. What is not open for debate is that Canadians felt a great sense of national pride at the time of the victory and subsequently. Canada, still a new country, gained a reputation, in its own right, on the world's stage. The *New York Tribune* wrote that Canada had fielded a better army than Napoleon's;[7] a French newspaper spoke of "Canada's Easter gift to France."[8] But the victory was secured at a great cost. Canadians suffered 90 percent of the casualties at Vimy.[9] Of the force Canada fielded, 3,598 soldiers never came home; 7,004 were wounded.[10] April 9, 1917, is still the bloodiest day in Canada's military history.[11]

At the start of the war, King George V made the following observation as the first Canadian troops arrived overseas: "I shall follow with interest the progress and work of my Canadians."[12] The King was as good as his word.

In the early morning of April 10, 1917, after most of Vimy Ridge had been captured the previous day, he wrote: "The whole Empire will rejoice at the news of yesterday's successful operations. Canada will be proud that the taking of the coveted Vimy Ridge has fallen to the lot of her troops. I heartily congratulate ... all who have taken part in this splendid achievement."[13]

The King visited combat zones on six occasions during the First World War. On each occasion he spent time with the Canadian troops. On July 11, 1917, three months after the battle, he visited Vimy. Despite considerable personal danger from enemy shelling, he spent an hour and a quarter, rather than the planned twenty minutes, in the field. He warmly praised the "splendid valor of the soldiers of the Dominion."[14] A photographer captured the moment when George V paused at the grave of Lieutenant Lionel Eliot. Eliot, from Goderich, Ontario, died in the April 9 assault. The graveside photo of the King, head bowed, was published in newspapers throughout the Empire and became a symbol of Canadian sacrifice. The next day, the King knighted Arthur Currie on the battlefield. Shortly after that, Sir Arthur Currie was made the new commander-in-chief of the Canadian Expeditionary Force, the first Canadian to be appointed to lead the Canadian Army.

Lieutenant-General Currie (middle) and His Majesty King George V (left) tour the Vimy Ridge battlefield in July 1917 with General Horne (right).

Of the four recipients of the Victoria Cross for gallantry in the face of the enemy at Vimy, only Captain Thain MacDowell, from Brockville, Ontario, survived the war. With the assistance of two runners, and by giving the impression that he had with him a superior force, he entered a dugout and held two enemy officers and seventy-five of their men. For this, he received his Victoria Cross from King George V at Buckingham Palace in the summer of 1917.

William Johnson Milne was one of the three soldiers who received his Victoria Cross posthumously. Earlier in the war, he had enlisted as a twenty-four-year-old Scottish immigrant and labourer from a farm west of Moose Jaw, Saskatchewan. At Vimy, crawling on his hands and knees, he captured two enemy machine guns and killed their crews, with total disregard for his own safety.

One of those injured at Vimy was a Japanese fisherman, Sachimaro Morooka, who had settled in British Columbia and had enlisted in 1916 to avoid racial prejudice. Morooka was hospitalized for his injuries in England. When George V and Queen Mary visited the hospital in 1917, the King was fascinated by Morooka's background and asked him many questions: "Are you Japanese? Can you speak English? How is your wound? When did you join the Canadian army?"[15]

Four years later, in 1921, George V appointed the former commander-in-chief of the Canadian Expeditionary Force, Julian Byng, by then 1st Viscount Byng of Vimy, to be Canada's twelfth governor general. Also in 1921, George V selected red and white when he assumed separate Royal Arms for the Dominion of Canada. These colours, symbolic of blood and bandages, were meant to honour the sacrifices of Canadian soldiers during the First World War.[16] In 1965, they were adopted as the colours of the new Canadian flag.

For Canadians, Vimy is more than a defining moment, stained into a bloodied battlefield. It is also an eternal memory, sculpted into a limestone monument. The Vimy memorial is dedicated to the sixty thousand soldiers of the Canadian Expeditionary Force who never came home from the Great War. It is thought by many to be the most beautiful of the combatant nations' memorials.[17] The monument stands on Hill 145, the highest point on Vimy Ridge. Other battle sites were suggested, but Prime Minister

Mackenzie King believed Vimy to be "hallowed ground."[18] The 250 acres of surrounding fields were ceded in perpetuity by the Government of France in gratitude for the sacrifice made by the Canadian soldiers. The construction cost the immense Depression-era sum of approximately $1.5 million — more than $26 million in 2017 Canadian dollars.

Most war memorials consist of one central structure.[19] Vimy consists of two pylons, one with a carving of a maple leaf representing Canada, the other with a carving of a fleur-de-lis for France. A representation of it can be seen on the back of Canada's current $20 bill. The pylons reach 120 feet into the sky. They are visible for thirty-five miles from the French Douai plain once held by the enemy.

The design for Vimy was submitted in a competition won by Walter Allward in October 1921 from 160 entries. The second-place design, subsequently used for a Canadian war memorial at Ypres, was submitted by a Regina sculptor, Frederick Clemesha. The Vimy monument took fourteen years to build. The first two years were spent clearing the fields of undetonated shells, mines, and human remains. Unusually, Vimy is constructed of white stone. The much more common practice was to construct war memorials from grey stone, considered to represent the colour of battlefield terrain. The twenty sculptured figures making up the memorial do not glorify war. Instead, they represent justice, hope, charity, honour, faith, truth, and knowledge. Peace, the highest figure on the monument, reaches upward with a torch, reminiscent of the passing of the torch in John McRae's poem, "In Flanders Fields."

The monument includes one especially beautiful, especially haunting, sculpture. It is carved out of a single thirty-ton block of limestone. "Canada Bereft," also called "Mother Canada," stands alone on the northeastern wall of the monument. Her head rests gently on one hand. She stares downward at an empty sarcophagus. Her expression is one of indescribable tenderness and inconsolable grief. The folds in her gown flow toward the base of the monument where the names of 11,285 Canadian soldiers are carved. They went missing in action in France; they have no known graves.

The dedication of the monument took place on July 26, 1936. It was the centrepiece of a grand, national act of remembrance. The Canadian Legion organized a pilgrimage of 6,200 Canadian veterans and their families, at that time the largest peace-time movement of people from Canada to Europe.[20] The pilgrims were issued Vimy pilgrimage medals, souvenir berets, and special passports stamped on their covers with the words "Vimy Pilgrimage." Five ocean-going steamers left Montreal on July 16, 1936, accompanied by two Canadian naval destroyers. The flotilla docked in Le Havre, France, on July 24 and 25. When the pilgrims arrived at the dedication site on July 26, they were joined by a crowd estimated to have been between fifty thousand and one hundred thousand people. The spectators included other Canadian, British, and French ex-servicemen and their families; widows and mothers of those killed; French school children; and local residents.

King Edward VIII dedicated the memorial. During the war, while Prince of Wales, he had been on the staff of the Canadian Corps in France. Now he was present as King of Canada, prominently wearing a Vimy medal on his suit lapel and flanked by Mounties in scarlet dress uniform. This was his first official engagement since the death of his father, George V. It was also one of his few official engagements prior to his abdicating the throne. The King was at the height of his popularity. When he appeared, one veteran told that he was greeted by the veterans with "such a roar [as] you never heard in war or peace."[21] The King walked among the veterans. He stopped at one point to offer comforting words to a Canadian Silver Cross mother, Mrs. C.S. Wood, from Winnipeg. She had had eleven sons in service, eight of whom had not survived. Holding her hand, the King said, "I wish your sons were all here."[22]

In his speech of dedication, the King asked for remembrance: "Though the mortal remains of Canada's sons lie far from home, yet here where we now stand … their immortal memory is hallowed upon soil that is as surely Canada's as any acre within her nine provinces." Then the words of the King, like the monument that he was dedicating, called upon his listeners to turn their thoughts from the "cannonade which beat upon this ridge" to the splendor of the sacrifice of the fallen. He added the following words: "Around us here today there is peace and the rebuilding of hope."[23]

The presence of the King made the dedication an Empire-wide event. The ceremony was broadcast live to Canada by the Canadian Radio Broadcasting Commission, using the shortwave facilities of the British Broadcasting Corporation. The BBC used those facilities to transmit the

Dedication and unveiling of the Canadian National Vimy Memorial by King Edward VIII on July 26, 1936.

ceremony to the world. Hundreds of thousands listened; millions more read the newspaper stories. In the days following the ceremony, the pilgrims were entertained at a garden party at Buckingham Palace. The monument, the pilgrimage, and the ceremony, all underlined by the royal star-power of the King of Canada, rekindled the pride of Canadians in what they had accomplished at Vimy and the place that the young nation could now command in the world.

By 2002 the monument was showing signs of serious deterioration. The Canadian government committed $20 million to its restoration. The meticulously repaired memorial was rededicated by Queen Elizabeth II on April 9, 2007, the ninetieth anniversary of the battle. The Queen was joined by Prince Philip and the largest crowd since the 1936 ceremony. Military, Royal Canadian Mounted Police, twenty thousand veterans, and four thousand high school students were in attendance. This was the first time in years that the Canadian government had asked Her Majesty to act as Queen of Canada in an international setting.[24]

In her address, the Queen rededicated the monument "to all those who would serve the cause of freedom." Looking back to the battle itself and the original construction of the monument, she signalled Canada's place in the world: "Those who seek the foundations of Canada's distinction would do well to begin here at Vimy." She, too, focused not on war but on the future: "In capturing this formidable objective, the Canadian Corps transformed Vimy Ridge from a symbol of despair into a source of inspiration."[25]

On April 9, 2017, the one hundredth anniversary of the Vimy battle, the royal family again used its presence to draw the world's attention to Canada's accomplishments at Vimy and to underline the sacrifice for freedom that her forces made. The Prince of Wales, Prince Charles, together with his sons and thirty thousand pilgrims, nearly half of whom were high school students, recalled the stand taken a century earlier by thousands of Canadian soldiers who fought against tyranny and oppression.

Prince Charles spoke of the four divisions of the Canadian Corps serving together for the first time. "This was and remains the single bloodiest day in Canadian military history," he said. "Yet Canadians displayed a strength of character and commitment to one another that is still evident today. They did not waver. This was Canada at its best. The Canadians at Vimy embodied the true north, strong and free."[26] Charles's sons, both of whom have served in the forces, each laid a pair of soldier's boots on the memorial to complete a collection of boots, one pair for each of the 3,598 soldiers who had died.

The story of Vimy, the battle and the monument, illustrates perfectly the role, and the dedication, of Canada's monarchy. It shows the Crown as Canada's willing partner, there to assist, in good times and bad, as the country develops its distinct national identity. It shows the Crown as Canada's steadfast witness, there to speak to the country and the world of who Canadians are and what they aspire to be. It also shows the Crown as this country's enduring conscience, there to remind its citizens of those who sacrificed for peace and their freedom — "Lest We Forget." Willing partner, steadfast witness, enduring conscience: these are royal commitments that will make bright Canada's next 150 years.

Notes

1. A version of this article was originally presented at the annual Queen's Birthday Luncheon sponsored by the South Saskatchewan Branch of the Monarchist League of Canada, Regina, on May 13, 2017.
2. Useful accounts of the Battle can be found in: Ted Barris, *Victory at Vimy: Canada Comes of Age, April 9–12, 1917* (Toronto: Dundurn, 2008), and Tim Cook, *Vimy: The Battle and the Legend* (Canada: Allen Lane, 2017).
3. Corporal Gus Sivertz, 2nd Canadian Mounted Rifles, as cited in Barris, *Victory at Vimy*, 92.
4. "Canadian National Vimy Memorial, France," *The Great War 1914–1918*, www.greatwar.co.uk/french-flanders-artois/memorial-canadian-national-vimy-memorial.htm.
5. Robert Everett-Green, "Vimy Ridge: Birthplace of a Nation — or of a Canadian Myth?" *Globe and Mail*, March 31, 2017.
6. National Post Staff, "Cowboys, Immigrants, First Nations and Hockey Players (Of Course): The Canadian Soldiers at Vimy," *National Post*, April 9, 2017.
7. CBC Learning, "Pride at Vimy Ridge," in *Canada: A People's History*, www.cbc.ca/history/EPISCONTENTSE1EP12CH1PA3LE.html.
8. Ibid.
9. J.L. Granatstein, "Vimy Ridge Myth #1: Only Canadians Fought in the Defining Battle," *Maclean's*, Video Clip, April 4, 2007, www.macleans.ca/news/canada/vimy-ridge-myth-1-only-canadians-fought-in-the-defining-battle/.
10. Brian Bethune, "A Century Later, Remembering the Hard Win at Vimy Ridge," *Maclean's*, December 15, 2016, www.macleans.ca/news/world/a-century-later-remembering-the-hard-win-at-vimy-ridge/#.
11. Brian Bethune, "How Canada's Bloodiest Day at Vimy Defined Great War Sacrifice," *Maclean's*, March 27, 2017.
12. "The King to His People: Being Speeches and Messages of His Majesty King George the Fifth Delivered Between July 1911 and May 1935," in *Royal Observations: Canadians and Royalty*, Arthur Bousfield and Garry Toffoli, eds. (Toronto: Dundurn, 1991), 204.

13. Libraries and Archives Canada, "His Majesty the King to Field-Marshal Sir Douglas Haig, April 10, 1917," *War Diary, 4th Canadian Infantry Brigade, April 9–12, 1917*, RG 9, series III, Vol. 4881, folders 236–39, www.collectionscanada.gc.ca/firstworldwar/025005-1300-e.html.

14. "King George Visits Vimy Ridge and Views Battlefield," *Streetsville Review*, July 19, 1917, https://mississaugaatwar.wordpress.com/news-from-1917/king-visits-vimy/.

15. The Vimy Foundation, "#100 Days of Vimy," February 27, 2017, www.vimyfoundation.ca/100daysofvimy-february-27-2017/.

16. Arthur Bousfield, "King George V, 1910–1936," *Canadian Royal Heritage Trust*, 2013, http://crht.ca/king-george-v-1910-1936/.

17. Brian Bethune, "Vimy Ridge, April 9, 1917: Like a Scene out of Dante," *Maclean's*, www.macleans.ca/news/canada/vimy-ridge-april-9-1917-an-unheard-of-inferno-like-a-scene-out-dante/.

18. Bethune, "A Century Later," *Maclean's*, December 15, 2016, www.macleans.ca/news/world/a-century-later-remembering-the-hard-win-at-vimy-ridge/.

19. A detailed description of the memorial can be found in "Canadian National Vimy Memorial, France."

20. A detailed account of the pilgrimage can be found in Eric Brown and Tim Cook, "The 1936 Vimy Pilgrimage," *Canadian Military History* 20, no. 2 (2011): 39, www.canadianmilitaryhistory.ca/wp-content/uploads/2012/03/5-Brown-and-Cook-Vimy-Pilgrimage-v-2.pdf.

21. Bethune, "A Century Later."

22. Brown and Cook, 47.

23. "Vimy Ridge monument ceremony — Edward VII's address," YouTube video, 6:00, originally aired on July 26, 1936, posted by "easyplex," March 16, 2008, www.youtube.com/watch?v=6ZgddY086gg.

24. Lynne Bell, Arthur Bousfield, and Garry Toffoli, *Queen and Consort: Elizabeth and Philip: 60 Years of Marriage* (Toronto: Dundurn, 2007), 142.

25. "A Speech by The Queen at the 90th Anniversary of the Battle of Vimy Ridge," *The Home of the Royal Family*, April 9, 2007, www.royal.uk/90th-anniversary-battle-vimy-ridge-9-april-2007.

26. "A transcript of Prince Charles's speech at Vimy," *Maclean's*, April 9, 2017, www.macleans.ca/news/canada/a-transcript-of-prince-charless-speech-at-vimy/.

PART 2
THE CROWN AND INDIGENOUS PEOPLES

4 |

The Crown and First Nations in British Columbia: A Personal View

Steven Point

When I was asked by Prime Minister Stephen Harper to become the twenty-eighth lieutenant governor of British Columbia in 2007, I was more than reluctant. After all, it was in the name of the Crown that so many of our Indigenous people were arrested by police for withholding their own children from the "Indian" agent wanting them for residential schools. The land that we never lost in a war or signed away in a treaty was now called Crown land, and we needed permission to take trees for our own use from our own lands. It was the governor who, in the name of the Crown, made promises to our chiefs in 1864 at New Westminster, on the Queen's birthday — promises that were never delivered on, but were forgotten. I had been a chief myself, elected, mind you, but nonetheless a representative of the Skowkale Band, for fifteen years. I knew well about the poverty of our people under the wardship of the federal government. The elders called it "throwing chicken feed at us to fight over." Government funding was always too little too late for "Indian" problems.

I grew up at a time, in the fifties, when housing was accomplished by sending lumber to a family to build a home. I was one of ten children. My parents had a small bedroom and the rest of us slept in one other room. It was crowded. We had no indoor plumbing. We had a good life, though. I had no idea that others thought of us as poor.

So when the phone rang and my wife, Gwen, said that it was the prime minister, I remember asking her as I grabbed the phone, "What is his name?" She said "Stephen Harper." As I spoke with him, I could not help feeling uneasy — as if I was collaborating with the other side. I wondered what my elders would think of me representing the Crown. When my wife and I talked about this appointment, I expressed my reluctance to accept and she said, "It might be a good thing for our people."

On the day I was to be sworn in to office, I was dressed in ceremonial garb and seated in the back seat of a white Lincoln. Gwen and I were being driven to Parliament Hill. As we approached the majestic buildings, I could see a familiar sight: protests going on in the front. They were Indigenous people with signs and drums pounding. Familiar, because I myself had demonstrated against government policy many times in the past. I had slept in the Museum of Anthropology for a weekend during the constitutional talks in 1982. We had occupied the museum at the request of George Manuel, then president of the Union of British Columbia Indian Chiefs. I recognized a well-organized protest in progress — and my own brother was among the protesters! As we approached the building, however, they stopped the drums and put down the signs, and I could see them waving at me as we passed. They could not pass up a chance to protest just because I was being sworn in to office. I just smiled and waved back.

After the ink was dry on the papers that I had to sign, and the police escort had returned Gwen and me to Government House in Victoria, I saw eagles circling the House. The staff said that they had been there all day. I took it as a good sign. Eagles are well respected by traditional Indigenous Peoples, who know the meaning of an eagle feather. It was the eagle that flew high in the sky to stop the rain, with a promise to the creator that he would be the teacher to the Indigenous Peoples. It is an old story.

My duties as lieutenant governor began in earnest just a day or so later, with visits to schools, speeches at parades, and all kinds of different events imaginable. My first visit to an Indigenous community was going to tell me whether or not I had made a mistake. It was a sunny day and we were going to a West Coast village near Port Alberni. Again I saw signs being held by the people outside. At first I thought, *Oh no, a protest*; but then I read one of them and it said "Welcome." I was relieved to be treated really well by the elders and the people. Some of the elders had tears in their eyes in seeing me. They later told me how surprised they were that an Indigenous person had been appointed to such a high position. They were proud. And so it went: everywhere I travelled in "Indian Country" I would get the same response. The people were so happy about the appointment. At least I never witnessed any malcontents. A cartoon that appeared in the *Vancouver Sun* seemed to sum it all up. It showed me shaking hands with the premier. The premier said, "You have come a long way," and my response was, "So have you."

I was pleased to be so well received wherever I went in British Columbia. Every community, Indigenous and non-Indigenous, treated me very well. I quickly learned, however, that most people had virtually no idea what my role as lieutenant governor was. Many people thought I was the governor general! I was constantly explaining to them what my role was and why it was an important function in Canadian political life. Those who had some notion of the job seemed to think of it as a ceremonial position that hosted tea parties on the lawn every day.

I must admit that before the appointment I knew nothing about the role of lieutenant governor. Gwen and I had to look it up on the Internet to glean some inklings. What I learned is that in Canada the Crown is often seen as old-fashioned, outdated, a throwback to colonial days — something that did not fit with modern ideas about democracy. In 2009 Prime Minister Stephen Harper, struggling with the prospect of a non-confidence vote in Parliament, went to the governor general, Michaëlle Jean, to ask her to prorogue Parliament. There was some question raised in the media as to why the prime minister had to ask the governor general to do this in the first place.

This is democracy in Canada. The offices of the governor general and the lieutenant governors have been likened to a fire extinguisher that stands idle until needed in a crisis. The media is naturally very interested in the prime minister. He or she is the very visible representative of Canada who travels abroad to speak on behalf of Canadians. The media is less interested in the so-called ceremonial role of the governor general, that is, the Crown, because of the fire-extinguisher identity. This person does not speak out about political matters, which are the purview of the prime minister. So the Crown in Canada is not so much misunderstood as ignored by Canadians — ignored, not out of disrespect, but rather because Canadians generally know very little about the country's constitutional governance model.

This brings me to Chief Theresa Spence, who went on a fast in 2012 to protest the treatment of Indigenous people in Canada. She insisted on speaking, not with the prime minister, but rather with the governor general, that is, the Crown. Chief Spence was probably smiled at by federal politicians, who may have thought she was just not clear about who really ran Canada. But in this particular case Chief Spence was very clear, in my view. She well understood the long, historical relationship that the Crown has had with the Indigenous Peoples in Canada. After all, it was the lieutenant governors, like Alexander Morris (lieutenant governor of Manitoba, 1872–77, and of the North-West Territories, 1872–76), who came to the Indigenous Peoples to negotiate numbered treaties on behalf of the Crown. First Nations, now and especially then, viewed themselves as other nations who would open diplomatic relations with another head of state. At the time of contact, when Europeans first met with the Indigenous Peoples, the latter were always viewed as other nations. As in any such high-level meetings, the representatives of the Crown always sought out their Indigenous equivalents — namely the chiefs. Gifts were an important element of these parleys, another common feature of diplomacy in "Indian Country."

These negotiations were carried out in a very public manner, with the band on one side and the governor on the other. Only the chiefs participated on behalf of their respective nations. While the British, and later Canadian, negotiators created written records and treaties to record these meetings, the First Nations gave far more weight to the words that were spoken (including the actions, tones, and other inflections that accompany the spoken word). It was noted in Morris's negotiations report that the First Nations employed a member of their side to simply memorize everything that was said during the talks. The European side put more stock in the written words of the treaties and somehow forgot about many oral promises that never made it into the final drafts.

As time passed, the Indigenous people became fewer in number than the Europeans and therefore less significant. While Indigenous populations dropped drastically due to contact with Europeans, the "whites," as they called themselves, quickly increased. As Indigenous people became dependent on the government for food and shelter while living on reserves, so there began a policy by the government to watch over them. The expectation was that the Indigenous Peoples would soon become like the Europeans. The assimilation policy was viewed by governments and churches alike as inevitably necessary for the survival of the Indigenous Peoples. It laid the way for later policies that would steal children from their parents to be raised in Christian residential schools all across Canada. Wardship is the shadow of genocide, and Indigenous people in Canada have lived this reality and its consequences for a very long time.

Historical Perspective

In British Columbia, some treaties were negotiated by James Douglas (governor of Vancouver Island, 1851–64, and of British Columbia, 1858–64), as they were in the Prairie provinces, to divest the First Nations of their homelands in order to make way for white settlement. They covered the land on the southern part of Vancouver Island. There was also Treaty 8 in the northeast corner of British Columbia. Other than these small exceptions, there were no treaties with the First Nations in British Columbia until the Nisga'a Treaty in 1985.

Modern treaties are now being negotiated under the British Columbia treaty process. The land that is generally on the table is Crown land. First Nations in British Columbia have had reserves set out for them, but without first having the government purchase title to their lands prior to settlement, as had been Canadian policy stemming from the Royal Proclamation of 1763. After the War of 1812, the border of the lands between Canada and the United States was finalized by the Treaty of Oregon. Just prior to this, the Hudson's Bay Company decided to move its operation from the Columbia River north to Vancouver Island. In a ship called the *Beaver*, Governor James Douglas landed at a place called Camosun, named after the famous camous plant, near what is now Victoria.

James Douglas brought with him the values and beliefs expounded by humanist organizations like the Aborigines' Protection Society.[1] This organization had deep roots in the anti-slavery movement in Britain and, once slavery had finally been made unlawful there, they took up the cause of the Aboriginal people of the so-called new world. Douglas was a good company man, who could be trusted to run a fur-buying station while the chief trader was away. He moved quickly to the top levels of this organization because of his work ethic and trustworthiness. He was a religious man, too, who often took up the task of conducting Sunday prayers for company men at the trading post.

When Douglas became chief trader of the Fort Victoria trading post, he already had extensive experience in trading with the First Nations and in running a complex trading post that had to be self-sufficient, secure, and profitable. Vancouver Island had first been granted to the Hudson's Bay Company by way of Royal Charter for a period of ten years commencing in 1846. It became an official colony of Britain in 1849. The colony's first official governor was Richard Blanshard, who arrived in March 1850 from England and stayed for only eighteen months. The only significant event that can be attributed to his tenure is the naval bombardment of two Kwakiutl villages for failing to deliver suspected murderers to the colonial authorities.

James Douglas became the second governor of the colony of Vancouver Island in 1851. His "Indian" policy was a reflection of his beliefs and attitudes. He was a humanist thrust into a new world where realities on the ground dictated otherwise. He therefore disagreed with Blanshard's handling of that incident, and for the most part Douglas's use of military assistance was minimal. Douglas's views were reported as follows:

> Like all other fur traders, Douglas was not at all happy about Blanshard's treatment of the Newitty, and as governor he considered it downright dangerous. He described the action "as unpolitick as unjust"; poorly conceived as well as badly executed. "In all our intercourse with the natives," wrote Douglas, summarizing the fur traders' view, "we have invariably acted on the principle that it is inexpedient and unjust to hold tribes responsible for the acts of individuals."[2]

Upon the occasion of his elevation to governor of the colony, Douglas wrote a letter to the colonial secretary, Earl Grey. It was reported that "it was clear that Douglas had an agenda as he began his gubernatorial career, because in his acceptance letter he also informed Grey that one of his first priorities would be to improve the condition of the aborigines of Vancouver Island, whom he considered 'highly interesting people … worthy of attention.'"[3]

The Douglas Treaties

Douglas set out trying to purchase First Nations' lands by treaty for white settlement. He made fourteen such treaties on Vancouver Island between the years 1850 and 1854, then stopped. These first treaties saw the purchase of lands generally held by the First Nations.[4] The First Nations were paid in supplies made available at the Hudson's Bay store. The chiefs would sign on behalf of their people. The question arose some time later as to whether these were legal documents; in the case of *R. v. White and Bob*,[5] it was determined that they were lawful treaties per section 88 of the Indian Act.[6]

This is the genesis of the principle of wardship or fiduciary responsibility for the First Nations in British Columbia. This created a parental relationship for the First Nations, first with the colonial government, then with the federal government at Confederation. Lands were to be held in trust for the First Nations by the government to prevent them from selling their lands privately. The general concern was that Indigenous people would become victims to unscrupulous settlers or traders who would swindle their lands for whisky. Alcohol had been used by traders since the very early times of their contact with the Indigenous Peoples and had become a real health concern.

James Douglas considered two things: one was the safety and security of his employees, and later that of arriving settlers, from the real threat of an "Indian war"; the other was the survival of the First Nations. There is no doubt that he believed that the First Nations would benefit from the positive influences of white settlers, like education and farming, but he was also concerned that they not become a financial burden on the colony.[7]

Douglas was aware that he had a duty to protect the First Nations by setting aside reserve lands for them, but the question was the process. He had initially purchased their lands generally and set aside reserves from their territories. Later on he had dropped the process of purchasing title for a process of simply laying out reserves. He would go to the First Nations seeking their input as to where they wanted lands to be set aside. He allowed village sites, potato fields, graveyards, fishing sites, and favourite sites.

This process was in stark contrast with what was happening on the Canadian plains and in the United States. There, the government came in, called for negotiations and, through treaty, purchased the lands generally and in the treaty document specified what lands were to be designated as reserved to the Indians (the term that was and still is commonly used in the United States to refer to Indigenous Peoples).

There are fourteen treaties in all in British Columbia, with very simple wording. The curious title is "Conveyance of Land to Hudson's Bay Company by the Indian Tribes." Each document begins by identifying the particular tribe, specifies the date of the document, states that the chiefs of the people have signed the document and with these works, "so consent to surrender, entirely and fore ever, to James Douglas, the agent of the Hudson's Bay Company in Vancouver Island, that is to say, for the Governor, Deputy Governor, and Committee of the same...."[8] The land to be conveyed is then described. Conditions of the conveyance are listed, then the document is signed. What is interesting is that, although the land so described is conveyed to James Douglas, it becomes the "... property of the white people forever ...,"[9] with the exception of village sites and enclosed fields and with the proviso that the signatory First Nations are "... at liberty to hunt over the unoccupied lands, and to carry on our fisheries as formerly."[10] A sum of money is stated as being paid to the First Nations in consideration of their lands so conveyed to Douglas. So although James Douglas is a conduit mentioned in these documents, the land is being sold by the chiefs of the tribe to the white people. This is not a sale between individuals; it is a sale of land from a group or tribe to another group. It is a treaty.

Crown and First Nations Today

When I think of a relationship, I think of two or more people coming together. It is a social situation that involves communication back and forth. It is not always rosy and happy, but nevertheless it is a relationship.

If you grow up on a reserve, as I did, there was no relationship with the Crown that I recall. In towns, people speak about the mayor or council members or school board members, but on the reserve it is the chief who people talk of. The chiefs interacted with the "Indian agent." For all intents and purposes, the Indian agent was the Crown. There were times when royalty would arrive and the band members would be called upon to dress up and become visible, but for the most part we were invisible people. Reserves like Skowkale were ghettos, holding impoverished people. The reserve was a wasteland where we lived and it seemed that nobody cared for any kind of relationship with us.

Then the Second World War happened. Indigenous persons like my uncle signed up to fight for Canada. However, when they returned, they were treated differently from other veterans. Although they did not receive their medals like other returning soldiers, their sacrifices did not go unnoticed. It was only after the war that the Indian Act was amended to allow Indigenous persons to vote in all elections. New political organizations were formed to fight for Indigenous rights and to improve social conditions on reserves.

I still remember my first meeting with the Union of British Columbia Indian Chiefs. The meetings seemed to be dominated by consultants. Generally the chiefs were quiet. There was talk of court cases and funds needed to fight the government. I was twenty-three years old. I decided to speak at the microphone. My knees were shaking. I knew of no relationship with any Crown at that time. The plight of Indigenous people was a distant problem to be solved by philanthropists — perhaps. We had been marginalized to the edge of Canadian society, forgotten people on vacant reserves. In these meetings, we passed wordy resolutions meant to bring about change. No change happened. For Indigenous people to be noticed, it took legal action even to get Canada's attention. The Lovelace case in

2000 and the Drybones case in 1970 were examples of legal action that brought results. The other thing that brought results was direct action, like the 1990 Oka Crisis in Quebec.

Another Canadian birthday was celebrated in 2017 and Canadians had parties with balloons and fireworks, while we First Nations people stood aside and wondered what there was to celebrate. Chief Dan George said it best: Canada should be ashamed of what it has done to First Nations. It is not enough to simply acknowledge the damage of the past. Rather, there must be real change in a relationship that has been born in colonialism, simmered in ignorance, and burned by racism. We need a new relationship with Canada.

But how does a new relationship begin? One needs to influence government policy changes. In my role as lieutenant governor I learned that government representatives have ears and listen to people of influence inside their respective ridings or electoral districts. I recall one instance when members of the royal family were coming for a visit. The lieutenant governor, who is second in precedence to the Queen, had not been invited to the events surrounding the visit. It took a phone call from a wealthy citizen to change this oversight.

If it is true that the public, that is, voters, have power over government policy development, then in order to bring about positive change in that policy one would have to somehow change public opinion. As lieutenant governor of British Columbia, I tried to do just that. I am not so sure that I was successful. Any change in people takes a long time to ripen into government policy change. It is very difficult, after all, to change what has become common-sense policy. Changing an aspect of one's view of the world is frightening. We have become complacent, comfortable, and secure in our collective belief in current relations with Indigenous Peoples.

But I must say that my becoming the twenty-eighth lieutenant governor of British Columbia did have some impact. For one thing, I think it showed those non-Indigenous people who wanted to help but were before afraid of backlash from their own people that they could step forward without fear.

Suggestions for Future Representatives of the Crown

Victoria's Government House, the residence of the lieutenant governor, reflects the important place that Indigenous people have in the life of the province. From the 2008 installation of the fourteen-foot healing pole in the foyer to the raising of *Hosaqami* (meaning "You, the face of authority") totem pole in 2012, the home of the Crown in British Columbia has reinforced the fact that the lieutenant governor is deeply interconnected with Indigenous Peoples. Our stories are enmeshed, and Indigenous people can go to Victoria's Government House and see themselves reflected and know that they are respected as partners.

If we are to be a country that recognizes nation-to-nation relationships, there should be spaces in each Government House (or vice-regal office, for those provinces that have lost their Government Houses) that honour the Crown's relationships with Indigenous Peoples. It must go further than simply hanging Indigenous art on the walls — these places should honour ancient protocols that once happened between the governors and the chiefs. Grievances and petitions can be brought to these places where they can be accepted respectfully before being passed to the government.

The Crown has been here with the Indigenous Peoples since the beginning of European settlement, but most Canadians are not fully aware of that, which should not come as a surprise, since many of our vice-regal offices do not reflect their ancient relationships with Indigenous people. The governors need to become vehicles for education around what the treaties really mean and the relationships they established. It's in their DNA, so to speak.

A new relationship for Canada is not complicated, nor is it unrealistic. It begins with reconciliation — that is, to acknowledge the past, *then* to apologize and start anew. While the government's responsibility is to create a level playing field with enough resources for Indigenous people to survive off their lands on their own terms, it is the Crown — the governors — who ensure there is an atmosphere in this country of mutual respect and understanding. We can get there. It is possible. And I think that the Crown, and the office of lieutenant governor, provide a channel to do just that.

Notes

1. This society had written a letter to Colonial Secretary Sir Edward Bulwer Lytton expressing their humanist beliefs with regard to the First Nations of British Columbia, published in *Papers Connected to the Indian Land Question 1850–1875* (Victoria: Richard Wolfenden, Government Printer, 1895), 12.

2. Robin Fisher, *Contact and Conflict: Indian-European Relations in British Columbia, 1744–1890* (Vancouver: UBC Press, 1992), 53.

3. Ibid., 85.

4. It is important to note that the land could be described only in geographic terms, since the land had not been surveyed.

5. *R. v. White and Bob* (1965), 52 D.L.R. (2d) 481 (S.C.C).

6. Indian Act, RSC 1951 s. 88.

7. Governor Douglas's letter of March 14, 1858 to Sir E.B. Lytton sets out his plan for the First Nations. He assures Lytton that he will not be following the American example where the Indigenous people became totally dependent on the government.

8. *Papers Connected to the Indian Land Question*, 5.

9. Ibid.

10. Ibid.

5 |

Decolonizing the Crown in Canada: Restoring the Queen at the Council Fire[1]

Nathan Tidridge

> As the representative of The Queen, the highest office in this province, I am privileged to fulfil my duty of kinship with Indigenous Peoples in Treaty. It is a sacred trust as relevant as my duty to ensure the province always has a functioning government.
>
> *The Honourable Elizabeth Dowdeswell, lieutenant governor of Ontario, honours and commits to the family relationship between the Crown and Indigenous Peoples.*
> *Lakehead University, Thunder Bay, Ontario*
> *February 15, 2017*[2]

In 2015, the Truth and Reconciliation Commission released its final report. Recalling over two centuries of disruptions to the relationships that had served these lands well when settlers first began arriving, the commissioners issued the following call to action: "(#45) We call upon the Government of Canada, on behalf of all Canadians, to jointly develop with Aboriginal peoples a Royal Proclamation of Reconciliation to be issued by the Crown. The proclamation would build on the Royal Proclamation of 1763 and the Treaty of Niagara of 1764, and reaffirm the nation-to-nation relationship between Aboriginal peoples and the Crown." The report goes on to describe this as necessary in establishing what it calls "an action-oriented Covenant of Reconciliation."[3]

"Two Ottawa Chiefs Who with Others Lately Came Down from Michillimackinac Lake Huron to Have a Talk with Their Great Father the King or His Representative," ca. 1813–20, artist unknown.

The original Royal Proclamation was issued in the name of King George III following the defeat of New France in 1763, and is often held up as the "Indian Magna Carta" by the Government of Canada because, after much negotiating, it recognized "Indian Nations," placing them under the protection of the Crown. During the 250th commemorations of the Royal Proclamation of 1763 at Rama First Nation, near Orillia, Ontario, Justice Murray Sinclair reflected, "I love the Royal Proclamation and I hate the Royal Proclamation,"[4] as he reminded the audience gathered there that the Indigenous Peoples did not require a far-off king to affirm their existence.

Following the defeat of the French, British Governor General Jeffery Amherst attempted to treat King Louis XV's western Indigenous allies as if they had also been conquered, rather than concluding separate peace treaties with them. Amherst's methods of imposing British interests over the peoples of the Great Lakes region included the use of blankets laced with smallpox, one of the first uses of biological warfare on the continent. The governor general's efforts triggered widespread rebellion, coalescing under the leadership of Pontiac of the Odawa Nation. With mounting military losses, General Amherst proved to be incapable of negotiating peace, much less executing the British administration of the continent that was being framed back in England.

It was an Irishman, Sir William Johnson, superintendent of Indian Affairs, who successfully lobbied the Imperial government to accept the idea that, in order for the Royal Proclamation to be accepted, a partnership needed to be kindled in these lands on Indigenous terms, employing Indigenous diplomacy. By late 1763, Amherst was recalled to London, replaced by acting commander-in-chief Thomas Gage, who wrote to Johnson from New York on December 1, 1763, of the king's proclamation formalizing British control over North America. Informing Johnson of what we now know as "The Royal Proclamation of 1763," Gage commented:

> ... I received several copies of His Majesty's Proclamation to make known the Arrangements which His Majesty had thought proper to make in Consequence of the Cessions made to the Crown of Great Britain in America.... I think it right to inclose [*sic*] you one of the Said Proclamation, for your Information of the Regulations which have been made, & particularly as they are So very favorable to all the Indian Tribes, a proper Explanation of the Articles which concern them, I imagine Must have great Influence over their Minds, and induce them to a Conviction that His Majesty is well disposed to favor & protect Them.[5]

In another letter to Johnson from Gage, dated December 26, the acting commander-in-chief wrote, "I submit for your Consideration the best Manner of Making Peace with Indians. Whether by Assembling the Several Nations together; or treating as much as with each of Them Separately ...," initiating a correspondence on the matter that would stretch into the new year.[6] In a letter from Johnson Hall (northwest of Albany), Sir William laid out his plan for securing peace in the Great Lakes region. Suggesting the Niagara peninsula as an appropriate and central location for a great council, he wrote: "At this Treaty wheresoever held we should tye [*sic*] them down [in the peace] according to their own forms of which they take the most notice, for Example by Exchanging a very large belt with some remarkable & intelligible figures thereon."[7]

Gage agreed, and Johnson was authorized to hold a council with some twenty-four Indigenous nations along the shores of the Niagara River during the summer of 1764. Over the month of July, Sir William negotiated separately with each nation and, after weeks of exchanging wampum and other gifts on behalf of the Crown, left Fort Niagara and crossed the Niagara River on July 31, 1764, to address the Western Nations gathered along its banks:

> Brothers of the Western Nations, Sachims, Chiefs, & Warriors —
>
> You have now been here for several days, during which time we have frequently met to Renew, and strengthen our Engagements, & you have made so many Promises of your Friendship, and Attachment to the English that there now only remains for us to exchange the great Belt of the Covenant Chain that we may not forget our mutual Engagements. —
>
> I now therefore present you the great Belt by which I bind all your Western Nations together with the English, and I desire you will take fast hold of the same, and never let it slip....[8]

The wampum belt, described by Johnson's secretary as "... the great Covenant Chain, 23 Rows broad, & the Year 1764 worked upon it,"[9] embodied what become known as the Treaty of Niagara. The treaty extended the Silver Covenant Chain of Friendship, first established with the Haudenosaunee Confederacy in the seventeenth century, into the interior of North America. King George III was now bound to the Indigenous nations of the Great Lakes region in a relationship of equality, respect, and

The author of this essay (left) holds a replica of the 1764 Covenant Chain Wampum with Ken Maracle in his home on the territory of the Six Nations of the Grand River. Completed by Maracle in 2015, this replica will be gifted by Queen Elizabeth II to her Chapel Royal at Massey College in 2018.

familial love that continues to this day. The Treaty of Niagara ratified the Royal Proclamation of 1763 along Indigenous terms and perspectives, and was intended by Indigenous and non-Indigenous delegations to be the foundation of future negotiations between the Crown and First Nations.

The very existence of the Covenant Chain Wampum tells us that the settler population "got it," because it was created by the king's representative and presented on His Majesty's behalf. This wampum is not an Indigenous artifact; rather, it is a vice-regal one — a diplomatic device employed by the king's representative to, in the words of John Borrows, ensure "… some principles which were implicit in the written version of the Proclamation were made explicit to First Nations in these other communications."[10] Nearly 250 years later, the wampum was invoked by Governor General David Johnston, speaking at the 2012 Crown–First Nations Gathering in Ottawa, who acknowledged that the Covenant Chain presented by Sir William Johnson represented the core of the Crown's relationship with its First Nations allies.[11]

When looked at holistically, the Royal Proclamation *and* the Treaty of Niagara can properly be seen as one of the many "Magna Cartas" that continue to live and grow in these lands. This relationship was intended to inform future treaties, including the numbered treaties and modern treaties formed with the Crown. The Silver Covenant Chain of Friendship also reinforced the notion that the treaty relationship was a personal one — a kinship — with the king, regardless of the government or political developments of the day.

"Treaty" is a verb and not a noun. If treaties are understood to be relationships, certain descriptors come to mind as the parties articulate what qualities must exist in order to ensure their success: trust, honesty, communication, integrity, and love (the most important ingredient of all). Love must be understood to be the foundation of all treaties. Addressing members of Lakehead University in 2016, Elizabeth Dowdeswell, lieutenant governor of Ontario, explored the idea of "love" woven into every treaty. "The love that is meant is often described as kinship. The Crown is bound in kinship with Indigenous Peoples," the lieutenant governor remarked, in an important speech that refocused the relationship between the Queen's representatives and Indigenous Peoples. Dowdeswell continued, "Relationships, particularly those between family members, have a flexibility that allow for disagreements and even estrangement. However, no matter the conflict, with family there is always a path left open for reconciliation. Such relationships must have elements of the abstract if they are to work properly."[12]

Treaty is abstract, but that is the point. Relationships are complex and often ill-defined; they have to be, in order to evolve and survive. Indigenous and non-Indigenous people are very different, with, for example, distinct languages and concepts of time and space. Treaties must live in the abstract in order for such differing, and sometimes opposing, world views to coexist — they give their members a chance to evolve toward one another. Governor General David Johnston, attending the 2016 Treaty Four Protocol ceremony with the lieutenant governor of Saskatchewan, defined treaties as "… living, breathing documents. They are forward-looking. They matter to all of us, because they lie at the heart of the relationship between Indigenous and non-Indigenous Canadians."

The governor general went on to remark, "Treaty Four is fundamental to the relationship between the Crown and the First Nations you represent. Our relationship flows from this treaty, and today we have a chance to strengthen and reinvigorate that relationship."[13]

Not just abstract, the Crown also exists in the metaphysical realm, making it a preferred conduit through which we are bound in treaty. The monarchy, like treaty, requires us to use words that are far more allegorical, imbued with subtle meanings and histories. As Lieutenant Governor Dowdeswell remarked at Lakehead University, "Our constitutional monarchy, which has evolved over a thousand years, requires us to have an understanding of symbolism and words that often stray into an abstract realm and are imbued with history and subtleties. Exploring the institution of the Crown often steers us toward the same language that must be used in order to properly describe Treaty."[14]

A concrete definition of the Crown must always remain just beyond our reach. For the Crown, through the process of trying to define what it is, the institution naturally becomes a reflection of society, a reflection that is constantly changing. To paraphrase the Queen herself, the Crown is defined not so much by what it does, but by the fact that it exists.[15] The same can be said for treaty. Daniel K. Richter notes in his book *Beyond the Covenant Chain*, "[T]he process of treaty making was always far more important to Indians than the results enshrined in a treaty document."[16] Even while the Treaty of Niagara was being negotiated, the power of King George III as monarch was being curtailed by the emergence of what English political writer Walter Bagehot called the "Dignified Crown" (the king) and the "Efficient Crown" (powers now exercised by elected ministers, including the prime minister). This reality, as understood by the British, was never articulated in the treaties.

Beyond 1764, the gulf between the Dignified and Efficient Crowns grew larger in British political life. The crystallization of the convention of responsible government, and the emergence of Canada as a distinct political entity through Confederation in 1867, served to displace the very foundations of our treaties. The 1931 Statute of Westminster legally created a distinct Canadian Crown, albeit with a shared monarch, independent of its British counterpart. When Elizabeth II ascended the throne in this country in 1952, she did so as Queen of Canada, a title formally bestowed on her by the Parliament in Ottawa the following year. Since the establishment of our first treaty relationships, non-Indigenous people have repeatedly re-imagined the Crown in these lands without consulting, or seeking the consent of, the Indigenous Peoples that are bound with it. For many Indigenous people, their relationship is still with the British Crown, and the Canadian Crown is nothing more than an interloper. This remains a major hurdle to be resolved.

However, rather than focusing on the political and constitutional con-tortions brought about with the Crown over the last century and a half, we should instead return to the very roots of the treaty relationship — the kin-ship between the sovereign and Indigenous Peoples, where indispensable roles for the Queen and her representatives are revealed.

Constitutionally, the Queen is the embodiment of the Canadian state. Her Majesty, and her representatives, remain at the apex of our constitu-tional government. Indeed, understanding the delicate bonds holding this federation together is impossible without encountering its constitutional monarchy. What Canadians need to realize is that the kinship between the sovereign and Indigenous Peoples is separate and distinct from that which exists between the sovereign and other Canadian subjects — it is the for-mer relationship that is at the heart of any treaty. Eliminating the sovereign from treaties breaks down a familial relationship distinct from the Crown's place in Canada's political framework, removing the medium required for Canadians to realign themselves as "Treaty People." For many Indigenous nations, a vice-regal representative is important not because that person represents the Queen of Canada in a particular jurisdiction. Rather, the governor general and lieutenant governors are significant because they stand in for the Queen herself, what Philippe Lagassé calls "the Hereditary Crown,"[17] within the treaty relationship. For many Indigenous people, fed-eral and provincial incarnations of the Crown in Canada have little mean-ing because, in treaty, the personal relationship is paramount.

A mandate letter in 2016 instructed the minister of immigration, refugees, and citizenship to collaborate with the minister of indigenous and northern affairs in making changes to the oath of Canadian citizen-ship to reflect the Truth and Reconciliation's calls to action. This is an important step in educating Canadians about one of our most significant relationships. Notably, the Truth and Reconciliation Commission recommended retaining the Crown, as well as adding Indigenous treaties into the oath: "I swear (or affirm) that I will be faithful and bear true allegiance to Her Majesty Queen Elizabeth II, Queen of Canada, her heirs and successors, and that I will faithfully observe the laws of Canada, including treaties with Indigenous peoples, and fulfil my duties as a Canadian citizen."[18]

The retention of the Queen in the oath is as important as the inclusion of treaties, because the very act of swearing allegiance to the sovereign engages new citizens in the relationships that Her Majesty is bound with. The Queen remains the conduit for new Canadians to enter into treaty relationships with Indigenous Peoples and the new oath would serve as a reminder to Canadians, new and old, of the important role played by the Crown on their behalf. Just as the Queen frees Canadians from swearing allegiance to a particular ideology with regards to governing the state, Her Majesty also keeps treaty relationships above the political fray. While subject to the political will of the government or of the day, the relationships established by treaty can never be removed — kinship with the Crown indicates their permanence. This is often reflected in the assertion that treaties are with the Crown, not the government. As a medium for a true nation-to-nation relationship, the Crown provides stability and permanence above the political arena.

Until 2017, Queen Elizabeth II had only two chapels royal (ecclesiastical bodies appointed to serve the spiritual needs of the sovereign) outside of the United Kingdom. Both of the Queen's Canadian chapels can be found on Indigenous territory: Her Majesty's Royal Chapel of the Mohawks (Six Nations of the Grand River) and Christ Church, Her Majesty's Chapel Royal of the Mohawk (Mohawks of the Bay of Quinte First Nation). In 2017, the Queen established a new chapel royal — the first on Anishinaabe territory — in partnership with Massey College at the University of Toronto and the Mississaugas of the New Credit First Nation. Named Gi-Chi-Twaa Gimaa Kwe, Mississauga Anishinaabek AName Gamik (meaning "The Queen's Anishinaabek Sacred Place"), the chapel includes a mural depicting the 1764 Council of Niagara by Phil Cote and a mosaic window featuring the Covenant Chain Wampum executed by Sarah Hill. A key protocol observed between the sovereign and Indigenous people is reflected in the chapel's practice of offering tobacco to Indigenous visitors. Tobacco is a sacred element, and the Queen's Tobacco Bundles recall the ancient and enduring Silver Covenant Chain of Friendship and the family relationship it established.

The centrepiece of the Chapel Royal is a replica of the Covenant Chain Wampum presented by Sir William Johnson at the Treaty of Niagara. The wampum is a gift from Queen Elizabeth II and housed in cedar within the sanctuary of the chapel.[19] By presenting such a gift to the chapel, Elizabeth II polishes the Silver Covenant Chain of Friendship anew, elevating the wampum itself from a vice-regal to a royal document. Such an act of reconciliation emphasizes that the chapel, founded in the twenty-first century during the sesquicentennial of Confederation, is a space committed to the future of Canada and its relationships with Indigenous Peoples — a contemporary space intimately linked to relationships first established in the seventeenth century. Massey College's chapel manifests the cyclical relationship woven into the Covenant Chain, emphasizing the Crown as a medium linking contemporary Canada with the ancient relationships that were meant to be the foundations of our society. The Crown manifested in this space will be uncorrupted, representing our very best intentions as a society.

Offering support for the project, as well as underscoring its significance, Chief R. Stacey Laforme of the Mississaugas of the New Credit First Nation wrote:

> The Royal Proclamation cannot be properly interpreted unless it is combined with the Treaty of Niagara, and treaties cannot be understood without acknowledging the relationship Indigenous Peoples have with the Queen and her family. This chapel will serve to remind Canadians of these truths.
>
> My people's ancestors were at Niagara when the Silver Covenant Chain of Friendship was extended into these lands over 250 years ago. It is in the spirit of that gathering that this chapel will serve as a place to gather regularly and polish the chain for this and future generations.

Confederation set aside our treaty relationships, beginning a very dark chapter in the relationships between Indigenous and non-Indigenous Peoples on these lands. The establishment of this Royal Chapel — a space to reflect, learn and reconnect — by Her Majesty and the Massey College community 150 years later is a profound act of reconciliation. It will become, in effect, a new council fire for our peoples to gather around in love and friendship.[20]

Examples of the Crown's official representatives reinterpreting and re-engaging with their relationships with Indigenous Peoples can be found across the country. In 2013, at Fort Qu'Appelle, Vaughn Solomon Schofield, lieutenant governor of Saskatchewan, took part in a sweat lodge ceremony. The lieutenant governor's participation in such a personal event was a healing moment for an office that could trace its roots back to Edgar Dewdney, the controversial lieutenant governor of the North-West Territories who was active in the — self-described — "Policy of Reward and Punishment" with regard to Indigenous Peoples of the plains.[21]

Recounting the meeting where the invitation to a sweat lodge was extended to Schofield, an observer mentioned that "It felt like a meeting of family as we sat in a circle, ensconced in Her Honour's receiving room."[22] When asked to articulate her vice-regal role in relation to Indigenous Peoples, the lieutenant governor referred to her time in the sweat lodge: "I feel very privileged to have participated in a sweat lodge, and to walk among the elders, chiefs, and veterans in a pow wow grand entry; through these remarkable experiences and my visits to Indigenous communities, I have viewed my role as one of listening and sharing, as we move forward in healing and reconciliation."[23]

In rediscovering the intended relationships that are the hallmarks of treaty, governors general and lieutenant governors are realizing the potential of their offices, realigning them with their intended purposes as conduits through which non-Indigenous Peoples can connect with their Indigenous brothers and sisters. Speaking in 2015 at Government House in Fredericton, New Brunswick, at an event to honour residential school survivors, Lieutenant Governor Jocelyne Roy Vienneau offered the following definition for her vice-regal office:

> My office is a direct and symbolic link to our democratic process. But it is also a physical link, extending to the people and to the Province itself — the territory, the ground, the land — to Mother Earth. I so respect you, your cultures, your customs and traditions.
>
> I believe, as much as it is important to have strong roots and a notion of where we come from, it is also important to know where we are going — wherever it may be, it will always be toward the future. Today, we are moving ahead, with open hearts.[24]

Vienneau invoked this role again the following year when she welcomed Indigenous leaders from across New Brunswick to Government House: "We must better understand each other — and learn to appreciate our differences, but also what we share in common. We all sit under one tree — the Tree of Life — enjoying its beauty, and giving thanks to Mother Earth and to the Creator. We can all gather under that tree to find wisdom, power, healing, reconciliation, peace and friendship. We need to learn to understand one another, to tolerate, to have respect — for one another, and for our relationships."[25]

Much work was done by John Grant, lieutenant governor of Nova Scotia from 2012 to 2017, to rehabilitate one of the more contentious relationships in Canada. Nova Scotia's vice-regal office, one of the oldest in the country, included Edward Cornwallis, founder of Halifax and author of the infamous Scalping Proclamation of 1749. Grant's decision to host a ceremony to commemorate the treaty relationship at Government House in 2016 was commended by Mi'kmaq Grand Chief Sylliboy, who said "The Mi'kmaw treaties will continue to be integral in the future relationship between Nova Scotia and the representative of the Queen," adding, "We are convinced that the relationship the treaties represent can guide the way to a shared future in Canada and Nova Scotia."[26] Speaking at the ceremony, where one of the first written Peace and Friendship Treaties (Treaty of 1725) was on display, Grant shared the following interpretation of the Crown in Nova Scotia:

> A key concept that we should keep in mind when considering the importance of Treaties, and indeed all citizens' relationship with the Constitution and government in a broadest sense, is what is known in Mi'kmaq as "Elikewake," which translates as the King in our house. It is the concept that the Sovereign is an ally, and not an oppressor, but a protector and friendly ally. This Mi'kmaq concept is centuries old, and it dovetails nicely with the modern concept of the Crown as an institution that reigns but does not rule.[27]

Grant continued his exploration by differentiating the relationship between the Crown and the province from that of the Crown with Indigenous Peoples, saying "It is often easy to see the Crown and our Queen as a far-off and detached symbol. Yet beyond the role I play as the sovereign's representative in Nova Scotia, there is a very special connection that exists between the Mi'kmaq Nation and Her Majesty."[28]

The following year the premier, grand chief, and other dignitaries gathered at Halifax's Government House to witness the granting of a pardon to Grand Chief Gabriel Sylliboy by Lieutenant Governor Grant, which recognized that his conviction ninety years earlier for hunting out of season had violated Mi'kmaq treaty rights. While the pardon was the initiative of the government of the day, its issuance by the representative of the Queen underscored its importance to the Mi'kmaq as well as Nova Scotian society. Working within the conventions of responsible government, the lieutenant governor used the moment to emphasize the importance of the treaty relationship and the need for dialogue. "Talking and listening, and sharing and dreaming together — that is how we heal — and that is how we will move toward reconciliation," Grant remarked. "Today's event and the Free Pardon are an element of the broader conversation which involves everyone." Pronouncing the pardon, the lieutenant governor articulated the unifying role that the Crown holds in modern society, even while operating within the strictures of responsible government. Only an apology from the lieutenant governor could extend the weight and dignity necessary in order to make it meaningful: "The Crown, which I represent on behalf of Her Majesty The Queen, exercises the duty at the direction of the democratically elected government of our province. Crown, Mi'kmaq, government, and all Nova Scotians join this action. For those of us on this side of the table, we apologize for past injustices and undertake to atone for these misdeeds...."[29]

During the 2016 royal visit by the Duke and Duchess of Cambridge to British Columbia, a remarkable description of the Crown's relationship with Indigenous Peoples was provided in the itinerary released by the Department of Canadian Heritage. Detailing an event where the duke would add a "Ring of Reconciliation" to the province's Black Rod, the official press release highlighted "... the historic relationship of the Sovereign as the guardian and protector of the Aboriginal Peoples...."[30] Such a description echoes the Royal Proclamation of 1763, as well as the sentiments of David Onley, lieutenant governor of Ontario (2007–14), when he said at a 2011 gathering of the Truth and Reconciliation Commission of Canada that "there is a historic, legal, and ethical obligation between the vice-regal office and Aboriginal People in Ontario."[31] All of this suggests an active role for the Crown in Canada with regard to its relationships with Indigenous Peoples, especially in light of the "rights of the Crown" articulated by Walter Bagehot in *The English Constitution* and claimed by the vice-regal offices of Canada:

- The right to be consulted
- The right to encourage
- The right to warn[32]

Along with these rights should be included the unique and non-partisan power of the Crown to *convene*. On June 21, 2016, National Aboriginal Day, Elizabeth Dowdeswell, lieutenant governor of Ontario, was joined by the governor general in touring the "Mush Hole," a former residential school in Brantford. Afterward, both representatives of the Queen in Canada acknowledged what happened at that school and the legacies it had left in its wake. In her address to the assembled dignitaries and members of the public that day, the lieutenant governor said: "One of the greatest privileges I have as Lieutenant Governor is the power to convene. By bringing people together, the institution of the Crown is able to spark new relationships and encourage innovative partnerships. And there is no more important conversation than how we will live together, sustainably and equitably. How we can reimagine a country that is true to its values and strong in its diversity."[33]

If the Crown's role is that of a guardian and protector, and the Queen and her representatives in this country still retain the rights outlined by Bagehot, then they find themselves intrinsic to reconciliation efforts in this country. There is a long history in these lands of the Dignified Crown convening council fires so that both sides could meet together in peace and friendship. That convening power, while long-dormant with regard to vice-regal relationships with Indigenous Peoples, is being renewed.

Since the Queen and her representatives occupy the very heart of Canadian democracy, they are routinely immersed in active symbolism. Symbols are important elements in our rapidly changing times. In fact, many of our most important national and provincial events, as well as those from our own personal lives, are filled with symbolism and ceremony — they are dynamic ways to present our history and values as a society while at the same time inviting its members to participate and reinterpret their meanings. Nova Scotia Lieutenant Governor Grant remarked on this important royal and vice-regal role in 2016, saying "We must not underestimate the importance of these symbols and documents — nations and communities are founded upon ideas, symbols, and covenants."[34] Whether on purpose or due to decades of neglect, the symbolic aspects of the Crown have been grossly under-used in this country — particularly concerning its place within the treaty relationship.

A unique feature of our constitutional monarchy is that the federal and provincial Crowns allow Her Majesty's relationships to adapt to meet the needs of specific regions and Nations. However, the protocols and relationships being developed by vice-regal offices, in consultation and with the consent of their Indigenous partners, need to transcend individual governors general or lieutenant governors by becoming embedded in the very heart our constitutional monarchy.

For many vice-regal offices across the country, the incoming official representative directs what themes will be supported and ceremonies attended. In many ways, the Dignified Crown resets itself with every appointment. This continual resetting contrasts sharply with the radically different approach to time and history taken by Indigenous Peoples. The lack of institutional memory in regards to Indigenous relationships must be remedied. Maintaining and actively participating in the historic and personal relationships between Her Majesty and Indigenous Peoples are increasingly included among the official and publicized duties of the representatives of the Crown in Canada — key and contemporary responsibilities as important as their duty to ensure there is always a prime minister or premier in place (Ontario Lieutenant Governor Elizabeth Dowdeswell underscored this important evolution in an address quoted at the beginning of this chapter).

Government Houses and/or offices are becoming regular gathering places — "safe spaces" — for Indigenous and non-Indigenous peoples to come together in community, observing such ancient protocols as receiving

The first gift from the Dignified Crown to the Chapel Royal at Massey College, Toronto, was tobacco presented by Lieutenant Governor Elizabeth Dowdeswell to Elder Garry Sault of the Mississaugas of the New Credit for a Sacred Fire lit on October 27, 2017. Hugh Segal, Principal of the College, looks on.

petitions, gift-giving, sacred fires, feasts, and other ceremonies specific to the particular Nation gathered at that time.

The Crown provides Canadians who are looking for ways to engage with their treaty partners with such a vehicle. With their unique ability to create community, connect with government, and be seen as above the political fray, the Queen and her representatives are as relevant today as they were when treaty relationships were first established. The Crown in Canada has historic and specific relationships needed for meaningful reconciliation. To put it simply: they are family. A government, restricted by a four-year election cycle, can never hold such a place. A message by Judith Guichon, lieutenant governor of British Columbia, expertly articulated this new vice-regal role:

> The words reconciliation, treaty and love are all verbs and therefore require ongoing action. The Vice-regal family, being connected by kinship, has the means to continuously work toward genuine reconciliation. There is no one end point to reconciliation. The vision must be of respectful relationships with ongoing responsibility to future generations. Just as the definition of the Crown remains elusive, so too the act of making treaty holistically will differ from nation to nation. However, with trust as a foundation, honesty, communication, integrity and love will be as constant as the Crown.
>
> Most would agree that real action is necessary to move reconciliation forward. Action is the way to heal injustice. The past injustices are part of our shared history, and as such the healing of these wounds will become part of the fabric which weaves us together as a stronger nation.[35]

As demonstrated in the important work of the Truth and Reconciliation Commission, the Residential School Program sought to destroy Indigenous languages and replace them with those that included concepts such as ceding, property ownership, and land surrenders. If we see the violence committed through the Residential School Program through the lens of our treaty relationships, it becomes an attack on members of our family and in particular their children.

The lack of education about Canada's foundational institutions, such as the Crown, has contributed to the gulf between non-Indigenous Canadians and First Nations. Part of reconciliation includes a re-engagement by Canadians in the mediums that once allowed for communication between our peoples, as well as the gathering of diverse communities together in peace and friendship.

In 2017, Canada commemorated the 150th anniversary of Confederation, a moment in history that redefined non-Indigenous settlement on these lands. Confederation, and the federal and provincial governments it established, subsumed and attempted to forcibly replace treaty relationships across this land. Confederation also opened the door to the establishment of the Indian Act and the Residential School Program that flowed from it. The Indian Act remains the law of the land to this day. These are some of the truths we need to face before reconciliation can begin.

The Queen and her representatives are integral to this journey. After all, they are family. The vice-regal representatives of Canada are re-engaging with their treaty partners across the country, restoring a symmetry that once existed at the heart of Indigenous and non-Indigenous coexistence on these lands. As the Duke of Cambridge said in his address to the Haida Nation in 2016, "The historic link between the Crown and the First Nations people is strong, and something that I hold dear to my heart."[36] It is a relationship key to the continued evolution of the Canadian state, linking its most ancient institution to the promise of a future filled with peace, friendship, and respect.

Notes

1. I am indebted to the offices of the lieutenant governors of Ontario, Nova Scotia, New Brunswick, British Columbia, and Saskatchewan for their assistance in researching this chapter. I would also like to thank Nick E. Bridges and Michael Jackson for their invaluable notes.

2. Elizabeth Dowdeswell, "The Crown and Reconciliation in 2017" (speech, delivered at Lakehead University, Thunder Bay, Ontario, February 15, 2017).

3. *Final Report of the Truth and Reconciliation Commission of Canada* (Toronto: Lorimer, 2015), 1:196–201.

4. Justice Murray Sinclair, "Commemoration of the Royal Proclamation, Chippewa of Rama First Nation" (speech delivered at Rama First Nation, near Orillia, Ontario, October 7, 2013).

5. Alexander C. Flick, *The Papers of Sir William Johnson* (Albany: University of the State of New York, 1925), 4:255–56.

6. Ibid., 279.

7. Ibid., 330–31.

8. Milton W. Hamilton, *The Papers of Sir William Johnson* (Albany: University of the State of New York, 1925), 6:309–11.

9. Ibid.

10. John Borrows, "Wampum at Niagara: The Royal Proclamation, Canadian Legal History, and Self-Government," in *Aboriginal and Treaty Rights in Canada: Essays on Law, Equality, and Respect for Difference,* Michael Asch, ed. (Vancouver: University of British Columbia Press, 1998), 155–72.

11. David Johnston, "Crown–First Nations Gathering," Ottawa, 23 January 2012, www.gg.ca/document.aspx?id=14404.

12. Dowdeswell, "The Crown and Reconciliation in 2017."

13. David Johnston, "Treaty Four Protocol Ceremony" (speech delivered at Fort Qu'Appelle, Saskatchewan, September 13, 2016).

14. Dowdeswell, "The Crown and Reconciliation in 2017."

15. Sir Anthony Jay, *Elizabeth R: The Role of the Monarchy Today* (London: BBC Books, 1992), 236.

16. Daniel K. Richter, "Indian-Colonist Conflicts and Alliances," in Daniel K. Richter and James Merrell, eds., *Beyond the Covenant Chain: The Iroquois and Their Neighbors in Indian North America, 1600–1800* (University Park: The Pennsylvania State University Press, 2003), 225.

17. Philippe Lagassé, "Conclusion: The Contentious Canadian Crown," in D. Michael Jackson and Philippe Lagassé, eds., *Canada and the Crown: Essays in Constitutional Monarchy* (Montreal and Kingston: McGill-Queen's University Press, 2013), 271–87.

18. *Final Report of the Truth and Reconciliation Commission of Canada*, 1:196–201.

19. The Queen's Covenant Chain at Massey College is a national symbol of reconciliation. The wampum was initially donated to Her Majesty Queen Elizabeth II by the Tidridge Family of Waterdown, Ontario, in 2017. Created by Ken Maracle, a faith keeper of the Lower Cayuga Longhouse (Cayuga Nation), the wampum was completed on Six Nations of the Grand River territory on March 8, 2014. Once it was cut free by Ken Maracle, the wampum was taken to the site of the Mohawk Institute, Canada's first "Indian residential school." Late that year, it was displayed at the reception for the Souharissen Natural Area in Waterdown, Ontario, attended by Lieutenant Governor David C. Onley and Mississaugas of the New Credit Chief M. Bryan Laforme on August 21, 2014. The wampum travelled across Canada from 2014 to 2016 and was witnessed by various representatives of the Crown, including Elizabeth Dowdeswell (Ontario), Frank Fagan (Newfoundland and Labrador), Judith Guichon (British Columbia), Lois Mitchell (Alberta), Steven Point (British Columbia), and Vaughn Solomon Schofield (Saskatchewan), as well as territorial commissioners Nellie T. Kusugak (Nunavut), Doug Phillips (Yukon), and George Tuccaro (Northwest Territories). The wampum was also witnessed by members of the office of the governor general of Canada, including secretary Stephen Wallace. On August 13, 2015, the wampum was displayed at the Canadian Museum for Human Rights and in 2016 shown to the Elders Council of the Treaty Relations Commission of Manitoba.

When not travelling, the wampum was displayed at Waterdown District High School and handled by countless students and other members of the community. A bead from the wampum was placed in the roots of *Shki Maajtaang*, a white oak tree planted in the Souharissen Natural Area.

20. Chief R. Stacey Laforme, letter to Chapel Royal Committee, 6 September 2016.
21. James William Daschuk, *Clearing the Plains: Disease, Politics of Starvation, and the Loss of Aboriginal Life* (Regina: University of Regina Press, 2013), 159.
22. Carolyn Speirs, "LG's Relationship with Indigenous Peoples," email to author, 17 March 2017.
23. Vaughn Solomon Schofield, "LG's Relationship with Indigenous Peoples," email to author, 17 March 2017.
24. Jocelyne Roy Vienneau, "A Day to Honour Residential School Survivors" (speech delivered at Government House, Fredericton, June 11, 2015).
25. Ibid.
26. The Government of Nova Scotia. "Ceremony to Commemorate our Treaty Relationship," Government House, Halifax, November 23, 2016.
27. J.J. Grant, "Ceremony to Commemorate our Treaty Relationship" (speech delivered at Government House, Halifax, November 23, 2016).
28. Ibid.
29. J.J. Grant, "Ceremony to Grant a Free Pardon to the Late Grand Chief Gabriel Sylliboy" (speech delivered at Government House, Halifax, February 17, 2017).
30. Day Three, Black Rod Ceremony held at Government House, Victoria, 2016, Royal Tour of the Duke and Duchess of Cambridge.
31. David C. Onley, "Truth and Reconciliation Commission of Canada 2011 Circle of Witness for the Revitalizing of Reconciliation in Ontario: A Cross-Cultural Dialogue" (speech delivered at Queen's Park, Ontario, September 28, 2011).
32. Walter Bagehot, *The English Constitution, and Other Political Essays* (New York: D. Appleton & Company, 1877), 143.
33. Elizabeth Dowdeswell, "National Aboriginal Day Address" (speech delivered at Woodland Cultural Centre, Brantford, Ontario, June 21, 2016).

34. Grant, "Ceremony to Commemorate Our Treaty Relationship."
35. Judith Guichon, "Reconciliation and the Vice-Regal Family" (speech, April 21, 2017, Government House, Victoria).
36. HRH The Duke of Cambridge, "Address to the Haida Nation" (speech, Haida Gwaii, September 30, 2016).

PART 3
THE CROWN AND CONTEMPORARY CANADA

6 |

The Crown in Canada: Is There a Canadian Monarchy?

Andrew Heard

Introduction

Canada's 150th anniversary celebrations in 2017 mark a singularly Canadian moment in time, as it is difficult to pinpoint when exactly in those 150 years Canada actually gained its independence. Canada's evolving relationship with the monarchy is emblematic of the transformation of the British North American colonies into the vibrant, distinctive, and thoroughly independent country that Canada is today. This chapter looks at Canada's evolution into an independent nation through the lens of its relationship with the monarchy. While one can easily define Canada as a sovereign nation, it is not clear how Canadian its sovereign is. Simply put, while Canada began as territory belonging to the monarch, does the monarchy now belong to Canada?

This chapter will explore these issues in several stages. Canada's emergence from colonial status provides a backdrop for discussing the tangible connections between Canada and the British monarch. In the process, we will see a deliberate creation of a Canadian identity for the monarch and an increasingly personal presence in Canada of the Queen and other members of the royal family. The Queen is now called, and refers to herself as, the Queen of Canada, as part of a process of localizing the monarchy and cutting lingering colonial ties to Great Britain. The political and cultural construction of a localized monarch has been successful to a certain degree, but it has not fundamentally altered the fact that the Queen *visits* Canada and *resides* in the United Kingdom. The degree to which the monarch was absorbed into Canada's constitutional structure became a lively legal issue with the move in 2013 to make changes to the laws of succession to the throne. A court case is working its way through appeal, which will effectively decide whether the whole monarchy and royal family are Canadian institutions, or whether our head of state is the monarch of the United Kingdom.[1]

Historical Evolution of the Monarchy in Canada

Canada emerged from its colonial origins in stages, some with formal legal milestones, such as the 1931 Statute of Westminster, which gave Canadian legislatures the power to amend or repeal Imperial legislation — even if it did not end Britain's power to legislate for Canada.[2] Many important milestones, however, occurred through changes in political practice, such as the decision taken at the 1930 Imperial conference to allow Dominion governments to advise the king directly on their own affairs; this power was most notably flexed in 1939, when the Canadian Cabinet asked the king to issue a separate declaration that Canada was at war with Germany. And yet even after the passage of the Canada Act, 1982, which ended the British Parliament's power to legislate for Canada and outlined a new process for Canadians to amend all aspects of our own Constitution for the first time, some questions linger about our remaining ties to the United Kingdom. The most visible of these ties is clearly Queen Elizabeth II, who serves as Canada's head of state.[3]

Canada's relationship with the monarchy has undergone tremendous changes since Confederation. In 1867, Canadians were British subjects, with their own self-governing "dominion." However, that dominion was very much part of the British Empire, which still controlled Canada's foreign relations. Canada's long socio-political evolution, from a colony into first an autonomous dominion and finally a fully independent nation, was marked by an evolution in how Canadians viewed the monarch and particularly the bilateral nature of Canada's relationship with the monarch.

The feelings that Canadians in 1867 held toward the monarchy in general and Queen Victoria in particular were those of British subjects belonging to a British Empire that spanned the globe at the time. As such, there would have been a mix of positive attachment, particularly among settlers of British origin, and possible resentment to a "foreign" monarch among some of those who were either Indigenous or rooted in other European nations. That said, attitudes toward the British monarchy reigning over Canada were complex by the late nineteenth century, and there was a range of views among French Canadians and Indigenous peoples.[4]

While Canadian sentiments toward the monarch began as those of British subjects toward the sovereign of the British Empire, by the late twentieth century Canadians were proclaiming their loyalty to and affection for Queen Elizabeth as the Queen of Canada. This cultural and political characterization of the Queen's relevance to us as our Canadian queen follows from the long process through which Canada became an independent actor on the world stage. More importantly, however, it exemplifies how Canadians went from being British subjects to a distinct multicultural nation living in its own sovereign state.[5] A milestone along the way came in 1953, when the Canadian Parliament passed a Royal Style and Titles Act to include reference to the Queen of Canada in her official title in Canada.[6] The new Canadian title helped launch a rebranding of the Queen as the Queen of Canada. In the process of evolving into a cultural nation, Canadian political leaders in the decades since 1953 have come to refer to the Queen almost exclusively as the Queen of Canada, downplaying the colonial origins of the relationship. And visiting members of the royal family have been welcomed as if they were "coming home" in some way. When the Queen came on a royal tour of Canada in 1973, she made the point that "It is as Queen of Canada that I am here."[7] After Canada created its own heraldic authority in 1988, the localization of the royal family took another symbolic step forward, with the design of unique personal Canadian flags for the Queen and several members of the royal family, to be flown when they are present in Canada.[8]

The emphasis on the Queen's local Canadian persona was accompanied by a dismantling of several royal symbols that stretched back to Canada's colonial past. In the years around Canada's centennial, conscious efforts were made to create unique Canadian national symbols that better reflected both its independent national status and its increasingly multicultural population.[9] Considerable controversy was generated by the Pearson government's move to replace the red ensign with the maple leaf flag in 1965.[10] Shortly after, the Royal Mail Canada was rebranded as Canada Post, while the Royal Canadian Navy and Royal Canadian Air Force were consolidated into a unified Canadian Forces (without any "royal" in the title).[11] Another important localization of national symbols occurred with the adoption of "O Canada" as the official national anthem in 1980, to displace the use of "God Save the Queen."[12] While the diminution of royal symbols may seem to run counter to the increasing embrace of the Queen as Queen of Canada, it is consistent if these particular symbols were seen as ties to Canada's colonial heritage and connection to Britain.

Tangible connections with the monarch and other members of the extended royal family have helped cement ties between Canadians and the monarchy, including numerous visits to Canada and even periods of residency here.[13] The nine years spent in Quebec and Nova Scotia by Prince Edward, Duke of Kent, between 1791 and 1800 created a considerable bond with this son of King George III. A royal visit some decades later by the Prince of Wales (to become King Edward VII) helped revive Canadian interest and sentiments toward the Crown.[14] This was followed up with the appointment of the Marquis of Lorne, Queen Victoria's son-in-law, as governor general (1878–83). He and Princess Louise were young at the time of their arrival in Canada (thirty-three and thirty, respectively) and did much to promote support for the Crown and to build Canada.[15] More royal visits followed, with Prince George, who would become King George V, travelling across Canada by train in 1891 and later visiting with his wife in 1901. These early royal visits set the stage for an increasing number and range of visits by members of the royal family as travel became so much easier in the twentieth century. In 1939, Canada received its first visit from a reigning monarch, when King George VI and his wife visited every province.[16] Another member of the extended royal family spent 1940–46 living in Canada, when the Earl of Athlone was governor general; his wife, Princess Alice, was a granddaughter of Queen Victoria.

The post-war period saw a tremendous increase in the frequency and variety of visits from the monarch and other members of the royal family. Queen Elizabeth II has made full use of the age of air travel, with twenty-three official visits to Canada.[17] A remarkable procession of members of the royal family have paid official and private working visits to Canada in the post-war period. Indeed, since 1951, twenty-four members of the extended royal family have visited Canada. And not a year has gone by since 1957 without at least one member of the royal family visiting Canada.[18] There is some irony in the fact that Canada has had far more contact with the royals since becoming a fully independent country than when it was an integral part of the British Empire.

However, this political and social portrayal of the monarch as something Canadian, divorced from the United Kingdom, is one that we must recognize as largely a cultural and political construction — and an incomplete one at that. Just as the Crown is a fictionalized legal persona, with

Princess Elizabeth square dancing in Ottawa during her visit in 1951, one year before she became queen.

distinct conceptions of the Queen in Right of Canada and each of the provinces, the Queen of Canada may be as much of a construction. To varying degrees, the same sort of process has been at work in the Queen's other realms as well, as nations attempted to localize their relationship with the monarch after gaining their full independence from Britain.[19] All fifteen overseas realms that have the Queen as their head of state refer in some way to the Queen as their own Queen, such as the Queen of Australia or the Queen of Papua New Guinea.

An important question arises: do these countries all share the part-time attentions of an individual who happens to be Queen in sixteen countries, or do they share a monarchy in which each country has a head of state who is simply the sovereign of the United Kingdom, exercising duties and powers under each state's constitution? To put the question more simply, does each of the realms have its own monarchy, or do they in some sense share the British monarchy? It is beyond the scope of this chapter to answer these questions for each of the realms, but an answer is attempted here for Canada's connection to the Queen.

The Issue of the Succession to the Throne

The interconnected relationships between the various realms and the monarch came into the limelight in recent years with the move to update some of the rules around the succession to the throne and royal marriages, which necessitated agreement and coordination among all the Queen's realms. Like Canada, fourteen other nations chose to retain the Queen as their head of state when they gained independence from Britain, and they shared a common interest in modernizing the laws governing succession to the throne.[20] The heads of government of the sixteen realms met in 2011 in Perth, Australia, and agreed that it was time to act. The question became more urgent when Prince William, second in line to the throne after Prince Charles, got married and his wife, Catherine, became pregnant.

Debates swirled over potential injustices if a girl was their first-born but one or more sons followed. In the modern age, it was seen as no longer socially acceptable to continue with the rules of male primogeniture,

Prince William and the Duchess of Cambridge were presented with personalized hockey jerseys in Yellowknife.

where male children take precedence in the line of succession over their sisters. The bar against the sovereign marrying a Roman Catholic seemed similarly antiquated.[21]

After the Perth Agreement, a United Kingdom House of Commons committee examined the issues, while negotiations were undertaken with the overseas realms on how they wished to implement the changes. In the end, the British government introduced legislation in December 2012, which received royal assent in April 2013 and came into full effect in 2015.[22] While New Zealand and Australia enacted their own domestic laws that mirrored the British legislation, Canada and the twelve other overseas realms essentially relied on the legislation in the United Kingdom to effect the changes. Assuming that all that was needed was respect for the convention embodied in the Statute of Westminster requiring its approval of changes to the laws of succession, Canada's Parliament passed a bill declaring that the British legislation "is assented to."[23] Barbados, as well as St. Vincent and the Grenadines, took a similar approach to Canada's, but with slightly different wording; each of their statutes "acquiesces to" the

British legislation.[24] Most of the other realms took no legislative action, however, believing instead that the legal changes in the United Kingdom were sufficient.[25]

Both New Zealand and Australia enacted their own equivalents to the British legislation.[26] In Australia, all six states adopted legislation to request the Commonwealth (federal) parliament to make changes under s. 51(xxxvii) of the Constitution, which were then embodied in the Succession to the Crown Act, 2015.[27] The assumption behind both countries' legislation was that they each had to take action to make the required amendments, since the British laws were incorporated as part of their domestic laws and any changes to them would have to be made by the local legislatures in order for them to have effect there. If they did not take action, it was believed that different individuals might succeed to the throne in the United Kingdom, in Australia, and in New Zealand.[28]

And therein lies the rub for Canada. Professors Geneviève Motard and Patrick Taillon launched a court case in Quebec because they believed that the relevant laws on succession had been fully incorporated into Canadian law and that no British legislation can have an effect on those laws' operation in Canada. In order for the changes to have effect in Canada, they would have to be made here and not in Britain — as the Australians and New Zealanders did. Furthermore, their argument is that these laws form part of the "office of the Queen," which the constitutional amendment procedures laid out in the Constitution Act, 1982 stipulate can be changed only with the unanimous agreement of the provinces.[29] The Quebec Superior Court decision on their case, made by Mr. Justice Claude Bouchard, did not support these arguments. He decided that all Canada's legislation did in effect was "recognize that the King or Queen in the United Kingdom, designated in accordance with the laws of the United Kingdom, is the King or Queen in Canada."[30]

In Justice Bouchard's view, the Canadian Constitution incorporates a "rule of recognition" that simply recognizes whoever is king or queen in the United Kingdom as the person who exercises the powers of the monarch in Canada.[31] Distilled to its essence, this perspective views the Canadian head of state as a legal abstraction, a collection of powers that are to be exercised by the King or Queen of the United Kingdom. The Queen may be given a local political and cultural mantle in Canada, which gives a more intimate Canadian connection to the sovereign, but that is different from the legal framework underpinning the Constitution. While the time and attention of the monarch is shared among her realms, and she exercises specific powers in each, the consequence of the *Motard* decision is that the monarchy as a larger institution remains British.

Alternative Views

However, these issues may well be decided differently on appeal and it is important to explore the alternative view. Clearly, Australians and New Zealanders have a belief in the monarchy as an institution now endogenously rooted in each country. In their view, a failure to enact local changes to the laws of succession could in years to come see different members of the royal family potentially acceding to the thrones of the different realms. Each country's connection to the monarch goes far deeper than a collection of powers that the British sovereign exercises with respect to Australia, New Zealand, or Canada. The entire legal edifice of the monarchy must now be viewed as being transplanted into each country, and each country can make whatever changes it wishes to those laws without effect in or on any other country. To ensure the same person reigns in all the realms, those nations should enact similar measures to keep the laws of succession in harmony. In effect, Australia has its own royal family, as do New Zealand and the United Kingdom; the same individuals in all three countries are now coincidentally lined up in the same order to accede to the thrones of Australia, New Zealand, and the United Kingdom. Peter Trepanier neatly sums up the gist of this position: "The Queen reigns separately and divisibly as queen of the United Kingdom, Canada, Australia, and New Zealand. The monarch is shared, but the institution of monarchy had evolved into separate constitutional entities."[32]

However, if the logic of Mr. Justice Bouchard's *Motard* decision prevails, Canada would continue to share the British monarchy with most of the other overseas realms. The sharing of the monarchy is emphasized in the royal style and titles, which across her realms make reference to her being queen of country X and "her other realms and territories." In Canada's case, her official title was changed by the Royal Style and Titles Act in 1953 to be: "Elizabeth the Second, by the Grace of God, of the United Kingdom, Canada and Her other Realms and Territories, Queen, Head of the Commonwealth, Defender of the Faith."[33] So the Queen was not viewed as belonging to a unique monarchy in each nation over which she reigns. Indeed, her Canadian title explicitly acknowledges that her reign extends elsewhere. Furthermore, in the debate on this bill in 1953, Prime Minister Louis St. Laurent told the House: "Her Majesty is now Queen of Canada but she is the Queen of Canada because she is Queen of the United Kingdom.... It is not a separate office ... it is the sovereign who is recognised as the sovereign of the United Kingdom who is our Sovereign...."[34]

K.C. Wheare has underlined how much the Canadian government at the time stressed the British element of the Crown.[35] For Canada, the Queen of the United Kingdom held executive authority over the uniting provinces both before and after Confederation. As noted earlier, the preamble to the Constitution Act, 1867 declared that the provinces would be united "under the Crown of the United Kingdom" and in section 9 it is stated: "The Executive Government and Authority of and over Canada is hereby declared to continue and be vested in the Queen." That this provision extended to the heirs and successors to the throne of the United Kingdom is also an established rule.[36] Canada's birth and original constitutional framework clearly situated the British monarch as the sovereign over Canada.

Separate Monarchies?

Originally, the British sovereign's authority over the British North American colonies flowed from the royal prerogative of the Crown over any overseas lands claimed for Britain. In exercising that authority, the monarch acted uniquely on the advice of British ministers. As the colonies became more settled and developed local institutions of government, they came to be governed by the legislative authority of the Imperial parliament in London. Some of those pieces of legislation, such as the British North America Act,

1867, explicitly stipulated certain powers for the monarch. In all instances it was understood that any actions by the monarch would be exercised only on the advice of British ministers. With the advent of responsible government in the Canadian colonies, the local governors would normally act on the advice of local ministers, but those governors were also subject to paramount instructions from the British government, to ensure that no colony acted against overall Imperial interests. While the local ministers could advise their own governors, they had no right at all to direct advice to the monarch. In Canada's case, advice from the prime minister would be given to the governor general, who would forward it to the government in London, which in turn would then determine what if anything to say to the monarch. The principal shift in Canada's evolution into independence occurred simply through a change in political practice, by changing which set of ministers could advise the monarch on Canadian affairs. The ability of different sets of ministers to advise the monarch depended on the development of new political conventions and separate legal personas in the Queen's different realms.

British Imperial governance initially operated on the principle of an indivisible Crown. As W.P.M. Kennedy wrote in 1922, "The Imperial crown is one and indivisible and is not broken up between the British Isles, the dominions, and the rest of the Empire."[37] The monarch acted uniformly across the Empire and only the British Cabinet could advise the sovereign.

The subsequent acceptance of a divisible Crown occurred in two dimensions, with the first being the recognition of distinct legal personas of the Crown within each jurisdiction, whether the Queen in Right of Australia or the Queen in Right of Canada. These personas were essential for conducting business as distinct legal entities in each jurisdiction. And with that division came the issue of which sets of Cabinet ministers would offer advice to the sovereign acting in each context. Initially, only the British government continued to advise the Queen when she was personally acting as the Queen in Right of Canada.

An important change occurred after the Imperial Conference of 1930, however, when it was agreed that henceforth the dominion governments would advise the monarch on their Dominion's unique affairs (such as appointing a governor general or signing an international treaty). However, that change did not in itself necessarily end the monarch's capacity to continue to act on behalf of the whole Empire, on the advice of British ministers. With the right of Dominion ministers to advise the king directly on their Dominion's affairs, the divisibility of the Crown became accepted. But that divisibility was of an abstracted collection of legal powers and of the choice of ministers to advise the king on exercising those powers. No one at the 1930 Imperial Conference would have thought that separate monarchies had been created for each dominion. Canada's original constitutional framework detailed only that the British monarch would exercise executive authority of Canada and stipulated some specific powers for the monarch with respect to Canada. And little has changed in law to alter those foundational facts.

Even the accession of King George VI after his brother's abdication in 1936 was not achieved as a result of Canadian legal action. While the Canadian Parliament weeks later "assented to" the United Kingdom's Abdication Act, this was entirely symbolic. There was no doubt that King George VI was Canada's sovereign from the moment he ascended to the throne in the United Kingdom; a proclamation was even issued at the time by the governor general to make the new sovereign known to his subjects in Canada.[38] The leader of the Co-operative Commonwealth Federation, J.S. Woodsworth, complained to the Commons that they were being asked to pass the abdication bill after they had approved a resolution congratulating the new king on his accession and assuring him of their loyalty.[39]

No substantive changes occurred to the Queen's position and powers in Canada prior to the passage of the Canada Act and Constitution Act, 1982. As noted above, Prime Minister St. Laurent emphatically stated in 1953 that there was "no separate office" distinguishing the Queen of Canada and the Queen of the United Kingdom. As a result, it would not have been possible in our constitutional law for there to be different individuals occupying the throne in the United Kingdom and being Queen over Canada. The 1982 changes did, however, make some potentially fundamental changes. The "office of the Queen" is now protected in s. 41 of the Constitution Act, 1982, which requires the unanimous consent of the federal parliament and the provincial legislatures for amendments.

Anne Twomey and others have argued that the relevant British statutes touching on succession have been incorporated into Canadian law, and that since the adoption of the Canada Act in 1982 the British parliament can no longer enact changes to those laws that would have effect in Canada.[40] As a result, local Canadian changes would have to be made in order to ensure that the same order of succession applied in Canada as in the United Kingdom and the other realms. If that were the case, then the changes would have to be made as a constitutional amendment under s. 41.

This argument, however, may be based on too broad a notion of the reception of law into the colonies and the subsequent consequences for amendment to those laws. Even after independence, the new national parliaments could have only limited powers over certain British legislation covering shared institutions. For example, the Canadian and New Zealand parliaments could and did abolish their own appeals to the Judicial Committee of the Privy Council after independence, but they could not legislate to determine who shall be appointed to the Privy Council in the United Kingdom or abolish the Judicial Committee itself. The institution they shared in the Judicial Committee is a British institution. According to the *Motard* decision, the existing constitutional law that is protected by s. 41 incorporates a rule of recognition — recognizing the current sovereign of the United Kingdom as the person to exercise executive authority over Canada, but not the entire edifice of British legislation relating to the monarchy and royal family.

The throne itself, and the royal family who surround and succeed the reigning monarch, are institutions of the United Kingdom, which other countries have chosen to continue sharing after gaining independence. The order of precedence has its principal effects on individuals born and permanently resident in the United Kingdom. Some might say it is impertinent for foreign countries to legislate for citizens of the United Kingdom about their right to succeed to the throne. Those foreign nations might properly legislate only if they possess their own endogenous monarchy and their own royal family; their monarch may just happen to occupy thrones elsewhere. After all, it has not been uncommon for members of European royal families to hold claims to several different thrones.

Conclusion

The issue comes down to whether there are separate monarchies in the overseas realms. But in the case of Canada at least, there has been no change to the legal framework that provided that the occupier of the British throne is sovereign over Canada. She may be called, among her many titles, the Queen of Canada, but no direct action so far has created a Canadian monarch or Canadian royal family. The "office of the Queen" protected by s. 41 is, strictly speaking, a collection of powers to be exercised by the Queen or King of the United Kingdom. Fundamental constitutional convention ensures that those powers are exercised only on the advice of Canadian ministers.

The ultimate judicial decision on the issues raised in *Motard* will settle which of the two competing views should prevail as a matter of law. For the judiciary to declare that the monarchy and the laws supporting it are Canadian and must be legislated for in Canada, however, may be an invention by judicial fiat of something that contradicts both constitutional history and common sense. The Queen and the royal family are British and not Canadian. Those in line to the throne and their spouses are neither citizens nor residents of Canada. This fact was brought home when a special exemption category had to be created for the Order of Canada before Prince Philip could be named to the Order in April 2013: only citizens of Canada are normally eligible.[41] The sovereign is undoubtedly part of the Canadian constitutional structure by definition,[42] but it is debatable whether those in line to the throne are part of the body politic. The whole extended royal family, with its rules on marriage and its line of succession to the throne, remains in true essence a British institution.[43]

Many Canadians claim an attachment to the Queen and members of the royal family, but that cannot void the Britishness of the royals. For years I have canvassed the students in my Canadian government class about the monarchy. In these very diverse Vancouver-area classes, a majority has always supported retaining the monarchy. If I ask whether they think of Queen Elizabeth as the Queen of Canada, virtually every hand is raised. But if I ask who views Queen Elizabeth as a Canadian, it is rare for even a single hand to go up.

The acceptance of this duality, however, does not undermine a real and positive relationship between Canada and the Queen. In the modern era, a majority of Canadians have supported continued links to the monarchy, with only fleeting swings toward republicanism.[44] Canada shares a link with the other fifteen realms that honours a common bond while celebrating the independence and diversity of the Queen's realms. Some might say that Canada should follow the example of Australia and New Zealand, emphasizing their independence from a colonial past and enacting local legislation governing the succession to the throne. But such an action risks creating a complete legal fiction, of a local monarchy and royal family that everyone knows is in reality British. Canada finds good company in most of the overseas realms, which are proudly independent nations and yet accept that the Queen of the United Kingdom acts as their sovereign. There is little need for Canada to go beyond a political and cultural localization that embraces the monarch without appropriating her.

Notes

1. This case was launched by two law professors at l'Université Laval. The Quebec Superior Court has given an initial decision, *Motard c. Canada (Procureure générale)* 2016 QCCS 558, and the matter is being appealed to the Quebec Court of Appeal at the time of writing this chapter. The issue is almost certain to be further appealed to the Supreme Court of Canada.

2. In a notable exception to the new powers of Canadian legislatures, the British North America Act became fully amendable in Canada only with the passage of the Constitution Act, 1982.

3. Other lesser known constitutional connections with the United Kingdom lie in sections 55 through 57 of the Constitution Act, 1867. Section 55 gives the governor general the option of reserving a bill passed by the two houses of parliament "for the Queen's pleasure." Section 56 requires that the governor general send copies of any acts of Parliament to the British government; the British government has the power to ask the Queen to disallow Canadian legislation within two years of its passage through the Canadian Parliament. In dealing with reserved bills, the British government has the option of advising the Queen to either give royal assent or not. However, constitutional conventions have nullified the governor general's power to reserve a bill, the duty to send copies of legislation to London, and the British government's powers of disallowance.

4. See D. Michael Jackson, *The Crown and Canadian Federalism* (Toronto: Dundurn, 2013), 38–54; Serge Joyal, "La Couronne au Québec: de credo rassurant à bouc émissaire commode," in *Canada and the Crown: Essays on Constitutional Monarchy,* D. Michael Jackson and Philippe Lagassé, eds. (Montreal and Kingston: McGill-Queen's University Press, 2013), 33–61; and Donal Lowry, "The Crown, Empire Loyalism and the Assimilation of Non-British White Subjects in the British World: An Argument Against 'Ethnic Determinism,'" *Journal of Imperial and Commonwealth History* 31, no. 2 (2003): 96–120.

5. Statistics Canada's inclusion of "Canadian" as a permissible option for Canadians describing their ethnic origins in the national census, surprisingly, dates only from 2006.

6. Royal Style and Titles Act, R.S.C., 1985, c. R-12, s. 2.

7. Department of Canadian Heritage, *A Crown of Maples: Constitutional Monarchy in Canada* (Ottawa: Government of Canada, 2012), 61.

8. Personal Canadian flags have been approved for the Queen, the Prince of Wales, the Duke of Cambridge, the Duke of York, the Earl of Wessex, and the Princess Royal. Government of Canada, "Canadian Flags of the Royal Family," http://canada.pch.gc.ca/eng/1445001063704.

9. An interesting insight into the willingness to embrace some royal and Imperial symbols by Canadians of non-British origin is discussed in Christian P. Champion, "Courting 'Our Ethnic Friends': Canadianism, Britishness, and New Canadians, 1950–1970," *Canadian Ethnic Studies* 38, no. 1 (2006): 23–46.

10. It should be noted that there was a backlash in some areas of the country, with both Manitoba and Ontario adopting their own provincial flags with variations on the red ensign in reaction to the adoption of the new national flag.

11. This localization of the military was reversed by the Harper government in 2011, when it reintroduced the Royal Canadian Navy and Royal Canadian Air Force as official names for the marine and air services. This was a curious move, since there had been little public debate or pressure for such a move for many years. The Harper government's renewed emphasis on the monarchy is discussed in Raymond B. Blake, "A New Canadian Dynamism? From Multiculturalism and Diversity to History and Core Values," *British Journal of Canadian Studies* 26, no. 1 (2013): 95–97.

12. Prior to 1980, "O Canada" had been increasingly used as an informal anthem, while "The Maple Leaf Forever" receded as an unofficial alternative to "God Save the Queen." Since 1980, "God Save the Queen" has been known informally as the royal anthem in Canada. It should be noted that prior to 1980 Canada did not have an official anthem, in the sense of being set out in statute or regulation; even "God Save the Queen" held its prime place only through tradition.

13. Arthur Bousfield and Garry Toffoli, *Home to Canada: Royal Tours, 1786–2010* (Toronto: Dundurn, 2010).

14. John G. Bourinot, "Royal Visits to Canada: A Historical Retrospect,"

Forum 32, no. 1 (1901): 40–52; Ian Radforth, *Royal Spectacle: The 1860 Visit of the Prince of Wales to Canada and the United States* (Toronto: University of Toronto Press, 2004, 2012).

15. Carolyn Harris, "Royalty at Rideau Hall: Lord Lorne, Princess Louise, and the Emergence of the Canadian Crown," in *Canada and the Crown: Essays on Constitutional Monarchy*, D. Michael Jackson and Philippe Lagassé, eds. (Montreal and Kingston: McGill-Queen's University Press, 2014), 17–32.

16. This was in fact the first visit by a reigning monarch to any part of the Commonwealth or Empire outside Britain.

17. The Queen paid an extended visit to Canada in 1951 with the Duke of Edinburgh while she was still a princess. Since ascending the throne she has made twenty-two official visits and nine unofficial stopovers. Government of Canada, "Past Royal Tours," http://canada.pch.gc.ca/eng/1445001961355.

18. Ibid.

19. Queen Elizabeth II is the head of state of Antigua and Barbuda, Australia, Barbados, the Bahamas, Belize, Canada, Grenada, Jamaica, New Zealand, Papua New Guinea, Saint Kitts and Nevis, Saint Lucia, Saint Vincent and the Grenadines, the Solomon Islands, Tuvalu, and the United Kingdom.

20. A comprehensive account of the laws of succession in the United Kingdom may be found in Noel Cox, "The Law of Succession to the Crown in New Zealand," *Waikato Law Review* 7 (1999): 49.

21. The prohibition against the sovereign being a Roman Catholic, however, has been maintained, because the queen is the supreme governor of the Church of England. As part of their coronation ceremony, a new British monarch also swears to "inviolably maintain and preserve the Settlement of the true Protestant Religion as established by the Laws made in Scotland"; "The Accession Council," Privy Council Office, accessed June 22, 2017, https://privycouncil.independent.gov.uk/privy-council/the-accession-council/.

22. Succession to the Crown Act, 2013, c.20. This law amended a range of legislation and common law, but the principal effects were to alter the Act of Settlement, 1701, and to repeal the Royal Marriages Act, 1772. The

legislation ended male primogeniture and the ban on marrying Catholics, and greatly reduced the number of members of the royal family who require the permission of the Queen to marry. Because of delays in securing the passage of companion legislation in Australia, the legislation came into force only on March 26, 2015. The Succession to the Crown Act 2013 (Commencement) Order 2015, 2015 No. 894 (C. 56).

23. Succession to the Throne Act, 2013, S.C. 2013, c.6, s. 2.

24. Each country's parliament enacted legislation with the title The Succession to the Throne Act, 2013.

25. The prime ministers of these realms had previously consented in principle to the changes, through the 2011 agreement reached in Perth.

26. The New Zealand legislation is the Royal Succession Act, 2013, 2013 No. 149.

27. No. 23, 2015. No future changes may be made to this act without the consent of all six of the states; see s. 12.

28. The Australian legislation contains a provision, s. 3, stating that its objective is "to change the law relating to the effect of gender and marriage on royal succession, consistently with changes made to that law in the United Kingdom, so that the Sovereign of Australia is the same person as the Sovereign of the United Kingdom."

29. See s. 41(a).

30. *Motard c. Canada (Procureure générale)* [2016] Q.C.C.S. 558, at para 155.

31. Ibid., at para 153.

32. Peter Trepanier, "A Not Unwilling Subject: Canada and Her Queen," in *Majesty in Canada: Essays on the Role of Royalty,* Colin M. Coates, ed. (Toronto: Dundurn, 2006), 143.

33. Royal Style and Titles Act, R.S.C., 1985, c. R-12, s. 2.

34. *Hansard,* February 3, 1953, 1566.

35. K.C. Wheare, *The Constitutional Structure of the Commonwealth* (Oxford: Oxford University Press, 1960), 167.

36. The application to the heirs and successors was directly stated in the original s. 2 of the Constitution Act, 1867, but this section was removed after an equivalent rule was included in the general Interpretation Act, 1889. See Mark D. Walters, "Succession to the Throne and the Architecture

of the Constitution of Canada," in *The Crown and Parliament*, Michel Bédard and Philippe Lagassé, eds. (Montreal: Éditions Yvon Blais, 2013), 267–73.

37. W.P.M. Kennedy, *The Constitution of Canada: An Introduction to its Development and Law* (Oxford: Oxford University Press, 1922), 379.

38. The proclamation is found at: *Canada Gazette*. 70, no. 25 (1936): 1578; www.collectionscanada.gc.ca/databases/canada-gazette/093/001060-119.01-e.php?image_id_nbr=290977&document_id_nbr=8061&f=p&PHPSESSID=85ur4qk8oun4a999449tde68t0.

39. *Hansard*, January 15, 1937, 13.

40. Anne Twomey, "Royal Succession, Abdication, and Regency in the Realms," *Review of Constitutional Studies* 22, no. 1 (2017): 33 at 44, n. 52.

41. Bill Curry, "Prince Philip Named to the Order of Canada," *Globe and Mail*, April 26, 2013.

42. *Chainnigh v. A.G. Canada*, [2008] F.C. 69.

43. The High Court of Australia has gone as far as determining that the United Kingdom is a "foreign power" and that citizens of the U.K. are barred from seeking election to the Australian Parliament under s. 44 of the Australian Constitution.

44. See David E. Smith, *The Republican Option in Canada, Past and Present* (Toronto: University of Toronto Press, 1999).

7 |

The Oath of Allegiance: A New Perspective

Serge Joyal

Introduction

According to Canada's constitution, Her Majesty the Queen, who is the head of state of the United Kingdom, is simultaneously the head of state of Canada. Indeed, the Queen is the head of state of fourteen other Commonwealth realms, as well as being acknowledged as "Head of the Commonwealth."

The multiple roles of the Queen have given rise to considerable misunderstanding in Canada. This misunderstanding is well illustrated by challenges that have arisen over the last fifty years to the oath of allegiance sworn or affirmed to the Queen. As a constitutional monarchy, Canada's oath of allegiance is framed in language focused explicitly on the Queen rather than on the constitution or the people of Canada. The oath states: "I do swear, that I will be faithful and bear true allegiance to Her Majesty Queen Elizabeth II." Taking this oath is obligatory before many public officials can assume their functions. It is required to be sworn or affirmed by all federal parliamentarians as well as their provincial and territorial counterparts. The oath is also taken by all judges, members of the armed forces, and many other senior officials and public servants.

The oath of allegiance can be a useful barometer of Canada's development from 1867 to today. The oath has changed from one that was focused on the person of the Queen to a more abstract concept that identifies the Queen, the Crown, as an ideal that embodies the values and principles of

THE CROWN AND CONTEMPORARY CANADA

Canada. Two events in particular helped in the transformation of the appreciation of the Crown: first, the rise of the Parti Québécois and the provincial government it formed in Quebec in 1976; and second, the patriation of the Constitution in 1982 that included a Charter of Rights and Freedoms.

In 1867, the oath was not only a requirement for assuming public office; it also provided evidence of Canada's attachment to the British Empire, whose identity was confirmed through the Queen. During this period, there was no attempt or thought to identify the Queen as the Sovereign or Queen of Canada. Queen Victoria was, as her title made clear, the Queen of the United Kingdom of Great Britain and Ireland. It was only after the First World War, when Canada became insistent on its rights to claim and exercise full sovereignty, that the question of the sovereign's identity over different member states of the emerging Commonwealth first arose. With the accession of Queen Elizabeth II in 1952, and the adoption of the Royal Style and Titles Act in 1953, the Queen was recognized explicitly for the first time as Queen of Canada.

Beginning in the mid-1970s, after the Parti Québécois came to power, the oath of allegiance was denounced as a colonial vestige that was no longer appropriate for Canada and especially for Quebec. Following the patriation of the Constitution in 1982 with the Charter of Rights and Freedoms, a new wave of challenges to the oath of allegiance arose in Ontario. Through nine different court cases, the oath of allegiance was questioned on various grounds, largely based on the Queen's identity as Queen of the United Kingdom. The response to both of these challenges has transformed the meaning and significance of the Crown and demonstrated its continuing importance to Canada's constitution and national identity.

The Oath of Allegiance to the Queen as a Person: 1867–1919

When the British North America Act (now the Constitution Act, 1867) came into force, there was no doubt in the minds of the Fathers of Confederation that the oath to "be faithful and bear true Allegiance to Her Majesty Queen Victoria" was addressed to the very person of the sovereign, the Queen of the United Kingdom of Great Britain and Ireland, as provided for in the preamble of the act, which federated the four original colonies under the British Crown: "Whereas the Provinces of Canada, Nova Scotia, and New Brunswick have expressed their Desire to be federally united into One Dominion under the Crown of the United Kingdom of Great Britain and Ireland, with a Constitution similar in Principle to that of the United Kingdom."

The language and form of the oath of allegiance included in the Constitution Act, 1867 replicated in fact the text of the new oath for British MPs enacted in the Parliamentary Oaths Act adopted one year earlier in Westminster, in 1866. This new British oath no longer included recognition of the supremacy of the sovereign, or the obligation to swear "upon the true faith of a Christian."[1] The oath in the Promissory Oaths Act states: "I, (name of the Member), do swear that I will be faithful and bear true Allegiance to Her Majesty Queen Victoria, Her Heirs and Successors, according to Law. So help me God."[2] As some analysts have noted, this simplified language is closely modelled on the text of the ancient feudal oath of allegiance required by medieval kings.[3] During the Middle Ages, as far back as King Egbert of Wessex (802–39), the "King of the English,"[4] allegiance was made to the person of the king, who, in exchange for the submission of the subject, would commit to protect him accordingly.

In 1867, Canadians were British subjects, part of a larger Empire, and they would remain subjects for more than a century. This situation did not change following the adoption of the first Citizenship Act in 1947, when an explicit mention in the first page of the new passport stated that "a Canadian citizen is a British subject," a declaration that persisted until 1977.[5] We abandoned our identity as "subjects" only after that year. This state of affairs was never seen as one that needed to be addressed urgently: it was in fact a process of gradual transition from being British subjects, to mixed identity subjects, and finally, exclusively Canadian citizens.

In 1867, and until the Balfour Report in 1926 and the enactment of the Statute of Westminster in 1931, the British Crown was one and indivisible: to be otherwise was unthinkable. The attachment to the person of the sovereign remained quite evident through the celebrations that marked the Golden and Diamond Jubilees of Queen Victoria in 1887 and 1897. It was also clearly expressed at the Coronation of King Edward VII in 1902: "He's the symbol of the thing — is the King. Britain's King, our King, One King. For the

Mug commemorating the coronation of King Edward VII and Queen Alexandra, "Coronation ... Souvenir 1902"; a world map indicates the various parts of the British Empire, with Queen Alexandra and King Edward VII on either side. Captions include "He's the symbol of the thing — is the King. Britain's King, our King, one King" and "For the Crown is our Communion — And the Seal of our free Union — Is the King." Enameled tin, 1902.

Crown is our communion and the seal of our free union is our King." These are the loyal sentiments expressed on a coronation cup distributed in 1902.[6]

Canada's participation in the First World War prompted the realization that Canada needed to be more fully sovereign and autonomous on the international level; in seeking this, there was no question about remaining loyal to the Crown. In 1919, when the House of Commons was debating whether Canada should sign, in its own name, the Versailles Treaty ending the First World War, it would have been difficult for most Canadians to imagine that they would have any other status than that of British subjects, having the benefit of a direct link with the king: "M. Louis-Joseph Gauthier (Liberal MP — St. Hyacinthe-Rouville, Quebec): We want to remain with Great Britain. And, may I be permitted to say, our only safeguards are His Majesty the King, the Union Jack and the British authorities. I have confidence in no other.... We will remain British subjects and we will remain faithful British subjects."[7]

In the context of the war, a Crown divided between Great Britain and Canada would have seemed to weaken the prestige conveyed by the British sovereign, a king and emperor,[8] reigning over an "empire on which the sun never sets."[9] The pride of belonging to the greatest empire in the world was manifest. Canadian troops fought for four years yelling the battle cry "For King and Country," and the honour of serving the king was palpable, inspiring, and a source of real pride.

A new situation developed during the course of the war. The Imperial War Conference that took place March 21–April 27, 1917, in London, adopted Resolution IX, whereby Imperial constitutional relations would be redefined "based upon a full recognition of the Dominions as autonomous nations of an Imperial Commonwealth," a status that would be formalized after the war.[10] By the end of the war, Canada's army was under Canadian command. Canada signed the Versailles Treaty in its own name under Great Britain, in recognition of the fact that Canada had attained a status equal to other dominions for its considerable war efforts.[11] The British Empire would progressively transform itself into the Commonwealth following the Balfour Report of 1926. The main clauses of the report were later enacted in 1931 as the Statute of Westminster. This statute confirmed the full sovereignty of Canada and its Parliament[12] as totally distinct from Great Britain, which would no longer claim the authority to make laws for Canada. The British sovereign became the head of state of two totally sovereign and independent countries, even though the bearer of the Canadian Crown happened to be the bearer of the British Crown. It was not deemed necessary in 1931 to amend the original text of the oath of allegiance: the perception that "allegiance and loyalty" were to the person of the sovereign continued to live on, thus maintaining a strong historical link to the constitutional origins of the country and to its royal roots, always embodied in the British Crown.

British Dominions Beyond the Seas

Changes in the royal title acknowledged the shift that was transforming the British Empire into the British Commonwealth, and later, the Commonwealth of Nations. As early as 1901, the title of His Majesty Edward the Seventh was "By the Grace of God, of the United Kingdom of Great Britain and Ireland and of the *British Dominions beyond the Seas* King, Defender of the Faith, Emperor of India."[13] The phrase "British Dominions beyond the Seas" recognized that these former colonies were fully sovereign and that their association in the future Commonwealth was linked to their common recognition of the king-emperor as their own sovereign. The title of the sovereign was, by statutes enacted in 1927,[14] also subject to adjustment by each realm in the Commonwealth. This adjustment became fully evident with the accession of Elizabeth II to the throne in 1952.

The Queen of Canada

The accession to the throne of Queen Elizabeth II marked a historic leap. In 1953, prior to the Queen's coronation and for the first time in the history of the country since 1534, the year Canada became part of the Kingdom of France, the Canadian parliament adopted a law on "royal style and titles." The preamble of that act stipulates that "recognizing that the present form is not in accordance with present constitutional relations within the Commonwealth … in the present stage of development of the Commonwealth relationship, it would be in accord with the established constitutional position that each member country should use for its own purposes a form suitable to its own particular circumstances but retaining a substantial element common to all."[15] This act reaffirms, at first glance, the dual sovereignty represented in the person of the Queen: "Elizabeth the Second, by the Grace of God, of the United Kingdom, Canada and Her other Realms and Territories Queen, Head of the Commonwealth, Defender of the Faith."[16]

The act officially recognizes Canada's sovereign with a title of her own. Canada was thus recognizing its own Queen, whose Crown was specific to Canada, distinct from the Crown of Great Britain. Elizabeth II is the Queen of Canada because she is first Queen of Great Britain, as was clearly emphasized by Prime Minister Louis St. Laurent at the time of the debate on the Royal Style and Titles Act:

> Her Majesty is now the Queen of Canada but she is the Queen of Canada because she is the Queen of the United Kingdom and because the people of Canada are happy to recognize as their sovereign the person who is

the sovereign of the United Kingdom. It is not a separate office. It is the recognition of the traditional development of our institutions; that our parliament is headed by the sovereign; who is recognized as the sovereign of the United Kingdom who is our sovereign and who is loyally and, I may say, affectionately recognized as the sovereign of our country.[17]

In the Canadian zeitgeist, there was a particular need to insist on the distinction between the two crowns that were worn by the same person. The sameness of the person called to wear both distinct crowns is what ensures the living continuity of the Canadian Crown. These convictions were expressed during the debate on the Royal Style and Titles Act: "The Hon. James MacKerras Macdonnell (Progressive Conservative MP — Greenwood, Ontario): The crown is a symbol of the unity which we all desire, without exception. I am confident that the bonds of unity will become stronger and more sincere because of everyone's attachment for such a young, beautiful and gracious Queen."[18]

With this duality of crowns worn by the same physical person, there seemed to be no need to revisit the text of the original oath of 1867. The oath continued to reflect the reality perceived at that time: namely, an allegiance to the person of the monarch, as had always been the case. The person of the Queen herself was intimately linked to the existence and continuity of the Canadian Crown.[19]

Political Challenges to the Oath of Allegiance

The Queen and her incarnation of the Crown of Canada maintained the perception that the allegiance, sworn or affirmed in the oath, is to the person of the Queen. This general perception first became controversial in 1970, following the election of the first separatist parliamentarians to the Quebec legislative assembly. They protested the obligation of swearing an oath of allegiance to Queen Elizabeth II, whom they deemed to be a foreign sovereign. They denounced the oath's colonialist pedigree.

Plate commemorating the Silver Jubilee of Queen Elizabeth II: Her Majesty Queen Elizabeth II of Canada, on the occasion of her Silver Jubilee in 1977, is surrounded by the four Canadian governors general who had served during her reign: Vincent Massey, Georges Vanier, Roland Michener, and Jules Léger. Fine porcelain, Mercian China — Burton-Upon-Trent, England, designed by A. Kitson Towler, DFA ATD, numbered 328/500; 1977.

The Quebec premier, Robert Bourassa, asked his justice minister, Jérôme Choquette, to study the implications of the possibility that separatist members of the National Assembly (MNAs) could refuse to swear the oath of allegiance to the Queen. According to Bourassa, "This oath of loyalty is obsolete because Canada is an independent country and the Queen has no real authority."[20] Bourassa attempted to appease the protesters and to gain time. The premier knew full well that article 128 of the Constitution Act, 1867, could not be easily amended and he certainly did not want to venture into that domain. Despite their protests, and anxious to take their seats, the Parti Québécois (PQ) MNAs swore the oath while conspicuously crossing their fingers, in an attempt to appease their republican convictions. The same scenario was repeated some years later when the PQ formed the Quebec government in 1976: crossed fingers kept up the perception that their convictions had not been compromised.

A way out was finally found in 1982, when the René Lévesque government introduced an act respecting the National Assembly, Article 15 of which states that an MNA must swear a second oath set out in Annex I: "I, (name of the Member), declare under oath that I will be loyal to the people of Québec and that I will perform the duties of Member honestly and justly *in conformity with the constitution of Québec."* [21] This second oath sworn by MNAs does not in fact contradict the oath required by section 128 of the Constitution Act, 1867, because it implies a commitment to respect the "Constitution of Quebec," the legislative sovereignty of which is enshrined in the status of the lieutenant governor,[22] the representative of Her Majesty in Right of the Province of Quebec. In fact, the second oath makes explicit what future court decisions would interpret as implicit in the first oath.

From time to time, there are proposals by Quebec politicians made during political campaigns to abolish the oath to the Queen. For example, one PQ leadership candidate asserted in 2014 that the oath of allegiance to the Queen is a "secondary, nonessential characteristic of the monarchy" and could be unilaterally amended by the Quebec legislature.[23] However, the oath is intimately linked to the existence of the status of the sovereign, who presides over the constitutional order as holder of the executive and legislative power in right of the province. An amendment to abolish the oath would affect "the office of the Queen, the Governor General and of the Lieutenant governor of a province" as provided by s. 41 (a) of the Constitution Act, 1982. Such an amendment cannot be adopted by a province alone.

Later, in 1990, when Bloc Québécois MPs were elected to the House of Commons, its members were required to swear the oath of allegiance like every MP since 1867. They did so after having publicly stated that they would follow René Lévesque's example by crossing their fingers in protest.[24] A point of order raised in the House of Commons challenged this gesture, alleging that it made a travesty of the oath of allegiance, since there was no intent to truly swear allegiance to Her Majesty the Queen. The Speaker ruled that "[y]our Speaker is not empowered to make a judgment on the circumstances or the sincerity with which a duly elected member takes the oath of allegiance" and "[o]nly the House can examine the conduct of its members and only the House can take action if it decides action is required."[25] The decision of the Speaker closed the matter and no further action was taken.

We can hardly be surprised that the person of Her Majesty was at the centre of protests by sovereigntist MPs, since the Queen herself is the expression of the Crown. The oath of allegiance remains the privileged moment where the existence and legitimacy of Canada's Crown are expressed and affirmed. The person of Her Majesty remains a powerful element of the constitutional monarchy, and one can certainly understand that sustained media coverage of her public activity by an abundant and curious press fosters her presence as a person in the minds of the people. In various court decisions, the Queen has also been recognized as having the same rights as any other person.[26]

These references to the person of the sovereign explain in large part why the oath of allegiance, in the minds of many, is still perceived as addressed to Her Majesty as a person, as had traditionally been the case since 1867.

Legal Challenges of the Oath of Allegiance Since Canadian Patriation and the Charter

Other precedents in case law have taken another direction and set aside the predominant public perception. Many court decisions have completely "depersonalized" the oath of allegiance, even though the original text remains unchanged. The great irony is that it is the Ontario courts that delivered these conclusions, in four distinct cases, each one more precise than the other, dating from 1992 to 2015. Nine legal proceedings were brought before the Ontario Superior Court of Justice, the Federal Court, the Federal Court of Appeal, and, finally, the Ontario Court of Appeal, whose judgment was confirmed by the Supreme Court's refusal to hear an appeal in 2015.[27]

It may be surprising that the oath of allegiance could stir up so many challenges in the last twenty-five years. These judicial decisions relating to the oath of allegiance were first triggered by its reference in the Citizenship Act and in the General Regulations of the Canadian Armed Forces. Several arguments were given to sustain the unconstitutionality of the oath as provided for in section 28 of the Citizenship Act: its incompatibility with section 2(a) (freedom of conscience and religion), 2(b) (freedom of expression), 2(d) (freedom of peaceful assembly), section 15(1) (equality before the law), and section 27 (the preservation of multiculturalism) of the Canadian Charter of Rights and Freedoms. As well, some arguments referred to Her Majesty as the head of the Church of England, a church with no official status in Canada, or to the fact that Her Majesty was the sovereign of a foreign state, the United Kingdom, and that she was not a Canadian citizen.

All of these allegations referred to the person of Elizabeth II: her identity, her dynastic ties, her personal origins, her rank, and the religion she practises. No one denied that these characteristics were tied to the person of Her Majesty.

The Oath of Allegiance and the Charter of Rights and Freedoms

It is revealing to briefly review the reasons of the nine judgments, which concluded that the oath of allegiance does not violate the provisions of the Charter and that, contrary to popular belief held until then, the oath of allegiance is not directed to the person of Her Majesty but rather to the "system of government" represented by the constitutional order that governs Canada. The judicial interpretation of the oath of allegiance reflects an adaptation to the socio-political realities that gradually emerged following the enactment of the Statute of Westminster in 1931 and, more recently, following the adoption of the Canadian Charter of Rights and Freedoms in 1982.

The first decision regarding the oath of allegiance was made in the Federal Court in 1979 by Judge Collier.[28] A citizenship candidate, a Mr. Heib, interpreted the oath as a promise binding him to bear allegiance to a living person, Queen Elizabeth II, and her successors. Heib contended that "he cannot bring himself to swear allegiance to any living person."[29] He asked to be excused from swearing the oath of allegiance required by the Citizenship Act. Heib's argument did not challenge the constitutionality of the substance of the oath itself, but rather asked the court that he be excused from swearing the oath. The judge suggested to Heib that "the oath can be regarded not as a promise to a particular person, but as a promise to the theoretical political apex of our Canadian parliamentary system of constitutional monarchy."[30] Despite the judge's attempt to accommodate Heib's reservations, Heib maintained his position and the judge concluded that it was impossible for him to obtain citizenship without swearing the oath.

This was the first time that a court proposed an interpretation other than the plain meaning of the words included in the oath of allegiance. Even though stated as an *obiter dictum* in the Federal Court decision, the approach adopted by Judge Collier would resurface in 1992 in a new challenge to the oath of allegiance, again related to the Citizenship Act.

In *Roach v. Canada*,[31] the litigant alleged that the "citizenship oath violates certain rights and fundamental freedoms guaranteed under the Canadian Charter of Rights and Freedoms … under section 2 (a) and (b) and that it is against his conscience to make oaths to all but the Supreme Being and to the principles of truth, freedom, equality, justice and the rule of law."[32] Furthermore, he argued that taking the oath would have the effect of hindering his freedom to express his republican sentiments. Finally, he argued that the oath violated his freedom of religion under section 2(a) "inasmuch as Her Majesty the Queen is supreme governor of the Anglican Church and he is not of that faith."[33]

The litigant also alleged that to compel "him to take the oath as a prerequisite to citizenship amounts to a violation of his s. 12 right against cruel and unusual punishment."[34] In addition, he contended that the oath "creates a distinction between native-born Canadians and naturalized citizens," contrary to section 5 of the Charter guaranteeing equality before and under the law and "that it sets a class of human beings, namely, the Royal Family or the House of Windsor, apart from others."[35] Finally, he argued that the oath "is contrary to the spirit of s. 27 of the Charter, which provides that the Charter shall be interpreted in a manner consistent with the preservation and enhancement of the multicultural heritage of Canadians."[36]

In his decision, Justice Louis-Marcel Joyal responded in clear terms to each and every allegation of Charter violations made by the litigant and rejected all of them. The judge recognized first that "since 1926 there exists a King or Queen of Canada, distinct at law from the British monarch and there is now a distinction between the king or queen of Great Britain and the king or queen as head of state for Canada."[37] "The Queen's presence as Canada's head of state is an integral part of our Constitution."[38] Justice Joyal continued: "In the Canadian [constitutional] context the Queen is equivalent to 'state' and 'Crown.'" In other words, the oath required in various acts of Parliament, regulations, or in the Constitution itself to Her Majesty Queen Elizabeth II, *Queen of Canada*, is an oath to the country's head of state.

There is a clear distinction to be made between Elizabeth II, Queen of Canada, and Elizabeth II, Queen of the United Kingdom, with all the history, conventions, traditions, practices, royal style, and titles that are an integral part of the essence and definitions of that particular position in the British constitutional order. In the Canadian constitutional order, these are not automatically transferred to the status of Her Majesty as head of state of Canada. The judge added: "The personified symbol of Her Majesty the Queen as head of state is not, in terms of our long constitutional heritage, a latter-day invention of some imaginative or manipulative spinner of tales but the result of constantly evolving constitutional principles which are cloaked in constitutional conventions in the United Kingdom and partly codified, in Canada, in the Constitution Act, 1982."[39]

In concluding, the judge stressed the following: "The head of state, as Her Majesty is so defined, is the very embodiment of the freedoms and liberties which the appellant has inherited and which he now enjoys. In a legal sense, the head of state legitimizes the laws of Canada which in concrete terms, provide for the peace, the order and the good government of its citizens."[40] The head of state reposing in the Queen is defined by the Canadian constitution and is not determined by the British context: "Canada is a secular state and although many of its laws reflect religious tradition, culture and values, they are nonetheless secular or positivistic in nature."[41] Canada does not have an established church and as such the Queen of Canada is not the head of a recognized church.

The Charter is an integral part of the Constitution as much as the Queen of Canada is head of state; one part of the Constitution cannot be alleged to negate another part of it. This principle is well established at law.[42] This decision of 1992 of the Federal Court in *Roach v. Canada* was upheld in 1994 in the Federal Court of Appeal by Justice J.A. MacGuigan:[43] "The oath of allegiance to the Queen as Head of State for Canada is binding in the same way as the rest of the Constitution of Canada so long as the Constitution is unamended in that respect."[44] This position is based on the fact that Canada is a constitutional monarchy operating in a parliamentary democracy: "Elizabeth II is the personal expression of the Crown of Canada. Even thus personalized, that part of the Constitution relating to the Queen is amendable,"[45] as provided in section 41 of the act itself. Justice MacGuigan stressed that the aim of the oath is to express "a solemn intention to adhere to the symbolic keystone of the Canadian Constitution, thus pledging an acceptance of the whole of our Constitution and national life."[46]

One would have thought that those two decisions from the Federal Court would have settled the law for good in relation to the oath of allegiance. But the issue resurfaced again in 2008 in the Federal Court in *Giolla Chainnigh v. Canada (Attorney General)*.[47] This time, the challenge to the oath was by a member of the Canadian Forces, teaching at the Royal Military College in Kingston. Captain Aralt Mac Giolla Chainnigh objected to the "outward displays of loyalty to an unelected monarch of foreign origin" (that is, Queen Elizabeth II) as head of state of Canada. His grievance started in 2001 and went through all the legal steps provided in army procedure before reaching the Federal Court. The claim was based on an allegation of violation of s. 2(a) freedom of religion and 2(b) freedom of expression of the Charter. The court applied the legal test provided in *R. v. Oakes*[48] and concluded that, whether the captain liked it or not, the fact is that the Queen is his commander-in-chief and Canada's head of state and represents the "hierarchical and lawful command structures ... within Canada's existing constitutional arrangements."[49]

This court decision was not the final word on the constitutionality of the oath of allegiance. In 2005, Charles Roach brought a new petition, this time for a class action against the oath of allegiance in the Ontario Superior Court. The request to file this class action was contested by the Attorney General of Canada, who argued that the issue had been decided in 1994. However, the court accepted the request[50] and in a subsequent decision allowed the application to proceed[51] as an action on its merit.

In its 2012 judgment, the court responded to the arguments alleging that the citizenship oath violates Charter provisions (sections 2(a), 2(b), and 15(1)).[52] The court analyzed the supposed violation of these sections of the Charter, but concluded that the citizenship oath to the Queen was "saved by S.1 as being a reasonable limit on the right of expression that is justifiable in a free and democratic society."[53] The successor to Roach in the class action, Michael McAteer, et al., appealed the decision to the Court of Appeal of Ontario.

In 2014, that court rendered a lengthy decision that made jurisprudence. It is worth examining its legal reasoning, considering it has become the law of the land. The Court of Appeal underlined the fact that the oath in the Citizenship Act is similar to the oath required by members of Parliament and the Senate under the Constitution Act, 1867. In that oath, "the reference to the Queen is symbolic of our form of government and the unwritten principle of democracy. The harmonization principle of interpretation leads to the conclusion that the oath in the act should be given the same meaning."[54] The Court of Appeal was very clear on the relationship of the oath with the Charter: "There is no violation of the appellants' right to freedom of religion and freedom of conscience because the oath is secular and is *not an oath to the Queen in her personal capacity* [our emphasis] but to our form of government of which the Queen is a symbol. Nor is the oath a violation of the appellants' equality rights when the correct approach to statutory interpretation is applied."[55] The Court proceeded to review the judicial decisions already given by other Canadian courts and added:

> Viewing the oath to the Queen as an oath to an individual is disconnected from the reality of the Queen's role in Canada today. During the heyday of the Empire, British constitutional theory saw the Crown as indivisible....
>
> However, as Canada developed as an independent federalist state, the conception of the Queen ... evolved.... [I]ts role in Canada is divided into three distinct roles....
>
> [T]he Queen of Canada fulfils these varying roles figuratively, not literally....

The court quoted Justice Bora Laskin: "Her Majesty has no personal physical presence in Canada.... [O]nly the legal connotation, the abstraction that Her Majesty or the Crown represents, need be considered for purposes of Canadian federalism." The court concluded: "The oath to the Queen of Canada is an oath to our form of government, as symbolized by the Queen as the apex of our Canadian parliamentary system of constitutional monarchy."[56] The court clarified the ambiguity between the physical person of the Queen, and the abstract notion of the monarchical element in the oath: "Although the Queen is a person, in swearing allegiance to the Queen of Canada, the would-be citizen is swearing allegiance to a symbol of our form of government in Canada.... It is not an oath to a foreign sovereign."[57] The court made it very clear: the oath of allegiance required by parliamentarians is the same and to the same effect:

> Inasmuch as the oath to the Queen is a requirement in the Constitution for members of Parliament and is seen as an oath to our form of government, the harmonization principle supports the conclusion that the oath to the Queen in the *Citizenship Act* be given a consistent interpretation. This interpretation of the oath, as a symbolic commitment to our form of government and the unwritten constitutional principle of democracy, is supported by the legal norms of rationality and coherence.[58]

This unambiguous decision of the Court of Appeal of Ontario eliminated all doubts about the meaning of the oath of allegiance to Her Majesty. Not satisfied, the applicants, McAteer et al., sought leave to appeal the judgment to the Supreme Court of Canada, but their application for leave was dismissed by the Supreme Court in February 2015.[59]

The decision of the Ontario Court of Appeal stands now as the definitive interpretation of the meaning of the oath of allegiance in Canadian law. It has removed any personal association with Her Majesty. It is essentially an oath to our parliamentary system of democratic constitutional monarchy, which promotes Charter values. It finally brings years of litigation and confused interpretation to an end. It also makes obsolete past initiatives to amend the oath in various new formulations in the Citizenship Act, the Constitution Act, 1867, or in the Parliament of Canada Act. Many attempts have been made over the past twenty-five years by members of the House of Commons or the Senate to seek changes or to add a second oath of "allegiance to Canada," but none has succeeded.[60]

Conclusion[61]

The interpretation given by the courts to the meaning of the oath of allegiance confirms that the loyalty and allegiance sworn is to our form of democratic constitutional monarchy. However, it will tend to make the person of the sovereign appear more remote from the operation of our system of government. The bond between the monarch and her subjects will seem looser over time. The emotional, affectionate element of the oath between the Queen as a person and the one who pledges his/her allegiance will tend to fade away, making the sovereign an abstract concept, devoid of any humanity. In the United Kingdom, where the Queen resides, the impact may not be the same.

The question might rise again when the Indigenous Peoples of Canada have to determine which form of the oath of allegiance they could be requested to take, following their newly recognized rights, considering the personal link they always claimed to have with the sovereign in a covenant as old as the European presence in the land of Canada.

These court decisions have revealed how the constitutional monarchy of Canada has developed since 1867 and has produced an understanding of government that is quite original. The Canadian Crown has distinctive characteristics that make it significantly different from the Crown of the United Kingdom. The text of the Constitution, the evolution of particular customs, the exercise of prerogatives, the development of conventions, and, in particular, interpretations given by Canadian courts over the years have given us a monarchical system quite distinct from the British system. A large part of its original text has remained unchanged over the last 150 years, but Canadian courts have elaborated a theory of constitutional monarchy unique to Canada, the principles of which are linked to our form of federal government and parliamentary democracy.

The Crown is not a static institution: it has evolved and regularly adapted to prevailing circumstances. Over 150 years, the Canadian Crown has secured a status and function that must be understood if we are to shape its evolution and better respond to future needs. Ignorance or indifference regarding an institution that is intimately woven into our constitutional fabric distort the proper understanding of how Canada's system of government functions, and how it is reflective of new perspectives and flexible for contemporary needs.

Notes

1. Parliamentary Oaths Act, 1866.

2. Promissory Oaths Act, 1868, Section 2.

3. Michael Everett and Danielle Nash, "The Parliamentary Oath." Briefing Paper, The House of Commons Library, CBP7515, February 26, 2016, 25.

4. "The Royal Style and Titles Act. Change in Form of Titles for use in Canada," *Debates of the House of Commons of the Dominion of Canada*, 21st Parliament, 7th Session, Vol. 2, February 3, 1953, 1568. Although Prime Minister Diefenbaker referred to King Egbert (Ecgberht in Old English) as the first "King of the English," his grandson Alfred is actually considered to be the first "King of the English" and Alfred's grandson Athelstan was the first to declare himself "King of England." See https://en.wikipedia.org/wiki/Egbert_of_Wessex.

5. The phrase remained unchanged until the adoption of the Citizenship Act of 1976. Thus the reference was repeated in all passports issued between 1947 and 1976.

6. Enamel Coronation Cup (likely Russian-made), author's personal collection. It is a promised gift to the Canadian Museum of History.

7. "Debate Resumed on the motion of the Prime Minister to approve of the Treaty of Peace," *Debates of the House of Commons of the Dominion of Canada*, 13th Parliament, 3rd Session, Vol. 1, September 11, 1919, 210–11.

8. The title Emperor/Empress of India used to designate the British sovereign for that country dates from 1876.

9. The term was originally used by the Spanish Empire during the sixteenth and seventeenth centuries and started being used by the British Empire in the nineteenth century.

10. Arthur Berriedale Keith, *Speeches and Documents on Indian Policy, 1750–1921* (London: Oxford University Press, 1922), 2:132–33.

11. Serge Joyal and Serge Bernier, eds., *Le Canada et la France dans la Grande Guerre 1914–1918* (Montreal: Art Global, 2016), 117ff.

12. Except for the ability to amend the British North America Act, which

would last until such time as Canada and the provinces agreed on an amendment formula. S. 7(1) of the Statute. The provision was in force until the patriation of the Constitution in 1982, s. 2 by the Canada Act.

13. Our emphasis. *An Act to enable His most gracious Majesty to make an Addition to the Royal Style and Titles in recognition of His Majesty's dominions beyond the seas*. 1 Edw. 7. c. 15 [17 August 1901]; and the *Order in Council Approving Proclamation making an Addition to the Style and Titles Appertaining to the Imperial Crown of the United Kingdom and its Dependencies*, London, November 4, 1901.

14. An Act to provide for the alteration of the Royal Style and Titles and of the Style of Parliament and for purposes incidental thereto (short title: The Royal and Parliamentary Titles Act 1927). 17 Geo. 5. c. 4 [12 April 1927].

15. Royal Titles Act, 1953, 1 & 2 Eliz II, c. 9, Preamble.

16. Royal Style and Titles Act R.S.C., 1985, c. R-12.

17. "The Royal Style and Titles. Change in form of titles for use in Canada," *Debates of the House of Commons*, 21st Parliament, 7th Session, Vol. 2, February 3 1953, 1566.

18. "The Royal Style and Titles Act. Change in form of titles for use in Canada," *Debates of the House of Commons*, 21st Parliament, 7th Session, Vol. 2, February 3, 1953, 1572.

19. Frank MacKinnon, *The Crown in Canada* (Calgary: Glenbow-Alberta Institute/ McClelland & Stewart West, 1976), 69.

20. "Ce serment de fidélité comporte un « aspect désuet » puisque le Canada est un pays indépendant et que la Reine ne détient pas une autorité réelle"; Gilles Lesage, "Le serment de fidélité: une coutume désuète," *Le Devoir*, May 21, 1970.

21. Our emphasis. A-23.1 — Act respecting the National Assembly, 1982, c. 62, Annexe I (article 15).

22. Judicial Committee of the Privy Council, *Maritime Bank of Canada (Liquidators of) v. New Brunswick (The Receiver General of)*, [1892] A.C. 437.

23. "Caractéristique secondaire et non essentielle de l'institution monarchique"; Robert Dutrisac, "Alexander Cloutier promet d'abolir le serment à la Reine," *Le Devoir*, December 10, 2014.

24. Charles Lynch, "Bloc Québécois: Members Make Oaths of Office Seem Ridiculous," *Ottawa Citizen*, July 29, 1990, A.9.

25. "Privilege. Oath of Allegiance — Speaker's ruling." *Debates of the House of Commons*, 34th Parliament, 2nd Session, Vol. 11, November 1, 1990, 14970.

26. *Verreault (J.E.) & Fils Ltée v. Attorney General (Quebec)*, [1975] S.C.R. LII 179(Can.).

27. *Michael McAteer, et al. v. Attorney General of Canada*, [2015] S.C.R. LII 8563.

28. Heib (Re), [1979] F.C. LII 2693 (Can.).

29. Ibid., para. 7.

30. Ibid., para. 8.

31. *Roach v. Canada (Minister of State for Multiculturalism and Citizenship)*, [1992] 2 F.C. T.D. 173, LII 8551.

32. Ibid., para. 2.

33. Ibid.

34. Ibid., para. 3.

35. Ibid., para. 4.

36. Ibid., para. 5.

37. Ibid., para. 10.

38. Ibid., para. 11.

39. Ibid., para. 15.

40. Ibid., para. 16.

41. Ibid., para. 20.

42. *Motard c. Canada (Procureure générale)*, [2016] Q.C.C.S. 588, para. 154; *Canada (House of Commons) v. Vaid*, [2005] 1 R.C.S. 667, CSC 30, para. 30; *New Brunswick Broadcasting Co. v. Nova Scotia (Speaker of the House of Assembly)*, [1993] 1 S.C.R. 319, 373, 390.

43. *Roach v. Canada (Minister of State for Multiculturalism and Citizenship)*, [1994] 2 F.C. 406, Can LII 3453.

44. Ibid., 7.

45. Ibid., 8.

46. Ibid., 9.

47. *Giolla Chainnigh v. Canada (Attorney General)*, [2008] F.C. 69 (Can LII).

48. *R. v. Oakes*, [1986] 1 S.C.R. 103, Can LII 46.

49. *Giolla Chainnigh v. Canada (Attorney General)*, para. 50.

50. *Roach v. Her Majesty Queen Elizabeth II* [2007], 860 R (3d) 101.

51. *Roach v. AG of Canada* [2009], O.N.S.C. Can LII 7178. Later, another court decision refused the defendant's motion to dismiss for delay.

52. *McAteer, et al. v. Attorney General of Canada*, [2013] O.N.S.C. 5895 (Can LII).

53. Ibid., at para. 111.

54. *McAteer v. Canada (Attorney General)*, [2014] O.N.C.A. 578, para. 6.

55. Ibid., para. 7.

56. Ibid., para. 50, 51, 52.

57. Ibid., para. 54.

58. Ibid., para. 62.

59. *Michael McAteer, et al. v. Attorney General of Canada*, [2015] S.C.R. Can LII 8563.

60. "Oaths of allegiance and the Canadian House of Commons," Parliamentary Information and Research Service, modified October 2008, 241.

61. As a final note, during the last twenty years there have also been legal challenges to the oath in the United Kingdom as well as attempts to amend it. See Michael Everrett and Danielle Nash, *The Parliamentary Oath*, no. 7515, (U.K.: House of Commons Library, 2016),17–18.

     As in Canada, none of these efforts succeeded. The legal challenges brought by Martin McGuiness (a Sinn Fein member) on August 12, 1997, went from the High Court of Northern Ireland all the way to the European Court of Human Rights (ECHR). The objections raised were mainly based on the right to freedom of expression, freedom of thought, conscience, and religion. In June 1999, the ECHR ruled among other things that "taking an oath of allegiance to the reigning monarch can be reasonably viewed as an affirmation of loyalty to the principles which support inter alia the workings of representative democracy in the respondent states (U.K.)," adding that "the oath did not require allegiance to a particular religion." See Ibid., 34–35.

     See also Randall White, "The Oath to the Queen in the Canadian Citizenship Act and the Charter of Rights and Related Experience in Other Commonwealth Realms and Other Jurisdictions with

Constitutionally Entrenched Bills of Rights," 6 November 2006 (referred to in *Roach v. Canada (Attorney General)*, [2009] O.N.S.C. Can LII 7178).

Even though the United Kingdom is leaving the European Union, one can reasonably expect that the substance of the decision of the ECHR will remain the accepted interpretation of the British Parliamentary Oath of Allegiance.

8 |

The Vulnerability of Vice-Regal Offices in Canada

Christopher McCreery

Although the offices of the governor general and lieutenant governors (the governors) are entrenched by the Constitution Act, 1982, the relationship between ministers, legislators, and the Crown's representatives in each jurisdiction has at times been uneven and largely dependent on personality as opposed to best practices. While the governors are the representatives of the Queen in Canada and usually act on the advice of responsible ministers, they are also, from time to time, required to evaluate the extent to which they are compelled to act on the advice of the government of the day in fulfilling their constitutional roles.[1] This necessitates an element of institutional independence, which has brought a number of governors into conflict with their heads of government. The subtle threat of withdrawal of resources has the potential of encroaching on the governor's independence from the government of the day, and by extension of impinging upon the prerogative powers exercised by the Crown's representative.

The history of the governors, their official residences, and administrative establishments is replete with examples of budgetary reductions and Government House shutterings. While these have nominally been cast in the context of fiscal restraint and a desire to limit the "flummery" of the state, such changes have occasionally found their root in a desire to influence or punish a particular vice-regal representative and his or her office. The resources provided to lieutenant governors in particular have served as a soft target for premiers in efforts to divert attention from other issues and be perceived as attacking the federal government or assailing ubiquitous elites — those whom Ontario Premier Mitchell Hepburn derisively referred to as the "smart set."[2]

The financial and administrative support afforded to the Crown's representatives varies in each jurisdiction and has at times been used as a mechanism to influence or control the activities of the governor general and lieutenant governors through the allocation of both human and financial resources. Lord Dufferin, governor general from 1872 to 1878, the first holder of that office to focus not only on the constitutional duties, but also on the social and public outreach aspects that we now consider part of the vice-regal function, noted that the lack of resources was "perpetually forcing [him] to give up doing many things which would be of the greatest public advantage."[3]

At the heart of any discussion surrounding the vulnerability of the vice-regal offices in Canada lies the question of the level of administrative independence that these offices have from the respective governments of the day. The governors serve as the arbiters in our political system and have some requirement for being treated as independent of the government of the day.

It is a paradoxical dichotomy that on one hand the governors are separate from the government of the day, while on the other hand, aside from security of tenure, salary, pensions, and other resources are provided through monies voted by the responsible legislature — and therefore fall within the purview and responsibility of their prime minister or premier. Under the system of responsible government that has developed in Canada, the head of government has an obligation to defend the governor. However, this practice has not been followed uniformly. This chapter recounts a few of the occasions when the administrative independence of the vice-regal offices has been jeopardized, examines the reasons why greater administrative independence of the various vice-regal offices is required, and offers some suggestions for how this could be achieved.

The offices that support the governors exist by tradition and not by statute, like much of the royal prerogative.[4] This means that the support provided to the governors is exceedingly malleable and subject to change at the stroke of a pen. To borrow from Walter Bagehot's dichotomy of the dignified and efficient functions of the Crown,[5] the vulnerability of the vice-regal offices comes in two forms:

- **efficient vulnerability**: the head of government removing functions of the governor; and
- **dignified vulnerability**: the removal of the governor's ceremonial functions and the reduction of resources and support.

The former vulnerability is almost unheard-of in Canada; however, it was practised with great aplomb by Eamon de Valera in the Irish Free State, which saw the near-complete marginalization of the Crown over a period of twenty-five years following the attainment of Dominion status in 1922, most notably with the innocuously titled External Relations Act, 1937. Every reference, symbol, and aspect of the Crown's presence in the functioning of the Irish Free State was removed or hidden.[6]

The dignified vulnerability has two subsections, the first related to the provision of resources and the second to what can be called the "presidentialization" of the role of the head of government — some have also called this the "regalization" of prime ministerial power.[7]

The provision of resources primarily relates to funding of administrative staff, outreach programming, travel, and the provision of an official residence. It ultimately comes down to the voting of funds to support the vice-regal office in its constitutional and ceremonial functions. The provision of funds, while voted by the legislature, is invariably controlled by the head of government in each jurisdiction, who has responsibility for the vice-regal office. The governor does not have the ability to appeal to the public for additional resources, nor can he or she turn to the leaders of the opposition parties for support.

The "presidentialization" of the functions and role of the head of government — not in terms of the legal/constitutional role, but rather in the symbolic and ceremonial discharging of certain duties — has the effect of taking away from the vice-regal function and presence. As the importance of the media in the life and woof and warp of politics has transformed display of authority into an almost entirely visual — rather than written — form, having the head of government perceived as discharging the duties of the state has become of even greater importance. This manifests itself in the head of government speaking for "all citizens" of a particular jurisdiction, rather than the more correct form of speaking on behalf of the *government* of the jurisdiction, and in making announcements of what he or she plans to advise the governor to approve (rather than waiting until after the governor has approved a recommendation of Cabinet). This encroachment on the various aspects of the symbolic and ceremonial elements of the state can do much to erode the perception of the Crown as the locus of authority and has the effect of marginalizing the governor and making him or her appear as little more than a ceremonial fixture and a rubber stamp.

In Quebec, this encroachment upon the Crown has become the norm since the 1960s, with the premier's role being presidentialized, while the functions of the Crown's representative have been habitually sequestered in quiet offices, away from the public and media. This has manifested itself in the installation of the lieutenant governor, which is undertaken in a small ceremony, eschewing the guard of honour, speeches, reception, and pomp that accompany the same state event in every other Canadian jurisdiction. (From 1945 to 1985, a similar pattern was followed in Saskatchewan.) The granting of royal assent is done in the privacy of the lieutenant governor's office or a meeting room in the National Assembly. The granting of provincial honours in Quebec does not involve the lieutenant governor in any way, the system being headed by the premier. In Quebec, the functions of the lieutenant governor have been chased into the shadows — away from the public eye, the pomp and protocol of the dignified state having been almost entirely eliminated in favour of a presidential premier.

The First Reduction

It is telling that one of the early post-Confederation debates to unfold in the newly established Parliament of the Dominion of Canada concerned the stipend provided to the governor general. Some members of Parliament felt that the £10,000 salary was too extravagant.[8] The second session of the first Parliament saw a bill passed, and reserved by the governor general,[9] reducing his salary by nearly a third, to £6,575. Despite Confederation and the new-found autonomy of the young Dominion, many legislators still wanted "Mother Britain" to pay for the upkeep of the head of state and her viceroy. As with so many debates surrounding financial support to the Crown's representative, it was only the amount of funding that was discussed, not precisely what it was being used for. In the case of the governor general, the £10,000 was not a salary in the traditional sense — it was in effect a subvention. All of Canada's governors general until the time of General Georges Vanier were either independently wealthy or able to draw upon other financial resources. Certainly, a few hoped that the salary would help to cover personal debts,[10] but all found the amount to be barely sufficient to maintain Rideau Hall and certainly not so generous as to allow for any financial gain or savings — there was of course no pension or annuity set aside for governors general until General Vanier's time in office. The funds were used to defray costs associated with the operation of Rideau Hall, personal staff, fuel, snow removal, official entertainment,[11] official gifts, and travel.[12]

Prime Minister Sir John A. Macdonald and the Colonial Office were both anxious to resolve the issue of the viceroy's salary,[13] despite government-wide austerity measures that saw the salaries of many public servants reduced.[14] The year 1869 saw passage of "An Act Respecting the Salary of the Governor General," which was again reserved and then granted royal assent by Her Majesty-in-Council on August 7.[15] This bill set the salary of the governor general at £10,000 (and specified that this meant $48,666.63 in Canadian dollars). It was a respectful debate that occupied a portion of the first three sessions of Parliament. It was, however, quite innocent, in that there was no attack upon the Crown or its representative; the root cause was concern for the ballooning Dominion budget and a desire for fiscal prudence. This was perhaps the most convivial of deliberations surrounding support for a governor; while periodic reductions in resources would become the norm in Canada, the cheery nature of the debate was not repeated.

Today, the salary of the governor general and an annuity are set out in the Governor General's Act, with a statutory provision for an annual increase. When the latest amendment to the act was made in 2012, it removed the tax-free status of the governor general, which had been in existence since Confederation. This also resulted in an increase in the salary to bring it more into line with what ministers of the Crown and federally-appointed judges earn, the base amount of $48,666.63 finally being superseded after being unchanged for nearly 150 years. The salaries and pensions for lieutenant governors are outlined in the Salaries Act, with provisions for an annual increase based on a formula applied to a number of other public office holders.[16] In addition to this, each of the lieutenant governors receives what is called a "named grant" from the Department of Canadian Heritage to cover the cost of certain expenses that are not covered by their provincial budgets, notably out-of-province travel to state events and an audience with Her Majesty the Queen, official gifts, and some hospitality. This amount is set by the minister of Canadian heritage, has been in place since 1951, and is used for operational expenses and not as a salary.[17]

Bricks and Mortar: The Closing of Government Houses

The salaries of the governors have not often been the subject of public discourse; rather, it has been the operating costs of Government Houses and other matters such as travel that have generated debate. The withdrawal of resources has most publicly manifested itself through the closure of Government Houses in New Brunswick, Saskatchewan, Alberta, Ontario, and Quebec — and proposals for the same have arisen in every jurisdiction across Canada on various occasions since Confederation. While the closure of official residences strikes against the Crown's symbolic presence, it is the manner in which the vice-regal representative is supported administratively that demonstrates the most profound risk to the independence of vice-regal offices. The closure of a Government House naturally results in a reduction of office resources, prestige, and the presence of the Crown and its representative. This erodes the dignity of the office in a tangible manner. No longer are citizens summoned to attend events at Government House. Instead, they trundle off to some rented venue, usually entirely devoid of history or dignity of the state — in the broadest sense of the meaning. The resulting symbolic imbalance can leave the premier with more impressive official surroundings than the lieutenant governor, especially when one considers that premiers have at their disposal a provincial legislature for official functions, something that a vice-regal representative invariably needs to negotiate permission to utilize.

Although three of the five Government Houses that suffered closure have subsequently been reopened, only one has returned as an official residence in which the governor lives — that in Fredericton. New Brunswick's Government House was the first to be closed (1890, reopened in 1999). Ontario's Premier Mitchell Hepburn announced his intention to close the palatial Chorley Park during the 1937 provincial election,[18] although the closure did not take place until 1938, after an extended and exceedingly complex dispute and series of negotiations between Hepburn, Prime Minister Mackenzie King, the lieutenant governor, and several vice-regal and senatorial candidates.[19] Alberta's bombastic premier William Aberhart would follow Hepburn's lead and not only announce but proceed with the closure of Government House, Edmonton, in 1937. Saskatchewan was next in the cascade of closing vice-regal residences in 1945, when Premier Tommy Douglas closed Government House in Regina.

The premiers of these three provinces stated that their desire to close their Government Houses was justified by reasons of economy, although this was really true only in the case of Saskatchewan. Hepburn's motivations, though complex, can be boiled down to a running battle with his political nemesis William Lyon Mackenzie King. Aberhart was seeking retribution against Lieutenant Governor John Bowen for refusing royal assent to three unconstitutional bills passed by the Alberta Legislature. Bowen was essentially evicted from Government House, following a reduction in the size of the staff and the cutting of electricity and telephone services. (This closure had first been proposed by the United Farmers of Alberta Party in 1925.) Quebec's Government House, Bois-de-Coulonge (formerly Spencerwood), burned in 1966 and was replaced by a parochial suburban residence, which was closed in 1997. The closure and sale of the post-1966 Quebec residence was undertaken by the separatist Parti Québécois, which had no desire to support the Crown or the federal appointee who filled the post.

Attempts have been made in at least three other jurisdictions to close Government Houses: Nova Scotia, Prince Edward Island, and Newfoundland and Labrador. The most recent musing about closing a Government House came during the 2015 Prince Edward Island general election, with the province's New Democratic Party leader, Mike Redmond, proposing that Fanningbank be converted into a museum.[20] With the NDP not having garnered a single seat in the provincial election, no change was made to the island's Government House.

It is natural to ask why an official residence is of any importance at all, especially when one considers that only a few public office holders other than the prime minister, eight vice-regal representatives, and the Speaker of the House of Commons have such a proverbial perk. The response is that official residences serve not only as a locus of official entertainment and hospitality for each jurisdiction, but in the case of the various Government Houses as an outward symbol of the Crown's presence and the authority of the state in the broadest sense. Heads of government, ministers, diplomats, and guests are invited to meet with the governor to be sworn in, to deliberate, to be celebrated and recognized with honours and awards. Government Houses also serve as places of political neutrality; unlike legislatures, where partisan deliberations and machinations unfold quite naturally as part of the political environment. In other jurisdictions, not just throughout the Commonwealth, but around the world, the heads of state and their representatives almost invariably have a place outside the legislature where they are able to carry out their constitutional and ceremonial duties.

Beyond Buildings

The closure of Government Houses has been the most overt and lasting of the incursions upon vice-regal independence and has also tended to be the most public. However, the ability for the government of the day to take decisions that directly touch upon the governor and his or her role extends well beyond official residences — important though they are. This ability has included selection of staff to work in vice-regal offices, removal of human resources and departmental support, and refusing to defend a governor when the governor has been acting on the formal advice of the head of government. In each Canadian jurisdiction, the human resources and financial administration components of the vice-regal offices conform to the public-service and financial regulations of the home jurisdiction — that is, the offices are required to follow the same rules, regulations, and directives as departments and agencies.

On the surface, this is not unlike judicial administrations in most provinces, which are attached to a department of justice or ministry of the attorney general. Although linked to a department of government for corporate-services purposes, judicial administrations have significant latitude over their own affairs and matters touching upon judicial independence, such as assignment of judges to cases, sitting schedules, and use of budgetary resources and human resources. While on paper they are not completely independent of the provincial government in the same way that the office of the federal commissioner of judicial affairs is insulated from the federal government (minister of justice), they have come to operate at arm's length from the government. The federal commissioner of judicial affairs supports the minister of justice in relation to judicial appointments, while support services to the Supreme Court are provided by the Office of the Registrar and to the Federal Courts by the Courts Administration Services — all of which operate at arm's length from the government of the day.

No head of government, minister of the Crown, clerk of the executive council, or public service commissioner would presume to direct or influence the operation of judicial administration, although there is occasionally tension around the provision of financial resources and allocation of space. This level of administrative independence is not duplicated in relation to any of the vice-regal offices, aside from the office of the secretary to the governor general. The provincial vice-regal offices are treated much more as an adjunct of a parent department, and this may cause conflict and tension that can have a deleterious effect upon the governor and vice-regal office.

The choice of a secretary to the governor general has on a few occasions been the source of friction between a governor and the head of government. One of the best recorded examples is that of Esmond Butler, who was appointed as secretary to Governor General Georges Vanier in 1959. Prime Minister John Diefenbaker had his own candidate for what he perceived as a plum position. Although this is a public service job with the nominal rank of deputy minister, it is recognized that the "appointment of the Secretary was made on the recommendation of His Excellency [the governor general] himself."[21] Vanier, being well aware of this and desirous to maintain the independence of the Crown,[22] outmanoeuvered Diefenbaker, having received the support of none other than the Queen for Butler's appointment — Butler having most recently served as Her Majesty's assistant press secretary at Buckingham Palace and media coordinator for the 1959 royal tour. Not having got his own way, and being unable to circumvent General Vanier or the Queen, Diefenbaker acquiesced and accepted Vanier's choice, but not before arranging to reduce the annual salary of the secretary to the governor general from $12,000 to $10,000.[23] This small, yet symbolically significant act would long remain in the mind of General Vanier, and with Esmond Butler throughout his career, as an example of the myriad ways in which the government of the day could act against the office of the governor general.[24]

In the federal realm, one of the more public assaults upon the vice-regal office came during Adrienne Clarkson's time as governor general. In September and October of 2003, the governor general undertook an official tour of several circumpolar nations in what was billed as the "Quest for the Modern North."[25] This was all undertaken at the behest of the Department of Foreign Affairs and with the support of then–Prime Minister Paul Martin. Opposition parties complained that the $5.3 million price tag of the tour, which saw the governor general and fifty-nine prominent Canadians travelling abroad to promote Canada, was an example of "excessive Liberal spending."[26] Rather than defend the governor general and the official travel that she was undertaking at the behest and with the express approval of the Government of Canada, the minister of foreign affairs, Bill Graham, publicly stated that it "would be unreasonable not to recognize that this was very expensive."[27] Prime Minister Martin made no effort to defend Clarkson. The throwing of the governor general under the proverbial bus went further when the government allowed the secretary to the governor general, Barbara Uteck, to be summoned before the standing committee on public accounts of the House of Commons to explain the travel and expenses. This was in fact the duty of the minister responsible for the governor general and the office of the governor general — the prime minister.

The most recent assault upon the administrative structure of a vice-regal office came in October 2016, when the position of private secretary to the lieutenant governor of Newfoundland and Labrador was merged with the position of chief of protocol of the province. On the surface, this might seem a natural innovation: both positions deal with ceremony and protocol and interact regularly with the lieutenant governor, premier, legislature, and diplomatic corps. The change did not, however, take into account the need for the private secretary to be an independent adviser to the lieutenant governor — or for the office of the lieutenant governor to be a separate organization from the protocol office, which is effectively an adjunct of the premier's office and focused on serving the premier as head of government. The province's newly elected Liberal administration made the changes under the rubric of eliminating fifteen assistant deputy minister positions in an effort to save the provincial treasury $2 million in salaries per annum.[28] There is no indication that this action was undertaken as part of a punitive attack upon the lieutenant governor; it seems instead to have been made on the basis of financial considerations. But it was certainly coloured by the fact that the incumbent private secretary, despite having served with aplomb for nearly five years, had in a previous career been chief of staff to the province's colourful Progressive Conservative premier, Danny Williams. The problems of having someone who reports to the lieutenant governor and is also responsible to the premier are significant and could become quite profound in the event of a minority government situation. How could any private secretary cum chief of protocol serve two masters if they were required to advise the lieutenant governor on matters of government formation, while at the same time being aware that they owed their job to, worked for, and were responsible to the current premier?

One cannot imagine an officer of Parliament being "double-hatted," at once being required to serve a neutral and arm's-length institution, while also reporting to the most powerful elected official in the jurisdiction. It would be an impossible position, even for the most seasoned private secretary. Such a private secretary would inevitably have to choose which of his or her two masters to serve, and this would ultimately be unfair to both the lieutenant governor and the premier — not to mention the mental health of the private secretary in question!

Other Jurisdictions

While Canada has not been immune from incursions into vice-regal independence, in other places, in the more extreme circumstances, the independence of vice-regal offices has been violated with Machiavellian creativity. Two of the more outrageous examples come from governors of British colonies that, although they had achieved responsible government and were on the cusp of achieving independence, were still under the nominal jurisdiction of the British government, which did little to aid them.

Sir Humphrey Gibbs, governor of Southern Rhodesia at the time of the infamous Unilateral Declaration of Independence, refused to acknowledge the illegal actions of Ian Smith's government. Gibbs was initially subjected to the same treatment that Alberta Premier William Aberhart meted out to Lieutenant Governor John Bowen, with the electricity and telephone being disconnected at Government House. Gibbs went on to have his water, official car, guard of honour, and funding for his staff discontinued, and was essentially made a prisoner in Government House, Salisbury. Smith's government also routinely presented him with rent invoices for his use of Government House!

Dame Hilda Bynoe, governor of Grenada shortly before that island nation achieved independence, was brought into conflict with her premier, Sir Eric Gairy, whose sexist attitudes did not enhance the relationship. Gairy routinely had the governor's correspondence intercepted and opened.[29] Dame Hilda even had difficulty soliciting balanced constitutional advice from her attorney general, Armand Williams, who was also a cousin and good friend, due to the creation of a culture of fear by Premier Gairy.[30]

While these are extreme examples, when the political stakes are high almost anything is possible, as demonstrated by Aberhart's actions in Alberta and even Diefenbaker's petulant reduction in the salary of the secretary to the governor general when his candidate was not selected.

Formalized Vice-Regal Independence

The nuances of the Crown's relationship with the government of the day are not entirely analogous to other arm's-length entities or offices. One should note that there is a significant difference between the function of officers of Parliament, who investigate, audit, and evaluate the executive and report to Parliament, and the role of the governor general and lieutenant governors, which is to formalize most government actions (except in those rare occasions when the advice is not binding or is otherwise inappropriate) and to carry out a diverse array of ceremonial and social functions, serving as the proverbial promoters-in-chief of their jurisdiction. Officers of Parliament lack any sort of dignified function, in the Bagehotian sense. They carry out only efficient functions on behalf of Parliament. Nevertheless, officers of Parliament, at the federal level particularly, demonstrate the ideal level of independence from the government of the day in terms of security of tenure and ability to manage human resources (within the broader public service regulations), and are afforded a predictable level of budgetary resources.

At first glance, it would be natural to default to the model of judicial independence that has developed with robust vigour in Canada since the 1970s,[31] with the near-complete insulation of the judiciary from intrusion of the government of the day through such institutions as the office of the commissioner of federal judicial affairs (established in 1978). Indeed, there are similarities, when one compares the institutional setting that lieutenant governors and federally-appointed judges find themselves in — despite the different aspects of their roles. Lieutenant governors, like federally appointed judges, have security of tenure, and security of salary and pension. This covers off two of the three "essential conditions" that were unanimously found in *R. v. Valente* to be required for judicial independence.[32] Indeed, these are also a feature of the officers of Parliament such as the chief electoral officer, commissioner of official languages, and auditor general, so it can be said that these are also the cardinal aspects of independent actors within our system of parliamentary democracy. Lieutenant governors differ from judges and officers of Parliament, however, in their control over the administrative aspects of their offices. Federally appointed judges have come to control the administrative decisions that "bear directly and immediately on the exercise of the judiciary function."[33] These matters include control over the assignment of judges, court sittings, court lists, allocation of courtrooms, and the direction of court administrative staff. In the context of the governors, this would touch upon such matters as the administrative office budget, human resources, travel, and support for programming. These are matters that the vice-regals currently have only limited influence over.

The interplay between the governor as head of the executive and the head of government as the chief advisor to the governor, and the head of government's responsibility to defend the Crown's representative while the governor agrees to act almost entirely on the advice tendered by his or her chief minister, is an essential tenet of the form of responsible government that has evolved in Canada since 1848. Placing the governor at too great a distance could have the unintended consequence of undoing this cardinal aspect of our system of constitutional monarchy and parliamentary democracy. The overall goal is to insulate the vice-regal offices and their principals from inappropriate intrusion by the government of the day, not to separate the governors from the democratically elected government to the point that they become either nothing more than a figurehead or so completely separate that they have the latitude to act like an absolutist monarch — without the potential for being held to account for their decisions.

At present, unlike Australia where, at the federal level and in several of the Australian states,[34] the administrative elements of the vice-regal offices are constituted through the Governor General Act 1974 and 1984,[35] none of the administrative elements of the vice-regal offices in Canada are constituted by a legislative act. Whereas the positions of the governor general and lieutenant governor are entrenched in the Constitution Act, 1982, the administrative office or establishment that supports the governor is not constituted through an act. While the Canadian Governor General's Act outlines matters related to salary and annuity, it does not delineate the establishment that provides administrative support to the governor general. The office of the secretary to the governor general enjoys nominal independence, but is treated as a "department" of the federal government under the Financial Administration Act. However, this is done to bring the office into the framework pieces of legislation for accountability purposes, not as an effort to exert inappropriate control over the office of the secretary to the governor general or the governor general's person.

The situation in the provinces is much less formal. At the present time, Ontario's lieutenant governor's office is treated as a separate agency and enjoys the greatest degree of independence. The private secretary reports through the clerk of the executive council and has a functional arm's-length relationship with the government of the day, even if this is not delineated through legislation. In the other nine provinces, the offices of the lieutenant governor are attached to a government department for budgetary purposes. The private secretaries report on a daily basis to their lieutenant governor and for budgetary and administrative matters to the clerk of the executive council or another official at the level of a deputy minister via a department, be it the executive council office, Intergovernmental Affairs, the Department of Finance, the Department of Transport, or Public Works.

The Crown's representatives and the office that supports them must have sufficient autonomy to fulfil the governor's role as the sovereign's representative and the neutral arbiter at the head of the political system. Having the governor's staff report to a government official or minister outside of the vice-regal office has the potential of exposing the vice-regal office to undue political influence. A minister or departmental head could exert this influence in a variety of ways, notably the reduction of budgetary or human resources, or the closure of an administrative office or Government House. There is a necessity for an arm's-length relationship between the person of the governor and the government of the day and the wider bureaucracy. This does not, however, mean that the proverbial arm is severed; a balance between autonomy and oversight is necessary.

The governors lack the level of independence or arm's-length relationship that other significant elements of the state have developed, noticeably the judiciary, chief electoral officers, auditors general, ombudsmen, and other offices that support the overall functioning of a fair and equitable democratic system and public service. As the importance of the perceived and actual independence of the judiciary and officers of Parliament has grown, there has been an increased understanding of the requirement for the provision of constant and predictable resources, the existence of a transparent reporting relationship, and a non-punitive approach to these institutions, even when they are brought into direct conflict with the government of the day.

Extending the "Length of the Arm"

As noted, it is Australia at the federal level that has achieved the greatest degree of administrative independence of the vice-regal representative from the government of the day via the Governor General Act 1974, while subsequent amendment has ensured an even greater degree of financial autonomy in the operation of the vice-regal establishment in Canberra. Such an innovation for the governor general of Canada would be a positive step forward in formalizing the nature of the relationship that already exists between the governor general, the office of the secretary to the governor general, and the government of the day in Ottawa. Given the level of functional administrative independence that the federal vice-regal office in Canada has already, such a measure may not seem necessary at this juncture. Nevertheless, with the events of the past fifteen years, federally and provincially, in relation to prorogation, issues surrounding the resignation of Quebec Premier Pauline Marois following the 2014 provincial general election, the merging of the private secretary and chief of protocol role in Newfoundland and Labrador, and the selection of a first minister most recently in British Columbia, there have been occasions when a greater degree of vice-regal independence would more effectively insulate the governors from potential retribution for discharging their constitutional duties.

As jurisdictions consider departing from the single member plurality voting system in favour of some form of proportional representation, the inevitability of near-perpetual minority governments will place the governors in a position of greater involvement in the messy business of government formation. This ultimately means that vice-regal representatives will be increasingly perceived as choosing political winners and losers, even if their decisions are largely dictated by convention and precedent. Politicians and partisans who lack understanding of the vice-regal role in such situations will look to the lieutenant governors as the cause of their loss or victory — when in fact they must be viewed as neutral arbiters in our system of responsible government.

In an ideal world, the provincial vice-regal offices would be afforded a greater degree of administrative independence from the government of the day in their jurisdiction. The author acknowledges that, while legislation at the federal level for the office of the secretary to the governor general is entirely feasible, it would be Pollyannaish to expect each province to adopt legislation to better insulate their lieutenant governors' offices as the principal mechanism to achieve a more stable arm's-length relationship. Rather, a less legislatively cumbersome option is the more palatable and realistic approach. There needs to be an acknowledgement by the governments in each jurisdiction of the necessity for a high degree of administrative independence for their vice-regal offices, which could be achieved through the development of a written policy or even a statutory instrument such as an order-in-council, which would be part of the public record. Such an innovation would also require the vice-regal offices to be more transparent in articulating precisely their activity level. While budgetary information is publicly available on each of the vice-regal offices, the example set by the office of the secretary to the governor general, and lieutenant governors' offices in both British Columbia and Ontario, where annual reports are released about the governor's activities, would have to be adopted in each jurisdiction.

Attaining a great arm's-length relationship does not mean striving for the level of administrative independence that the judiciary enjoys federally; however, it does require that ministers of the Crown and department heads not "reach into" vice-regal establishments to impose staff appointments, dictate the holding of events, reduce budgets other than as part of government-wide expenditure reduction (that is, across-the-board austerity), or direct the use of budgetary resources, beyond requiring the vice-regal offices to fall within the broad budgetary directives of their provincial governments. It also requires that the private secretaries in each jurisdiction have their primary relationship with the provincial government exercised through the clerk of the executive council, or whoever is the premier's chief bureaucratic advisor and confidant. It makes little sense to have the lieutenant governor's private secretary, who is the chief of staff, reporting through a more junior official. The question of stable funding to allow for the lieutenant governors to discharge their constitutional and ceremonial duties and the continuing operation of Government Houses is more difficult, yet the institution should be viewed by policy-makers and treasury boards as being integral to the functioning of the government writ large, both in a legal and constitutional sense, and with regard to the symbolic functions of the state.

The continuing attachment of the vice-regal offices to government departments for the purpose of human resources administration and provision of corporate services makes a great deal of sense, especially given the modest size of the vice-regal establishments in every province. As with the development of administrative independence for the judiciary and the various officers of Parliament, the evolution of the vice-regal arms-length relationship is likely to be achieved only via incremental advances, not a wholesale remaking of the system. This will require a detailed examination of the options for formalizing the arms-length relationship. One or two jurisdictions should be encouraged to take the lead in developing a robust package of best practices — something that does not currently exist in Canada in the provinces.

Notes

1. Andrew Heard, *Canadian Constitutional Conventions: The Marriage of Law and Politics*, 2nd ed. (Toronto: Oxford University Press, 2014), 40.
2. Neil McKenty, *Mitch Hepburn* (Toronto: McClelland & Stewart, 1967), 139.
3. Barbara Messamore, *Canada's Governors General: Biography and Constitutional Evolution* (Toronto: University of Toronto Press, 2006), 191.
4. R.A.W. Rhodes, John Wanna, and Patrick Weller, *Comparing Westminster* (Oxford: Oxford University Press, 2009), 48.
5. Walter Bagehot, *The English Constitution* (London: Chapman Hall, 1867).
6. As president of the executive council of the Irish Free State, Eamon de Valera introduced the Executive Authority (External Relations) Act, 1936. This act abolished the office of the governor general and effectively removed the Crown from most of the dignified and efficient roles. See Brendan Sexton, *Ireland and the Crown, 1922–1936: The Governor Generalship of the Irish Free State* (Ann Arbor: University of Michigan, 1989).
7. This is also what Philippe Lagassé terms "prime ministerial 'regalization,'" in "The Crown and Prime Ministerial Power," *Canadian Parliamentary Review* 20 (2017).
8. Constitution Act, 1867, s. 105. "Unless altered by the Parliament of Canada, the Salary of the Governor General shall be Ten thousand Pounds Sterling Money of the United Kingdom of Great Britain and Ireland, payable out of the Consolidated Revenue Fund of Canada."
9. Direction to reserve any legislation related to the salary of the governor general was included in the Instructions issued to the governor general upon appointment.
10. Messamore, *Canada's Governors General*, 12.
11. Ibid., 13.
12. Sir Alan Lascelles, "The Green Book," in *Government House Confidential* (Ottawa: King's Printer, 1935), 72–74.

13. The Colonial Secretary strongly recommended retaining the £10,000 salary. *House of Commons, Debates*, May 20, 1869.

14. The allotment was generous in the context that ministers of the Crown were earning $5,000 annually, while the lieutenant governors of Ontario and Quebec drew $8,000. However, like the governor general, they were expected to use a portion of this salary to defray such costs as official gifts, entertainment, and some Government House staff.

15. Earl of Granville, Colonial Secretary, to Sir John Young, Governor General of Canada, 25 August 1869; see *Canada Gazette*, October 2, 1869, 177. Her Majesty-in-Council approved the bill on August 7, 1869.

16. Prior to 1985 the salaries of the lieutenant governors varied by size of the jurisdiction — thus the Queen's representatives in Ontario and Quebec received a higher salary than those in provinces with smaller populations such as Nova Scotia and Saskatchewan. The base salary in 1985 was set at $69,000 and, via the formula set out in the Salaries Act, 1985, it now amounts to $142,500. The formula set out that "For the 1984 calendar year and for each calendar year thereafter, the salary of the lieutenant governor of each province shall be the amount obtained by multiplying the salary annexed to that office for the calendar year immediately preceding the calendar year in respect of which the salary is to be determined by the lesser of

    (a) the percentage that the Industrial Aggregate for the first adjustment year is of the Industrial Aggregate for the second adjustment year, and

    (b) one hundred and seven per cent."

17. *Manual of Official Procedure of the Government of Canada* (Ottawa: Queen's Printer, 1968), 1:319.

18. Colin Read and Donald Forester, "Opera Bouffe: Mackenzie King, Mitch Hepburn, the Appointment of the Lieutenant-Governor and the Closing of Government House Toronto, 1937," *Ontario History* 69, no. 4 (1977): 239–40.

19. For an excellent overview of the closure of Government House, Toronto, see Read and Forester, "Opera Bouffe."

20. Angela Walker, "NDP Leader Wants to Turn Fanningbank into Museum," *CBC News*, January 13, 2015, www.cbc.ca/news/canada/prince-edward-

island/ndp-leader-wants-to-turn-fanningbank-into-museum-1.2899206.

21. LAC RG 2, Cabinet Conclusions, 31 March 1952. Today the appointment of the secretary is a governor-in-council appointment legally made under s. 130 of the Public Service Employment Act, on the recommendation of the prime minister, who by convention acts on the advice of the governor general in relation to this specific appointment.

22. Robert Speaight, *Vanier: Soldier, Diplomat and Governor General* (Toronto: Collins, 1970), 376.

23. LAC RG 2, Cabinet Conclusions, 16 October 1959.

24. Father Jacques Monet, interview, June 7, 2016.

25. Office of the Secretary to the Governor General, "Quest for the Modern North: Governor General to Visit Circumpolar Countries," news release, July 3, 2003.

26. *CBC News*, "Opposition Slams Price Tag for Clarkson Visit," February 13, 2004, www.cbc.ca/news/canada/opposition-slams-price-tag-for-clarkson-visit-1.485225.

27. Ibid.

28. Government of Newfoundland and Labrador, Executive Council Office, news release, October 27, 2016.

29. Merle Collins, *The Governor's Story: The Authorized Biography of Dame Hilda Bynoe* (Leeds: Peepal Tree Press, 2013), 130.

30. Ibid.,132.

31. Heard, *Canadian Constitutional Conventions*, 179.

32. Ibid. See also *R. v. Valente* [1985]2 S.C.R. 672.

33. *R. v. Valente* [1985] 2 S.C.R. 673.

34. Queensland and Tasmania.

35. Sir David Smith, *Head of State: The Governor General, the Monarchy, the Republic and the Dismissal* (Sydney: Macleay Press, 2005), 41–42.

 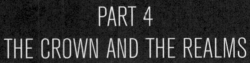

PART 4
THE CROWN AND THE REALMS

9 |
Australian Perspectives on a Shared Monarchy

Peter Boyce

This essay proceeds on the view that "Australia's system government more closely resembles that of Canada than that of any other nation."[1] The two federal constitutions of 1867 and 1901 offer the primary explanation for this happy parallel. The three constitutional features embraced by both the Canadian and Australian founding fathers were federalism, responsible government, and the Crown, and it is the third of these three elements of Canadian and Australian constitutional history that is discussed in the following pages.

Historical Overview

Historical accounts of the drafting of the Australian constitution during the last decade of the nineteenth century attribute only limited influence to the Canadian federal experience on Australia's federal debates, though a recent Australian revisionist study indicates a far stronger influence than previously acknowledged.[2] We do know that several of the key participants in the drafting process had either visited Canada or closely examined Canada's post-1867 federal experience. With respect to the status of the Crown, the critical divergence of the Commonwealth of Australia Constitution Act was the exclusion of the Crown in the six colonies from the purview of the new national constitution. This meant that the status of the Crown in the six self-governing colonies would be unaltered by federation. Five of the six Australian colonies had inherited responsible government in the mid-1850s, modelled on that bestowed on the Canadian colonies in the 1840s and 1850s, and Western Australia followed suit in 1890.

Australia's constitutional draftsmen were well aware of the British North America Act, 1867, and at the first constitutional convention in 1891 there seemed a real possibility of Canada's monarchical arrangements winning favour from colonial delegates. The most influential contributor to the 1890–91 draft constitution, Tasmania's Andrew Inglis Clark, recommended appointment of state governors by the governor–general-in-council, as well as a channelling of vice-regal communication to London via the governor general. But at the later conventions of 1897–98 (in which Clark did not participate), the Canadian system of subordinating the vice-regal office to the central government was rejected. The Australian founding fathers also rejected the Canadian nomenclature of "Dominion" for the new federal entity, preferring "Commonwealth."

The immediate and lasting consequence of excluding the Crown from the scope of federal government powers was the higher status enjoyed by state governors and the enhancement of state identity vis-à-vis the Commonwealth. Another serious consequence was the frequent necessity for state governors to exercise the reserve power to resolve deadlocks between legislative assembly and legislative council in a parliamentary system that remained largely unaltered by federation. This differed from the Canadian experience, where all provinces eventually became unicameral (while five provinces had appointed legislative councils in the nineteenth century, only two survived into the twentieth. Nova Scotia's was abolished in 1928 and Quebec's forty years later). Compared to their Australian counterparts, the Canadian legislative councils were infrequently brought into direct conflict with legislative assembly, and this meant the lieutenant governors were rarely faced with breaking legislative deadlock between the upper and lower houses.

The newly proclaimed federal Commonwealth found it very difficult to establish a high public profile for its governor general. This was in contrast with the experience in Canada, where the provincial lieutenant governors had a low profile for many decades after Confederation and were in no position to compete for prestige with the governor general. The Australian state governors were for many years wary of federal government attempts to reduce their status.[3]

For the first few years of Australian federation, the governor general, sometimes encouraged by the prime minister, sought to channel state governors' correspondence with Buckingham Palace through the governor general's office, but governors refused to comply with repeated requests. The states would win this particular contest, but within just two decades the process of judicial review of constitutional challenges would begin a steady shift of political influence to the Commonwealth. Canada's history of judicial review was rather different, with the provinces actually gaining relative authority for their Crowns from a number of judicial rulings since the late nineteenth century. Most of the cases supporting the rights of the provincial Crown were rendered by the Judicial Committee of the Privy Council in London, Canada's final appeal court until 1949.

The British government continued to select and appoint Australian state governors after federation, though it increasingly afforded state premiers the opportunity to comment on nominees to the office. By the 1920s several state premiers, notably those heading Labor governments, were demanding the right to nominate candidates for vice-regal office, and in 1933 the Labor premier of Western Australia refused to accept the British government's choice of governor, insisting on the retention of a home-grown lieutenant governor on a much lower salary. That lieutenant governor, Sir James Mitchell, remained in office for fifteen years until the return of a Liberal administration, which persuaded London to promote Mitchell to full status as governor. No similar precedent has arisen in the Canadian context, given the constitutional inability for the authority of a provincial lieutenant governor to be exercised by a deputy or administrator, once a lieutenant governor has vacated office. The Canadian provinces have never claimed a right to be consulted on the choice of vice-regal appointees, unlike their Australian counterparts.

Although republican sentiment did not establish deep roots outside the Labor Party during the first half of the twentieth century, Labor's official platform adopted a pro-republic plank, focused more specifically on the office of state governor than of governor general. Australianization of the Crown took a serious turn in 1931, when the Labor prime minister, James Scullin, insisted, against the wishes of King George V, that his nominee, Sir Isaac Isaacs, Australia's chief justice, be commissioned as the country's first native-born governor general. The significance of the King's resistance lay partly in the claim that he did not know Isaacs personally and partly in his conviction that a local appointee would find it difficult to think and act as a truly independent agent.[4]

Isaacs served dutifully and with dignity, but the British government was reluctant to make such concessions in the appointment of state governors. The next forceful challenge to London's claimed prerogative came from New South Wales in 1946, when the Labor premier, William McKell, rejected several British nominees for the state governorship, insisting on an Australian Second World War military leader, General John Northcott. The impasse was not broken for nearly a year, but Northcott's subsequent tenure was popular.[5] A similar impasse in Queensland was avoided a year later with the King's reluctant approval of another senior military figure, General John Lavarack.

Five years before Canada would receive its first native-born governor general, Vincent Massey in 1952, the Labor-led Australian government had persuaded King George VI to appoint a second local son to Yarralumla.[6] This was a particularly sensitive choice in that William McKell was a serving Labor premier. Robert Menzies, as leader of the Liberal opposition, was appalled by the move, but McKell adjusted to the role and, to the surprise of several Labor colleagues, exercised his discretionary power in the next Liberal government's favour when he granted Prime Minister Menzies's request for a double dissolution in 1951, following the Labor-controlled Senate's rejection of the Commonwealth Bank Bill.

Although their round of ceremonial and community leadership functions was less hectic for mid-nineteenth century British appointees to Government House than for later, locally recruited governors, they did not necessarily escape challenging constitutional tests.[7] Legislative councils could still block critical legislation and conservative party coalitions were not always rock solid.

The Exercise of Vice-Regal Authority in the Twenty-First Century

The monarch's representatives in Canada and Australia exercise identical constitutional responsibilities, but in both countries the political climate in which they are exercised has accommodated some changes. The three so-called "rights of the monarch" articulated by Walter Bagehot are still upheld, in theory at least, but some governors utilize them more confidently than others. At Yarralumla, governors general are left in no doubt that they are entitled to be consulted, to encourage, and to warn, and since the high drama of Sir John Kerr's 1975 dismissal of Prime Minister Gough Whitlam (following the Senate's protracted refusal to pass appropriation bills), they have sought to maintain a close and sometimes confiding relationship with their prime ministers.

However, the initiative for maintaining a pattern of regular private meetings between governor general and prime minister lies largely with the latter, and it would appear that very few prime ministers have sought to revive the tradition. Whitlam and Sir Paul Hasluck (1969–74) enjoyed regular confidential discussion at Yarralumla in the early 1970s, but even though later prime ministers maintained respectful relationships with the occupant of Government House, only the current (2017) governor general has successfully revived the practice of regular private meetings. Sir Peter Cosgrove meets privately with Prime Minister Turnbull for hourly sessions every six to eight weeks, and did so with Turnbull's predecessor, Tony Abbott, usually in the morning in the governor general's study or over breakfast.[8]

The Canadian experience of regular relaxed discussions between governor general and prime minister has been intermittent, with no consistency in the weekly meetings over a glass of whisky like those between Prime Minister Lester Pearson and Governor General Roland Michener in the late 1960s. While Governors General Georges Vanier and Jules Léger, like Michener, had regular meetings with their prime ministers, the practice subsequently fell into disuse and was not resumed until Prime Minister Stephen Harper revived it with his appointee, David Johnston, after 2010.[9] Prime Minister Justin Trudeau, however, discontinued the practice after taking office in 2015.

At the state governor level in Australia there has been no uniformity of practice and relatively few recent premiers have seen the need for a time-table of regular private discussion at Government House. This is similar to the Canadian experience: meetings between lieutenant governors and their premiers in the majority of provinces have been sporadic at best. Only in British Columbia, Saskatchewan, Nova Scotia, and Prince Edward Island have there been regular meetings between the two.[10]

In arranging their schedules of official activity, vice-royalty in both Canada and Australia have become more closely identified with worthy charitable causes in recent decades, as well as with solemn national or subnational anniversaries, lending support to the soubriquet of a "welfare monarchy." They are now patrons to an ever-growing list of voluntary associations, they present ever more prizes and trophies, and they receive ever more visitors, including school parties, at Government House. It might not be fair to suggest that the weekly schedule of state governors has become more hectic than for most of their Canadian opposite numbers, but their activities seem to be more widely publicized within their communities. The websites of state governors offer more detailed accounts of official activities than do most Canadian vice-regal websites, and all governors utilize social media. In two states, New South Wales and Tasmania, the governor's movements and hosting of visitors are still reported in a "vice-regal notices" column of the leading daily newspaper.

As former governor general Sir Paul Hasluck argued in his 1979 manual, accountability is strengthened when the general public knows who has been in receipt of a governor's hospitality or has sought an audience.[11] The hosting of dinners, lunches, or early evening receptions at Government House is more commonplace in Australia than in the Canadian provincial capitals. Visiting diplomats, delegates to international conferences, and members of organizations enjoying vice-regal patronage are often on the guest lists. The governor of New South Wales must make room in his diary for a heavy traffic of official calls from the consular corps and visiting foreign leaders; Sydney is reputed to host the world's second largest resident corps of career consuls. In Canada, only the lieutenant governors of Ontario (in Toronto) and British Columbia (in Victoria and Vancouver) would deal with anything comparable.

Meanwhile, state governors continue to be styled "Excellency," unlike the Canadian lieutenant governors, who are styled "Your Honour"; and they are entitled to a twenty-one-gun artillery salute, where their Canadian counterparts must be satisfied with fifteen. They are received by the monarch at least once and usually twice once during their terms, and are allowed to correspond directly with Buckingham Palace. Canadian lieutenant governors are received once, and that practice did not eventuate until nearly a century after Confederation. Under Section 4 of the Commonwealth Constitution and via letters patent pertaining to the office of governor general, the longest serving state governor assumes the role of administrator of the Commonwealth (with full powers) during the absence or incapacity of the governor general. In Canada the chief justice assumes that role.

Reserve Powers

The granting of self-government to the Australian colonies conferred on the colonial governor the full authority of the monarch's reserve power, and, unlike in the Canadian provinces, the Australian versions of responsible government necessitated frequent exercises of it. The primary reason was that all the new Australian legislatures were bicameral, with the legislative council invested with equivalent authority to the House of Lords. A second contributor to political instability and appeals for vice-regal intervention was the absence of political party allegiances, unlike the changing pattern of Canadian political life during the second half of the nineteenth century. Crisis situations arising either from the collapse of minority governments or conflict between the two legislative chambers and requiring discretionary decisions continued to occur in the Australian state legislatures well into the twentieth century.[12]

The governor general enjoys limited scope for discretion in responding to requests for a double dissolution of Parliament, when repeated deadlock between the Senate and House of Representatives on a proposed bill produces a general election for both chambers. Section 57 of the Constitution, which has no Canadian parallel, outlines conditions for a "trigger" that might justify the double dissolution, but the governor general is not bound by prime ministerial advice. Double dissolutions have been granted on seven occasions since federation, most recently to the Turnbull government in 2016.

Two areas in which a Canadian representative of the Crown may sometimes be tempted to exercise discretion in responding to a chief minister's request have had no parallel in Australian vice-regal experience. Prorogation of the legislature to postpone appropriations and requests for special warrants do not form part of Australia's constitutional history. The Harper government's grounds for requesting prorogation of Parliament in 2008 would not have been familiar to the Australian public; nor would the excessive use of special warrants for public expenditure by the Saskatchewan premier in the 1980s.

Executive Council

Governors general and their state counterparts must preside over their executive councils, and, unlike the Canadian system, there has been no attempt to establish a privy council. The state governor's chairmanship of the executive council is mandated by the state constitution or (in the case of Tasmania) by letters patent, and formal procedures for regular executive council meetings are spelled out in government manuals. At least two Cabinet ministers must attend meetings, which are held fortnightly in all states except New South Wales, where it is a weekly event. In most states the clerk must furnish the governor with the agenda and supporting papers at least three working days prior to an executive council meeting.

Although there appears to be general agreement that the governor is afforded very limited scope to reject a recommendation of Cabinet on the executive council agenda, some respected constitutional lawyers and vice-regal office holders, former governor general Sir Zelman Cowen and former Tasmanian governor Sir Guy Green among them, have argued that the chairperson is permitted to draw Cabinet's attention to perceived errors or irregularities in papers tabled or to withhold his signature until further information is provided to Council.[13] (It is not unknown for Canadian lieutenant governors to have pointed out errors in draft orders-in-council.)

The Range and Quality of Vice-Regal Appointees

The Australian national experience of vice-regal representation at Yarralumla has been largely successful. The second native-born governor general, Lord Casey, was a Cambridge-educated patrician anglophile, espousing a style and approach to the office not too dissimilar from those evident in Vincent Massey, his Canadian near-contemporary. The Labor opposition accepted Casey's acceptance of a life peerage without demur, but there was little attempt to Australianize the office. His successor, Sir Paul Hasluck, plucked by Prime Minister John Gorton directly from his Cabinet, sought to educate Australians about their history and national heritage, but he also issued a memorable and comprehensive public lecture, later expanded, on the protocol that should inform the vice-regal office.[14] He set a very high bar, which several of his successors were unable or unwilling to reach, but two of his suggested preconditions for holding vice-regal office have been taken seriously in Australia, though not, it would seem, in Canada.

First, Hasluck argued that all appointees should be able to claim prior experience of or close familiarity with the Constitution and with the machinery of government. This was one of the criteria for the vice-regal selection advisory committees established by Canadian Prime Minister Stephen Harper; another of the criteria was that the individual be at the end of a career of distinguished public service. However, these committees were discontinued by Harper's successor, Justin Trudeau. Second, Hasluck believed that no retired governor general should seek or accept further public office. He implied that his rules for vice-regal appointment were relevant also to state governors, though he was not explicit on that point.

Most governors general after Hasluck were drawn from the judiciary, had senior Cabinet experience, or had held senior military positions, and with one exception their departure from Government House spelled their exit from government employment. Sir Ninian Stephen (1983–89), a former High Court judge, was drafted as ambassador for the environment, then to a mediatory role in the Northern Ireland peace process, and as an ad hoc judge at the International Court of Justice. In the 1980s a later governor general, Sir Zelman Cowen, accepted election as provost of Oriel College,

Oxford, and was subsequently appointed as chairman of the British Press Council. Two former Canadian governors general, Edward Schreyer and Michaëlle Jean, both still relatively young on leaving office, subsequently re-entered public life.

The nomination of General Peter Cosgrove as governor general in 2014 was quite predictable, because Prime Minister Tony Abbott had publicly stated that he would favour a representative of the military or judiciary, and Cosgrove had enjoyed a high and positive public profile since his command of the international military force in East Timor. The Australian public would appear to be very accepting of military governors, perhaps more so than Canada. Unlike Australia, Canada has only rarely drawn upon military and judicial leaders to fill vice-regal office, the revered General Georges Vanier (governor general, 1959–67) being a conspicuous exception. Arguably, this has been a loss to the Canadian vice-regal offices.

The main sources of recruitment to state governorships since the 1970s have tended to be the judiciary and the military, and until the turn of the century they were mostly male. Sir Richard Trowbridge (1980–83) was the last imported governor, the Western Australian premier, Sir Charles Court, having invited Buckingham Palace to make a choice.[15] Although there have been no publicly identified advisory panels to assist the premiers in making their choices, the selections have generally been careful and prudent. Only one business leader has been recruited to a Government House, Sir Eric Neal to South Australia in 1996. Given the adequate remuneration paid to governors and their comfortable, subsidized accommodation, there has not been a perceived need to call on the services of affluent business-people. Without a doubt, South Australia has been the most experimental state in its selection of governors, with the first Aboriginal appointee, the first woman, the first business leader, and the first former Asian refugee in Government House. Senior military officers have been appointed in most states, the current governor of New South Wales having served as chief of the Australian Defence Force.

In Canada, where lieutenant governors are appointed by the federal government, women and leaders of community groups have been selected over a longer period than in the Australian states. Almost all Australian governors have enjoyed a high degree of public visibility from the outset and almost all would have satisfied the Hasluck prerequisite of basic familiarity with the Constitution and political process. Furthermore, most of them have been comfortable with formal ceremony and protocol.

Vice-Regal Residences

The possession of a grand vice-regal residence by each of the six Australian colonies from the mid-nineteenth century afforded them an advantage over their Canadian cousins, and Government House has remained an influential focus of vice-regal authority in the state capitals. In Canada, Ontario and Quebec make do without a Government House. While the historic Government Houses in British Columbia, Manitoba, New Brunswick, Nova Scotia, Prince Edward Island, and Newfoundland and Labrador are vice-regal residences, that in Saskatchewan is shared between the lieutenant governor's office and a museum, and Alberta's is now a government conference centre. Only British Columbia's grand Government House in Victoria operates on anything like the scale of its Australian counterparts. Each of the Australian state residences was constructed soon after the granting of responsible government, with only Queensland's original Government House having since been replaced. Royal visitors traditionally base themselves at Government House, investitures and public receptions are held there, and the surrounding gardens are splendidly maintained. In several states, royal assent to legislation is given on the premises, and private meetings between premier and governor will be held there.

By the late twentieth century, a more egalitarian ethos had swept through vice-regal residences. Greater public access was now expected, with dinner and luncheon guests likely to be more representative of the wider community. Furthermore, the daily round of vice-regal activities, including the identity of visitors and guests, is published daily on the Government House website and or in the daily newspapers. But Government House has remained the governor's place of work. The physical separation from Parliament and the government bureaucracy can be seen as a visual reminder of the Crown's separate constitutional power base. This is not the case in the Canadian provinces of Alberta, Manitoba, Ontario, and

Quebec, where the vice-regal office is located in the legislative building or, the case of Quebec, an adjoining government office building.

State practice varies as to how many official functions of the political executive are conducted at Government House. In most states, royal assent to bills is normally given at Government House, and in a few of them executive council meetings are held. New ministries are always sworn in at Government House. Investitures are held there, as are formal dinners or receptions for distinguished overseas visitors. The Queen is expected to stay at Government House and other royal visitors are normally accommodated there. Since the 1980s all foreign heads of mission making their first official visit to Tasmania have been invited to stay at Government House.

In only one short period of state history has the governor been required to vacate Government House as the official residence, unlike Canada, where lieutenant governors were forced to leave their residences in New Brunswick (1898, returned in 1999), Ontario (1937), Alberta (1938), Saskatchewan (1945 — the office returned in 1984), and Quebec (1996). Early in 1996 the New South Wales Labor premier, Bob Carr, closed Sydney's Government House, with the incumbent governor, Gordon Samuels, and his two immediate successors having to commute between their suburban homes and a small suite within the chief secretary's department in the city. At the time of closure an estimated twenty thousand protesters marched through Sydney streets. Government House remained available for a range of official functions. Bob Carr later confessed that the closure had been a mistake, and in 2011 the Liberal premier invited the serving governor, Marie Bashir, to re-occupy the nation's oldest vice-regal residence.

The Vice-Regal Establishment

During and since the colonial era Australian governors have been serviced by efficient and reasonably well-funded support staff, the most senior of whom has long been designated "official secretary." Despite some confusion in the first decade after federation as to whether the governor general's official secretary was primarily an agent of the British government or an official of the Australian government, the line of accountability had become unambiguous by the mid-1920s. The long tenure of David Smith (1973–90) helped professionalize the office. (On his retirement Smith was invested with a knighthood in the Royal Victorian Order.) Since then, official secretaries have generally served for shorter terms, most recently on leave from a senior foreign affairs posting or early retirement from the military. The official secretary in Canberra enjoys the rank of a federal department head and represents the interests of Government House in Senate Estimates hearings. Although a governor general can come to depend heavily on the official secretary, he or she is not supposed to become a source of policy advice. There would be no room for a latter-day Australian equivalent to Canada's long-serving and influential secretary to several governors general, Esmond Butler (1959–85)! Nevertheless, long service and a familiarity with Government House precedent and protocol can smooth the governor general's path.

Each of the state governors is assisted by an official secretary, a few of whom have served long terms, most notably Charles Curwen in Victoria (1984–2016). Australia-wide conferences of official secretaries were once held at intervals of about eighteen months, but in the twenty-first century they have been less frequent. This is in contrast with Canada, where the provincial private secretaries and the secretary to the governor general meet annually — as do their vice-regal superiors. The official secretary's office usually also includes a deputy official secretary, an appointments secretary, aides-de-camp drawn from the armed services, and a police officer. These Australian vice-regal establishments stand in contrast with their Canadian counterparts, the majority of which do not have anything near the level and size of the staff in the state Government Houses.

Links with Buckingham Palace

Given the sensitivity of Canadian monarchist observers to any signs of diminished direct links with the royal family and their suspicion of excessive Canadianization of the Crown, it is pertinent to note that the problem seems not to have arisen in Australia. During the 1990s, in the prelude to

Australia's national convention on the republic issue, the Queen's photograph was removed from the walls of several Australian embassies, but there was no deliberate removal of insignia or other symbols of the Crown from vice-regal residences. On the other hand, Australian governments, both Commonwealth and state, have not been as active as have some Canadian provinces in cultivating direct links with members of the royal family through visits (or "homecomings") or patronage appointments in the Canadian military. The Queen herself has visited Australia on sixteen occasions, as has the Prince of Wales, but visits by other members of the royal family have been infrequent in recent decades.

There has been no call in Australia for the appointment of an Australian secretary to the Queen (a role discharged in Canada on a part-time basis for royal tours for several decades and full-time from 2013 to 2017 by Kevin MacLeod), but Kevin Skipworth's appointment as Western Australia's agent-general in London listed liaison with Buckingham Palace as one of his duties. One sphere in which Australian links with the Crown have been preserved over a long period is the granting of patronage to major public hospitals. Each of the state capital cities can boast a large public hospital carrying the prefix "Royal."

Honours System

Canada preceded Australia in abandoning Imperial honours for its citizens and in establishing a home-grown national system in 1967. Imperial knighthoods had been abandoned in Canada from 1919 (apart from a brief revival from 1933 to 1935); some non-titular honours continued to be awarded, but sparingly and mostly in periods of war. Australia's Labor government (1972–75) led by Gough Whitlam was impressed by the Canadian example and modelled the Order of Australia closely on it in 1975.[16] It is not an exact replica of the Order of Canada, however. It contains four grades instead of three, with the most junior category (Order of Australia Medal) spared any quota on the number of recipients. Significantly, the Order of Australia Council, which reviews nominations twice a year, includes a representative of each of the six states. The Advisory Council to the Order of

Canada is differently composed and chaired by the chief justice, with no provincial representation. As with the Order of Canada, the chancellor of the Australian order is the governor general and the secretariat is located in Government House, Canberra. From the outset, the Order of Australia included recognition of service within the states, which, however, continued nominations for Imperial honours by the state premiers until passage of the Australia Acts in 1986. There was therefore no serious push for the establishment of state honours systems akin to the provincial honours systems in Canada.

Although the Order of Australia was generally well received by the public and major political parties, the national experience has not been altogether free of controversy. For its first fifteen years, the order co-existed with ongoing eligibility for the award of Imperial honours, including knighthoods, via direct recommendations from the six state premiers to the Foreign and Commonwealth Office in London. Conservative premiers were especially eager to reward major party donors or loyal lieutenants with knighthoods. The actions of two premiers in particular, Sir Robin Askin in New South Wales (during the 1960s) and Sir Joh Bjelke Petersen in Queensland (in the 1970s and 1980s), called the integrity of the Imperial honours system into question, but they were not alone. Askin was even accused of selling knighthoods, but never faced criminal prosecution.

The integrity of the Order of Australia has been compromised on two occasions since 1975, with a short-lived reintroduction of knighthoods by two Conservative Coalition prime ministers, Malcolm Fraser and Tony Abbott. The latter episode came at considerable cost to both prime minister and Cabinet. Within months of the Coalition parties' regaining office in the December 1975 federal elections, Prime Minister Fraser inserted knighthoods as the top tier of the Order of Australia, but his Labor successor, Bob Hawke, allowed the system to lapse. The next Coalition prime minister, John Howard, made no attempt to reintroduce knighthoods, but Tony Abbott, a dedicated monarchist who had served as national convenor of Australians for Constitutional Monarchy (ACM), chose to restore them in March 2014. His handling of the issue accelerated his fall from office by caucus revolt in 2015. Without consulting or informing Cabinet or his party caucus, Abbott had announced that he would nominate four knights or dames each year and that the governor general of the day would be one of the recipients. In seeking to justify this initiative, Abbott stressed that he wanted to make it easier for senior vice-regal office-holders to return to private life. The first recipient of the title "Dame" was the outgoing governor general, Quentin Bryce, a self-confessed republican. The second recipient was Professor Marie Bashir, who served a thirteen-year term as a very popular governor of New South Wales. Unfortunately for the monarchist cause, the veteran chairperson of ACM, David Flint, weakened his own authority by publicly championing Abbott's initiatives, in the course of which he also cast scorn on the Order of Australia, of which he is a member (AM).

When Malcolm Turnbull replaced Abbott as prime minister in a party-room coup, he immediately reassured voters that no further candidates for titles would be selected, an announcement that invited further denunciation from David Flint, who took to acerbic political journalism during 2016 as a sworn enemy of Prime Minister Turnbull, well remembered to Flint as former chairperson of the Australian Republican Movement.[17]

Monarchy's Prospects

Support for the appointment or election of a local citizen as head of state continues to be more widespread in Australia than in Canada, but there appears to be bipartisan agreement that no constitutional change will be launched during the current Queen's reign. In January 2016, all state premiers except Western Australia's Colin Barnett (though himself a republican) signed a declaration calling for an Australian head of state, and Prime Minister Turnbull said his commitment to that cause was "undiminished." The feisty convenor of the Australian Republican Movement (ARM), Peter FitzSimons, wanted swifter action, calling for a national vote before the Queen's death. "Never before," he declaimed, "have the stars of the Southern Cross been so aligned in pointing to the dawn of a new republican age for Australia."[18] Meanwhile, the ARM has reportedly gained many new members and attracted sizeable donations. But, as a senior columnist for the Murdoch press has warned, "The risk for republicans is that the crown passes to Prince William after a short reign of Charles. William and Catherine will inaugurate a new age of monarchy that may rival the Elizabethan age."[19] Meanwhile, in March 2017, the Parliamentary Friendship Group for an Australian Head of State was launched in Canberra, with both the prime minister and leader of the opposition as members.

Risky though it may be to predict mood swings by the electorate, one can be moderately certain that public support for the status quo is unlikely to depend heavily on the two pro-monarchy organizations that played such a prominent, even decisive, role during the referendum campaign in the 1990s. The convenor of Australians for Constitutional Monarchy is now publicly identified with right-wing elements within the Liberal Party, and the chair of the Monarchist League seems unable to address issues that might engage widespread public interest. Australia's two monarchist lobbies appear to be in competition and they differ in their public presentations. Whereas the ACM has generally stressed the Crown's strength in upholding a superior system of government, the Australian Monarchist League (AML) has been accused of "focusing too much on the celebrity status of young royals."[20] The executive director of ACM has referred to Monarchist League members as "the diamonds-and-pearls monarchists."[21]

During the 1999 referendum campaign, the ACM laid heavy emphasis on a claim that Australia was a "crowned republic" and even that the governor general was already head of state.[22] This argument is not likely to be effective in the next round of debates, because the issue is increasingly narrowed to one of the monarch's national identity, not so much her constitutional powers. For republicans, however, the major challenge will probably be how to gain acceptance of a model that preserves the essential elements of a Westminster-derived parliamentary system. That challenge reopens the question of whether the head of state should be appointed by a process involving Parliament, as recommended in the 1993 report commissioned by Prime Minister Keating, or be directly elected. Hitherto, most state premiers on both sides of the main political party divide have voiced opposition to direct election, but the general public so far has been overwhelmingly supportive. The monarchist campaigners will certainly revive their warning that this would ensure a "politicians' republic."

Australia can boast a more exhaustive examination of the political options for constitutional change than can Canada, which has been spared the exercise of a government-sponsored debate and constitutional convention on the future of its monarchy. On the other hand, there is no equivalent in Australia of the Canadian Institute for the Study of the Crown, which promotes research, conferences, and publications on the constitutional monarchy. Almost all vocal appeals for acceptance of the status quo are voiced by two lobby groups, which struggle to convey a fresh and convincing message: the Monarchist League of Canada, founded in1970, and its 1994 offshoot, the Canadian Royal Heritage Trust. As in Australia, the two organizations have an uneasy relationship and are sometimes in competition. In 2013, they took opposite approaches to the Canadian legislation for changes to the royal succession, the League supporting it and the Trust opposing.

Thus the Crown expresses or reveals itself differently in these two realms, especially in the manner by which governments and vice-regal representatives identify with the monarch and her family, but the shared successful experience deserves to be better known and understood.

Notes

1. Timothy D. Gassin, "Canada and Australia: Federation and Nationhood," (Ph.D. thesis, University of Melbourne, 2015), 1.

2. Ibid. See also Helen Irving, "Sister Colonies with Separate Constitutions: Why Australian Federationists Rejected the Canadian Constitution," in *Shaping Nations: Constitutionalism and Society in Australia and Canada,* Linda Cardinal and David Heaton, eds. (Ottawa: University of Ottawa Press, 2002), 27–37.

3. See Christopher Cunneen, *King's Men: Australia's Governors-General from Hopetoun to Isaacs* (Sydney: Allen and Unwin, 1983).

4. Zelman Cowen, *Sir Isaac Isaacs* (Melbourne: Oxford University Press, 1967), chap. 8.

5. Christopher Cunneen, *William John McKell: Boilermaker, Premier, Governor-General* (Sydney: New South Wales Press, 2000).

6. Cunneen, *William John McKell*, 193–294.

7. Nineteenth-century constitutional crises are well documented in Davis McCaughey, Naomi Perkins, and Angus Trumble, *Victoria's Colonial Governors 1839–1900* (Melbourne: Melbourne University Press, 1994); and David Clune and Ken Turner, eds., *The Governors of New South Wales, 1788–2010* (Sydney: Federation Press, 2009).

8. Troy Bramston, *The Australian*, April 4, 2017, 12.

9. See D. Michael Jackson, *The Crown and Canadian Federalism* (Toronto: Dundurn, 2013), 206–07.

10. Ibid., 160–64.

11. Paul Hasluck, *The Office of Governor-General* (Melbourne: Melbourne University Press, 1979).

12. Bethia Foott, *Dismissal of a Premier: The Philip Game Papers* (Sydney: Morgan Publications, 1968).

13. See especially Sir Guy Green's Sir Robert Menzies Oration, "Governors, Democracy and the Rule of Law," *University of Melbourne*, 29 October 1999, www.unimelb.edu.au/__data/assets/pdf_file/0011/1727561/19991029-green.pdf.

14. Hasluck, *The Office of Governor-General*, 46.

15. Sir Charles Court, interview by Peter Boyce.

16. See Malcolm Hazell, "The Australian Honours System: An Overview," in *Honouring Commonwealth Citizens: Proceedings of the First Conference on Commonwealth Honours and Awards,* Michael Jackson, ed. (Toronto: Ontario Ministry of Citizenship and Immigration, 2007), 38–51.

17. Especially in editorials of the *Spectator* (Australia) and letters to the editor in the *Australian* newspaper.

18. *ABC News,* January 25, 2016.

19. Troy Bramston, "Republicans Will Exploit Aversion to King Charles," the *Australian,* April 11, 2017.

20. For example, Tom Iggulden on ABC's AM radio, January 27, 2016.

21. Peter Munro, "The Royal We," *Sydney Morning Herald,* June 7, 2014.

22. See Sir David Smith, *Head of State: The Governor-General, the Monarchy, the Republic and the Dismissal* (Sydney: Macleay Press, 2005).

10 |

The Path to Nationalization: How the Realms Have Made the Monarchy Their Own

Sean Palmer

Queen Elizabeth II has the distinction, unique in the world at present, of serving as head of state for multiple independent countries. These sixteen nations[1] are collectively known as the Commonwealth realms. Elizabeth II is queen of each and her position in each is in no way dependent on her position in any of the others. This situation has been made possible, indeed quite successful, because of the legal, political, and constitutional concept of the "divisible Crown." This concept allowed the gradual evolution of the realms from British colonial possessions to self-governing territories and then to independent nation-states. It was the mechanism by which political authority and power was moved from Britain to each of the realms upon their independence.

Growing legislative authority in territories around the British Empire, beginning in Canada with the Durham Report of 1840 and quickly spreading elsewhere, saw an increased desire for domestic sovereignty. To meet this demand, the British Imperial Crown was made divisible and separated into the crowns of numerous other nations. The development of these localized monarchies has been extensively examined, particularly in the Canadian context. However, it would be an error to assume that the evolution of these monarchies ended in the first half of the twentieth century, with the Balfour Report of 1926[2] and the Statute of Westminster in 1931. While much constitutional work had been carried out to create these new monarchies, many social and cultural refinements had only just begun. The latter half of the twentieth century saw increased efforts to "nationalize" the monarchy. These were actions taken, not necessarily to affect the powers of the Crown, but to influence the perception of it, to distinguish the separate crowns from each other in culturally relevant ways. Nationalizing the Crown in this context has been a long and gradual process, which has proceeded at a different pace in each of the realms. These past and present efforts reflect not only the flexibility of this structure of government, and the ingenuity of those who work within it, but also hint at the directions in which the monarchy may evolve in the future.

Defining Differences

For centuries, it has been acknowledged that the Crown is personified by the reigning sovereign. Constrained by the reality that the sovereign, as a person, is inherently indivisible, the realms have worked to nationalize her persona as a way to adapt the monarchy to the cultural needs of each realm. These symbolic developments fall into three broad categories. The sovereign is represented in word through the use of her name and titles. She is represented in graphic symbols, most notably on her personal flags and various other armorial devices. Finally, she is represented in effigy, appearing on coins and medals, as well as in countless photographic or painted portraits. All of these categories demonstrate marked evolution over the course of the Queen's reign. From a relatively standard, mainly British, model used in the mid-twentieth century, a good degree of variation has developed among the realms. With each symbolic change, the sovereign and the wider monarchy have grown closer to the younger realms. This nationalization has allowed the monarchy to better reflect the cultural identities of the realms and has further enhanced its relevance and accessibility in those nations.

What's in a Name? The Sovereign's Titles

The titles of a sovereign in the British tradition are determined by Parliament through legislation.[3] Over the centuries they have changed as necessary to accommodate new territorial or political realities. However, when not deliberately altered by legislation, the titles apply to the sovereign regardless of the circumstances in which they were originally granted. For this reason, when a new sovereign is proclaimed at the start of his or her reign, the titles mentioned are often treated a little more flexibly. In 1952, for instance, the Queen was proclaimed sovereign in numerous places around the world. In the United Kingdom, she was declared "Elizabeth the Second, by the Grace of God, Queen of this Realm and of all Her Other Realms and Territories, Head of the Commonwealth, Defender of the Faith."[4] The reference to the Commonwealth was included in proclamations in Australia, Ceylon, New Zealand, and Pakistan, all of which were Commonwealth realms at the time.[5] In Canada and South Africa, the title "Head of the Commonwealth" was not included. This was a logical decision, as there was not, nor is there now, a stated policy that the title is hereditary. In fact, it has been suggested that the title may not be part of the proclamation of the next monarch until the position is resolved by the Commonwealth itself.[6] Whether or not the sovereign's legal title is used in the proclamation, the title itself is set by legislation. If that legislation is not changed in the realms, the title will pass to the Queen's successor unchanged, regardless of what the Commonwealth decides to do with the position. While the role of Head of the Commonwealth may not be hereditary, the title certainly is, at least in the Commonwealth realms. This is not the first time a title and its substance have diverged.

The title "Defender of the Faith," though entirely honorary, was originally conferred on Henry VIII by Pope Leo X in 1521 for his spirited defence of Catholicism in the face of the Protestant Reformation. When Henry repudiated papal authority in England in 1530, Leo's successor, Pope Paul III, revoked the title. In 1544, the title was re-established by the English Parliament and again granted to Henry and his heirs. Despite nearly five hundred years of history, the title remains far from universally accepted in the twenty-first century.

At present, the Queen carries the title "Defender of the Faith" in only Canada, New Zealand, and the United Kingdom. References to this title were queried by Ceylon, Pakistan, and South Africa as early as 1948, suggesting instead that it be replaced by a phrase such as "by the Will of the People."[7] Though this phrase was never adopted, these three countries did drop the religious title when all of the realms promulgated the Queen's updated titles on May 29, 1953. It is understandable that a realm with a Buddhist majority and another with a Muslim majority opted to exclude the phrase. As for South Africa, while it does have a large Christian population, the fact that most of it is not Anglican may have influenced the decision.[8] On the other hand, the possibility of alienating Roman Catholic Canadians does not seem to have affected the Canadian adoption of the title. The Canadian prime minister at the time, Louis St. Laurent, stated that he did not believe the title referred to an established church (as it does in the United Kingdom) but to a broader "Supreme Being" and that "there could be no reasonable objection from anyone who believed...."[9] Whereas Canada has not changed the letter of the law in terms of titles, in a single statement in the House of Commons the prime minister changed the meaning of that law. In doing so, he arguably created a more inclusive Canadian role for the Queen. It is by no means inclusive of everyone's beliefs, but it is inherently more inclusive than the position in the United Kingdom.

There is evidence that the substance of the title in the United Kingdom is being re-examined, not only by the public but by members of the royal family itself. Prince Charles has made several public statements of his preference to modifying the title to something more inclusive, such as "Defender of Faith."[10] This would bring the title into line with the sentiments expressed by Prime Minister St. Laurent. Furthermore, the Queen herself has expressed the view that her position in the established Church of England should not be interpreted as an effort to exclude other religions. At a British interfaith conference in 2012, she stated, "The concept of our established Church ... is not to defend Anglicanism to the exclusion of other religions. Instead, the Church has a duty to protect the free practice of all faiths in this country."[11] Whether the substance of the title has moved sufficiently far from the original meaning to warrant a change in the title itself is not clear; but, if it has, legislation will be needed to address the matter.

"Defender of the Faith" is not the only religious component of the Queen's titles that has potential for modification. In fifteen of her sixteen realms, the Queen is declared to be sovereign "by the grace of God." This phrase has been used in many monarchies, at least nineteen around the world at present, either as a tradition or to denote belief in the ultimate source of the monarch's authority. The phrase is not used in the monarchies of Belgium, Luxembourg, Monaco, Norway, Sweden, and Papua New Guinea, the latter being a Commonwealth realm. It is possible that this distinction may be the result of the manner in which the Queen acceded to the throne in that country. Papua New Guinea is the only realm to have explicitly invited the Queen to become its sovereign. This may have obviated any need to refer to divine providence in the title. It is interesting to note, however, that several other realms became independent after Papua New Guinea and yet none opted to replicate that county's approach to the title.

At a conference of Commonwealth prime ministers in 1952, it was agreed that the titles of the monarch could be changed to suit each realm, with the proviso that each should include two common elements, namely, references to "Her other realms and territories" and to the "Head of the Commonwealth." This decision directly contradicted the preamble to the Statue of Westminster, which, while not legally binding, had stipulated that the laws of succession and legislated titles should be uniform among the realms. While no Commonwealth realm has ever ended the personal union of the crowns by altering the succession, modification to the sovereign's titles began just over twenty years after the passage of the statute.

Initially, Canada was among the realms that preferred to exclude any reference to the United Kingdom in the sovereign's titles, while, in contrast, leaders from Australia were apparently insistent that it remain. Though the Australian position prevailed when the first changes were agreed, subsequent changes have been made by many realms independently. Ironically, Australia removed the reference to the United Kingdom in 1973, while it remains in the Queen's legal title in Canada to this day. Of the sixteen realms, the United Kingdom is now mentioned in the sovereign's titles only in Canada, Grenada, and the United Kingdom.

Counting Concerns — Regnal Numbers in the Realms

A significant element of the current sovereign's title is her "regnal number," the denotation that she is the second queen to bear the name Elizabeth.

From time to time throughout her reign, questions about this regnal number have been raised. It first became a point of contention in Scotland shortly after she succeeded to the throne.[12] There had been no previous queen of Scotland called Elizabeth, and indeed, there had been no queen of the United Kingdom of Great Britain and Northern Ireland by that name, either. Of course, the Kingdom of England, a state that had ceased to exist following unification with Scotland in 1707,[13] was once led by a very well-known Queen Elizabeth. However, some people were of the view that to use the regnal number "the second" implied a greater appreciation for the history of England than for that of Scotland. The matter ultimately became the subject of a court case in 1953, which determined that the courts did not have the authority to address the matter and the petitioners did not have standing to sue the Crown.[14]

Queen Elizabeth's reign was not the first time regnal numbers had become an issue. Indeed, their anomalous nature was first noticed during the reign of William IV, who was noted by some to be William I, II, III, and IV: of Hanover, Ireland, Scotland, and England, respectively.[15] (Strictly speaking, he would have been William I of the United Kingdom, if one were inclined to start the numbering again for that younger state.) However, the issue gained greater attention during the reign of Edward VII, to the point that his ordinal number was sometimes left off entirely to avoid controversy, even by the Church of Scotland. The issue re-emerged at the start of Queen Elizabeth's reign, with the added complication brought about by the new dominions, none of which had been independent political entities in the first Elizabethan age.

Ultimately, it was proposed by Winston Churchill that in future all monarchs of the United Kingdom would use "whichever numeral in the English or Scottish line were higher," in deference to history in that territory.[16] In essence, regnal numbers would reflect past monarchs who had reigned over various parts of what was now the United Kingdom. This solution was very practical and resolved the potential conflict between England and Scotland in an apparently impartial way. It also reflected convention in other monarchies where, for example, Victor Emanuel II of Sardinia became the first king of a unified Italy but retained his original regnal number.[17] In 1918, when the Danish territory of Iceland became an independent country, the Danish King Christian X changed the spelling of his name for Icelandic purposes to Kristján, but still kept the regnal number X.[18]

Churchill's solution to the ordinal issue was also useful among the growing number of Commonwealth realms and ensured the preservation of a common regnal number among these newly independent states. However, it could be argued that the principle underpinning the solution was not extended to include them as equal partners. Consider, for example, the next king, who is expected to be known as Charles III, because both England and Scotland have been governed by two Charleses in the past. Based on Churchill's solution, Canada would be expected to number the king likewise. However, from 1550 to 1574, King Charles IX of France governed New France, a territory that included parts of what is now Canada. If Churchill's solution is to be applied equally, not only to parts of the United Kingdom, but to all the realms, then an argument could be made that the next King Charles ought to adopt the highest regnal number used anywhere in the Commonwealth realms, and should be rightly known as Charles X. The principle also requires the recognition of Francis I and Francis II and Louis XIII through Louis XV should the names Francis or Louis ever be adopted by a monarch in the future. The only other realm where such sensitivities would need to be considered is Jamaica. An independent realm since 1962, it was governed as part of the Spanish Empire from 1509 to 1655, at which point it became part of the English (and, later, British) Empire. Regnal names that would need to be recognized in Jamaica include Joanna I and Philip II through Philip IV.

While interesting to consider, especially from a nationalization perspective, the situation in the United Kingdom is not exactly the same as that in Canada or Jamaica. Both England and Scotland were independent kingdoms in their entirety, whereas the former colonial possessions of Quebec and Jamaica were not. Nevertheless, their history is marked by the actions of monarchs beyond those of England or Scotland, and to completely dismiss those rulers is to fail to fully appreciate the nations' histories, in the same way that Scotland's history was perceived by some as being disregarded by a more pervasive anglocentric perspective.[19]

Raising Royal Standards – Representation in Symbols

Around the world, heads of state are often represented by a flag or standard. Royal standards, in particular, have represented sovereigns of many countries for many centuries. They are usually a heraldic device drawn from the individual's personal coat of arms or from their arms of dominion, that is, a coat of arms that denotes the territory over which the individual claims sovereignty. Records of the designs of the earliest royal banners have not survived to the present day, but a long chain of evolving designs has spanned British history and extends into each of the Commonwealth realms.

The coat of arms of the monarchs of the United Kingdom has not changed since 1837. These arms of dominion indicate that the monarch claims authority over England, Scotland, and (part of) Ireland, the three constituent components of the present kingdom.[20] It is these arms on which the present royal standard is based in the United Kingdom.

The oldest grant of arms to a British territory outside of the United Kingdom is that granted to Nova Scotia by King Charles I in 1625.[21] Following this grant, other territories, colonies, provinces, states, and dominions were granted arms, usually as a grant to the sovereign in right of the territory concerned. Canada received its first grant in 1867, heavily

The arms of the sovereign in right of the United Kingdom.

modified the design in 1921, and made a further substantive revision in 1957. There have been relatively minor changes since. A ribbon bearing the motto of the Order of Canada, *Disiderantes Meliorem Patriam* ("They Desire a Better Country"), was added in 1994, but the design of the shield itself has not changed since 1957.

The arms of the Queen in Right of Canada serve as the basis of her royal standard in this country. The first use of those arms as a standard was at the coronation of George VI in 1937. It was used again in 1953 at the most recent coronation.[22] It is interesting to note that Australia, Canada, and New Zealand were represented by banners of their arms, whereas the other dominions — Ceylon, Pakistan, and South Africa — were represented by their national flags.[23] Given that all six of these realms had coats of arms, it is surprising that the pattern did not prove to be universal.

In a departure from the traditional British process, in which the standard is an unmodified depiction of the coat of arms, the Canadian standard

The arms of the sovereign in right of Canada.

as used regularly since 1962 depicts the arms defaced (that is, superimposed) by a blue roundel with the initial E surmounted by a St. Edward's Crown and within a wreath of roses, all gold-coloured.

This pattern has been adopted in all of the Commonwealth realms that have produced standards to date. Australia, Canada, Jamaica, and New Zealand introduced these banners in 1962.

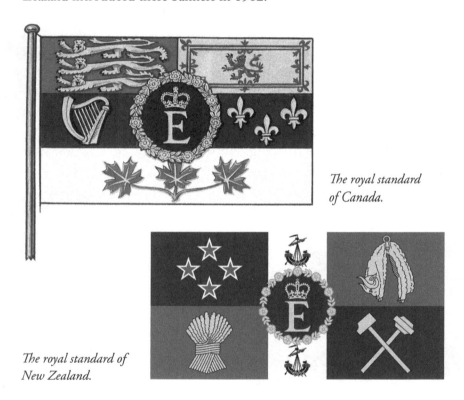

The royal standard of Canada.

The royal standard of New Zealand.

Barbados followed suit after receiving its independence from Britain in 1966. No other present Commonwealth realms have produced standards. Four former realms did use them: Sierra Leone (1961–71), Trinidad and Tobago (1966–76), Malta (1967–74), and Mauritius (1968–92), but abandoned them upon becoming republics.

There are precedents for the adoption of individual-specific royal standards, but they are relatively rare. Of the forty-two monarchies around the world at present, twenty-one use royal standards that do not change from one monarch to the next.[24] On the other hand, eight use a standard that does change with each monarch. Thirteen monarchies use no royal standard at all, including ten Commonwealth realms.

There are benefits to be had in both approaches. Monarchies that use unchanging royal standards enjoy an effective visual demonstration of the continuity of the Crown. The standard remains the same from one sovereign to the next, signifying that the "Crown never dies."[25] For this reason, it is never flown at half-staff.[26] It could be argued that this is an institution-oriented concept. The alternative is a more individual-focused concept, in which each sovereign bears a distinctive emblem uniquely suited to them. For example, the standard may bear their cipher or monogram, as is the case in Belgium and the Commonwealth realms. Such a design heightens awareness of the individuality of each sovereign and, perhaps more deliberately, the personal association each has with the realm in question.

Family Matters – Representing Other Members of the Royal Family

In Britain, members of the royal family are represented by their own coats of arms and fly these arms as banners when undertaking official functions. These banners (and the arms from which they are drawn) are modifications of the royal arms with minor differences assigned by the sovereign.

Though five of the current Commonwealth realms have distinctive flags for the Queen, only Canada has extended this concept to include other members of the royal family.

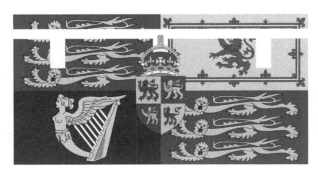

Personal standard for the heir to the throne of the United Kingdom.

Personal standard for the heir to the throne of Canada. "Royal Standard of the Prince of Wales (in Canada)."

Between 2011 and 2015, Canada produced six standards for various other members of the royal family.[27] It is difficult to determine how well these designs (or indeed the Queen's own design) are recognized by the public, but the symbolism of their production is clear. Through these standards, Canada is taking "ownership" of not only the Queen of Canada, but of the other members of her family as well. This is a particularly intriguing development, as there is no constitutional position provided to other members of the royal family anywhere in any of the realms.

Despite the lack of a constitutionally mandated role for them, the production of standards for multiple family members appears to affirm the concept of a "Canadian royal family," an entity as distinct as the Queen of Canada is from the Queen of the United Kingdom. However, whereas the latter is laid down in constitutional law, the former is a cultural element that has evolved organically. The development of a distinctive Canadian royal family is in itself a remarkable nationalization of the monarchy. While the concept is a logical one, it was not formally acknowledged until the Queen made reference to the idea in 2002. In an official visit to Nunavut, she stated, "I am proud to be the first member of the Canadian royal family to be greeted in Canada's newest territory."[28] The term has been used by other members of the family since then.[29] Nevertheless, it appears the concept has not been adopted in other realms and there are no official references to the Australian royal family or the royal family of New Zealand.

Toward a Non-Standard Standard – The Evolution of the Vice-Regal Flags

While considerable effort has been made to nationalize the Queen's standards in many of the realms, little has been done to do the same for her representatives. The governor general of each realm is entitled to fly a flag that takes precedence over all other flags in the realm with the exception of the sovereign's. Traditionally, these vice-regal standards displayed the crest (that is, the topmost portion of a coat of arms) of the British coat of arms, a crowned lion standing on a St. Edward's Crown, on a blue background. The only feature that distinguished one realm from another was a small scroll of text beneath the crown bearing the name of the realm.

The standard of the governor general of Jamaica.

This pattern was established in 1931 for two reasons. First, South Africa objected to the previous pattern, being a defaced Union Jack with the shield of the realm's arms at the centre, surrounded by a wreath of laurel leaves.

Second, some of the realms believed that a new design would better represent the new role of the governors general as personal representatives of the sovereign, following the passage of the Statute of Westminster.[30] The 1931 design was not popular with New Zealand's government or with the governor general at the time, Lord Charles Bledisloe, who declined to use it, preferring instead to remain with the defaced Union Jack. His successor eventually adopted the new design.[31]

The standard for governors general (pre-1931).

In 1978, on the independence of the Solomon Islands from the United Kingdom, Sir Baddeley Devesi was appointed as the country's first governor general and his standard was raised. This flag bore the traditional crest of the British royal arms, but beneath it, in place of a scroll, the nation's name was written on the yellow silhouette of a two-headed frigate bird, a shape used in their coat of arms. This was the first vice-regal standard (among the existing realms today) to deviate from the long-established pattern. It could be argued that the precedent for minor amendments had been established by South Africa at the inception of this pattern. As an officially bilingual nation, the English and Afrikaans names of the realm appeared on scrolls above and below the crest.

In 1981, Canada abandoned the traditional vice-regal standard, replacing the crest of the British arms, the standing lion, with the crest from the Queen of Canada's arms, a lion holding a maple leaf.[32]

The change could not be described as radical, as it maintained the same subject material, that is, the crest from the top of one of the Queen's coats

The standard of the governor general of Canada.

of arms; indeed, in this instance, the new crest was quite similar to that used previously. Nevertheless, the incorporation of a maple leaf, reminiscent of the maple leaf on Canada's national flag, made the new vice-regal standard distinctive and permitted the removal of the scroll bearing the name of the nation.

The only realm other than the Solomon Islands and Canada to have modified its vice-regal standard from the common pattern is New Zealand. This change occurred in 2008 and was a more radical departure than those made by the other realms, though the form may be recognizable to those familiar with the standards of the provincial lieutenant governors in Canada. Unlike that of many of the other realms, the crest atop the Queen of New Zealand's regnal arms is the St. Edward's Crown alone. Had designers followed Canada's pattern and simply replaced the British crest with New Zealand's, the flag would have consisted of only the St. Edward's Crown on a blue field. Such a flag may have represented a governor general rather well, but it would not have been distinctly of New Zealand. Instead, designers opted to display the entire shield of New Zealand's arms. From a distance, this vice-regal flag is by far the most distinctive of the fifteen in use today and naturally does not require the name of the nation to be written on it.

The standard of the governor general of New Zealand.

Precedent for the design of a vice-regal flag like this can be found as far back as 1950, when the Province of Quebec adopted a distinctive flag for its lieutenant governor. That flag bore the crowned arms of the province on a white disk on a blue background. Beginning in 1981, the other provinces began adopting distinctive flags for their vice-regal representatives, based on a common pattern proposed by the federal government.

The standard of the lieutenant governor of Ontario.

Those banners bear the crowned provincial shield of arms surrounded by a wreath of ten gold maple leaves on a blue background. The notable exception to the current pattern of lieutenant governor's flags is that of the Province of Nova Scotia, which still uses a design adopted in 1929, composed of a Union Jack defaced by a white circle bearing the shield of Nova Scotia surrounded by a circlet of green maple leaves. This is a design that would have been familiar to New Zealand's Lord Bledisloe.

Interestingly, although twelve of the fifteen realms with governors general use a common design for their flags, it appears that each flag is made locally according to the shared specifications. As a result, there is a surprising amount of variation in the execution of the designs. In Australia, for example, the crown is outlined in white.[33] In some realms the lion is simplified and monochromatic. In others, it is highly detailed. The variation does not appear to be deliberate, but a by-product of various local production techniques and budget requirements. This is particularly evident in Papua New Guinea, where the lion's face is almost cubist in appearance, though perhaps not deliberately so.[34] The last realm to gain independence, Antigua and Barbuda, did so in 1983. Despite nearly thirty-five years having gone by, and the realms routinely manufacturing their own vice-regal standards, only three have chosen to modify the design to stress their individuality.

It should be noted that the changes made to the vice-regal standards in Canada and New Zealand are reflected in other aspects of the offices. The lion bearing the maple leaf is used throughout the governor general's establishment in Canada, from formal letterhead to military uniform insignia to the official website. Similarly, the crowned shield of New Zealand is used on letterhead, printed promotional material, and staff uniforms. In

Australia, the symbol used in similar situations is a crowned sprig of wattle flowers. It would appear, therefore, that the need for some distinctive Australian vice-regal symbol has been recognized, but has not thus far been translated into a more distinctive flag.

Canada and New Zealand are the two realms that have paid the greatest attention to the nationalization of the visual symbols of the monarchy. Whether this has been a cause or an effect could be debated, but they are the only two realms to have modified the historic process by which coats of arms, flags, and badges are granted by the Crown. Historically, such emblems were granted by the College of Arms in London (or the Court of Lord Lyon in Scotland) on the authority of the Queen as exercised by numerous heralds. In 1978, it was decided that the Queen would create a new officer, "New Zealand Herald Extraordinary," who would advise the college in London on matters as they related to New Zealand. While innovative at the time, the constitutional appropriateness of this arrangement has since been contested.[35]

A decade later, Canada pursued a different pathway to patriation, creating a wholly Canadian authority to end reliance on the British bodies. The Canadian Heraldic Authority has been very prolific over the past thirty years and has been deeply involved in the further nationalization of the Crown through the development of other symbols reflecting the monarchy in Canada.

With Great Relief – The Queen's Effigy

The sovereign is represented visually, not only by graphic symbols, but also in effigy, that is, an image or artistic rendition of the Queen's likeness. For at least the past thousand years, British coinage has borne the portraits of the country's national rulers. This has also been true for most of the territories of the British Empire and for most of the current realms. It may seem somewhat obvious to consider the depiction of the sovereign on coinage, but the sheer scale of her presence in this medium warrants attention. Representations of Queen Elizabeth II appear on billions of coins around the world. The Royal Mint estimates the number of coins in circulation in the United Kingdom alone to be twenty-eight billion pieces.[36] With billions more circulating in other realms, the Queen is almost certainly the most frequently illustrated person in the world.[37] Innumerable artistic renderings have been produced for this purpose, mostly for small production runs of commemorative coins. However, the vast majority of coins bearing the Queen's image have been produced by eight artists over the past sixty-five years. Since 1953, British sculptors have produced portraits of the Queen for the coins used by most of the realms. The first two were used in virtually every realm (as well as in all of the territories that would eventually become realms). Barbados and Papua New Guinea did not use a portrait of the Queen on their coins following their independence, in 1966 and 1975, respectively. Jamaica removed her portrait from their coins in 1969 and the Bahamas did so in 1974. Otherwise, the Queen has appeared on all of the realms' circulating coinage.

For the first thirty years of the Queen's reign, the effigies sculpted for use on coins were used fairly consistently across the realms. The earliest of the realms to propose a break from this standard was New Zealand, which produced a distinctive portrait in 1979.

Effigy used on some New Zealand coins designed by James Berry.

The portrait, by naturalized New Zealand citizen James Berry, appeared on commemorative coins for several years, but was never used on circulating ones. It was not until 1990 that one of the realms, Canada, began circulating coinage bearing a distinctive portrait devised by one of its own citizens. In 1985, the United Kingdom replaced the nineteen-year-old portrait by Arnold Machin with a design by Raphael Maklouf. Australia did this in the same year and New Zealand followed in 1986. Smaller realms followed suit later, with Tuvalu making a change in 1994. The East Caribbean States, a monetary union of five of the realms, did not update their portrait until 2002. However, Canada never adopted the Maklouf portrait, continuing to use the Machin portrait until 1990, when sculptor Dora de Pédery-Hunt became the first Canadian to produce a portrait of the Queen for use on coins.[38]

De Pédery-Hunt's portrait bears a striking resemblance to Maklouf's, particularly in the choice of accessories. Both depicted the Queen wearing the George IV State Diadem and identical earrings and necklace. One might suspect that De Pédery-Hunt's mandate was to produce a new Canadian portrait that was not completely unlike those used in the other realms, but little information seems to be available. Whatever the case may be, by 2003, when Susannah Blunt was commissioned to update the portrait on Canadian coins, there was clearly no expectation that it should resemble those in use elsewhere.

Since the change in 1985, the United Kingdom has updated its portraits in 1998 and 2015. Australia and New Zealand adopted the first of these in 1999, but neither has yet adopted the 2015 design. Australia produced a "home-grown" portrait of the Queen in 2000. As in New Zealand, the portrait was used only on commemorative coins. Though the circulation was limited, Vladimir Gottwald was the first Australian since Sir Edgar Bertram Mackennal, who sculpted the 1910–36 effigy of King George V for all of the realms, to have his work on the obverse of an Australian coin.[39]

The nationalization of the portrait of the Queen used on Canadian coins and medals is remarkable among the realms. There is one further numismatic element that should be considered and is another area that exemplifies the nationalization of the monarchy in Canada. In 2008, on

Obverse-Avers   Reverse-Revers

Design of the Sacrifice Medal.

the new Sacrifice Medal, the Queen was depicted wearing a diadem of distinctly Canadian maple leaves and snowflakes.[40]

No such diadem physically exists, but this heraldic invention is a logical step in the continuing nationalization of the sovereign. The design has also been used on Canada's Operational Services Medal and the Polar Medal, and is included in the Diamond Jubilee window in the Parliament Buildings in Ottawa.[41]

There is clearly a significant role for accessories and other details to symbolize and demonstrate the nationalization of the Queen. While the snowflake diadem does not materially exist, there are other, physical symbols of the realms that the Queen does utilize from time to time to demonstrate her connection to each nation. Over the past few decades, she has been increasingly depicted in a variety of photographic portraits that clearly illustrate her different roles.

Portrait of a Nation – The Queen in Photographs

The easiest way to delineate the role the Queen is playing in any given photo is to consider the context in which she is presented. Surrounded by children waving Australian flags, opening the Parliament of New Zealand, or inspecting a guard of RCMP officers usually indicates the realm in which the Queen is working and thereby which sovereign she is currently serving as. Of course, public visits and events are not the only time the sovereign undertakes work for any given realm, and identification can be more difficult in other circumstances.

One of the most visible ways by which the realms have asserted their independence is through the development of unique honours systems, a process pioneered by Canada with the introduction of the Order of Canada in 1967.[42] They clearly demonstrate independence from the United Kingdom and do so with visible, culturally relevant designs. These systems have been examined extensively by a number of scholars, including Karen Fox in Australia, Christopher McCreery in Canada, and Brian Anderton in New Zealand.[43]

As the sovereign (or head) of each order, the Queen can use the insignia of these honours to provide an instantly recognizable indication of her role. Julian Calder, a British photographer, took a series of photos of the Queen and Prince Philip at Buckingham Palace in 2011.[44] Without visual indicators of some sort, it would be impossible to know whether the Queen was acting as the Queen of the United Kingdom, Canada, or any other realm. However, in each photo, the Queen's national office is demonstrated by the insignia she is wearing.

Just as it would be inappropriate for the Queen of the United Kingdom to open Parliament at Westminster wearing the Collar and Grand Cordon of the Order of the Chrysanthemum, which she received from the Japanese emperor in 1962, it would likewise be very improper of her to wear the

Portraits of the Queen in different national honours.

insignia of the Order of the British Empire while undertaking work in any of the Commonwealth realms.

Calder's portraits, and another similar series that preceded it, demonstrate that there are ways for the Queen to signal a nationalized persona regardless of her location. It is also interesting to note that in each of Calder's portraits (except the British one), the Queen wears an item of jewellery culturally specific to the realm she is representing. In Australia, she wears a brooch of jewels shaped to resemble a wattle flower, in Canada a silver maple leaf, and in New Zealand a silver fern. Each is a gift from a group within each realm, presented to either her or to her mother (in the case of Canada).[45]

Conclusion

The concept of the Queen of Canada or the Queen of New Zealand is an important legal and political reality. However, beyond these constructions the public understanding of the Crown in each realm is not necessarily robust.[46] In realms that have worked to present the sovereign as nationalized, the institution has been enhanced. It is not merely a political illusion or constitutional sleight-of-hand used to deftly avoid difficult realities that may arise from sharing a head of state. Nationalization, the use of distinctions in flags, coins, portraits, and other expressions of the monarchy, is the process whereby the divisibility of the Crown is made tangible. This process draws the Crown out of remote institutions such as parliaments and courtrooms to pervade society more widely.

While the constitutional division of the Crown made the independence of the realms politically possible, it is the cultural evolution of these separate crowns that is bolstering the relevance of the monarchy in each nation. The process has accelerated over the course of the Queen's reign and has been most visible in Canada over the last few decades. It is plausible to expect that this process will continue to develop, taking different forms and proceeding at different rates from one realm to the next. Indeed, if the past few decades are any indication, it is likely that significant new elements and further refinements may be expected during the reign of the Queen's successor, whenever that may occur.

Notes

1. Antigua and Barbuda, Australia, Barbados, Belize, Canada, Grenada, Jamaica, New Zealand, Papua New Guinea, Saint Kitts and Nevis, Saint Lucia, Saint Vincent and the Grenadines, Solomon Islands, the Bahamas, Tuvalu, and the United Kingdom.

2. The Balfour Report of 1926 was a communiqué released after a conference of Dominion Prime Ministers in which it was agreed that the Dominions were "... autonomous Communities within the British Empire, equal in status, in no way subordinate one to another in any aspect of their domestic or external affairs, though united by a common allegiance to the Crown." www.foundingdocs.gov.au/resources/transcripts/cth11_doc_1926.pdf.

3. "Eleventh Supplement to The London Gazette of Tuesday, 26th May, 1953," *London Gazette*, no. 39873, May 26, 1953, 3023; Royal Titles Act 1974, New Zealand Statutes (1974).

4. "Eleventh Supplement to The London Gazette of Tuesday, 26th May, 1953."

5. K.C. Wheare, "The Nature and Structure of the Commonwealth," *American Political Science Review* 47, no. 4 (1953): 1021.

6. Sam Knight, "Operation London Bridge: The Secret Plan for the Days After the Queen's Death," *Guardian*, March 17, 2017.

7. Anne Twomey, *The Chameleon Crown* (Sydney: The Federation Press, 2006), 105.

8. It has also been suggested that South Africa may have made this decision to highlight that the Queen holds her office by virtue of legislation. See Twomey, *The Chameleon Crown*, 107.

9. Rt. Hon. Louis St. Laurent, *Hansard*, February 3, 1953.

10. "Personal Faith," in *The Prince of Wales and the Duchess of Cornwall*, www.princeofwales.gov.uk/the-prince-of-wales/promoting-and-protecting/faith.

11. "The Queen Attends Multi-Faith Reception at Lambeth Palace," in *Dr Rowan Williams, 104th Archbishop of Canterbury*, February 15, 2012, http://rowanwilliams.archbishopofcanterbury.org/articles.php/2358/

hm-the-queen-attends-multi-faith-reception.

12. K.C. Wheare, "The Nature and Structure of the Commonwealth," 1023.

13. "Union with England Act 1707," www.legislation.gov.uk/aosp/1707/7/section/I.

14. *MacCormick v. Lord Advocate* (1953) S.C. 396 at 411 (Eng.).

15. George Croly, *The Life and Times of His Late Majesty, George the Fourth* (London: James Duncan, 1830), xlix.

16. "Royal Style and Titles," *Parliamentary Debates, House of Commons.* April 15, 1953, col. 199–201.

17. Denis Mack Smith, *Victor Emanuel, Cavour and the Risorgimento* (Oxford University Press, 1971).

18. Guðmundur Hálfdanarson, *The A to Z of Iceland* (Lanham, Maryland: Scarecrow Press, 2010), 23–25.

19. In 1973, Australian Prime Minister Gough Whitlam discussed with the Queen the prospect of dropping references to the United Kingdom in her Australian title and removing her regnal number, "as there had never been two Queens named Elizabeth in relation to Australia" (Twomey, *The Chameleon Crown,* 109).

20. The Principality of Wales is not included, but it is acknowledged in the arms and banner of the Prince of Wales. See "Royal Standard," at www.royal.uk/royal-standard.

21. *Public Register of Arms, Flags and Badges of Canada,* 5: 160, http://reg.gg.ca/heraldry/pub-reg/main.asp?lang=e.

22. *Illustrated London News* 222, no. 5955, Coronation Ceremony Number (June 6, 1953).

23. Ibid.

24. Non-specific Royal Standards are used in Bahrain, Brunei, Cambodia, Denmark, Japan, Jordan, Lesotho, Lichtenstein, Luxembourg, Malaysia, Morocco, Netherlands, Norway, Oman, Spain, Saudi Arabia, Swaziland, Sweden, Thailand, Tonga, and the United Kingdom. Personalized Royal Standards are used in Australia, Barbados, Belgium, Canada, Jamaica, Monaco, New Zealand, and Vatican City State. No Royal Standard is used in Antigua and Barbuda, The Bahamas, Belize, Bhutan, Grenada, Kuwait, Papua New Guinea, St. Kitts, St. Lucia, St. Vincent and the Grenadines, Solomon Islands, Qatar, and Tuvalu.

25. Andrew Tettenborn and Robert Blackburn, *Halsbury's Laws of England,* 5th ed. (UK: LexisNexus UK, 2014), vol. 29.

26. "Royal Standard," at www.royal.uk/royal-standard.

27. *Public Register of Arms, Flags and Badges of Canada*, 6:70, 483, http://reg. gg.ca/heraldry/pub-reg/project.asp?lang=e&ProjectID=2282, http://reg. gg.ca/heraldry/pub-reg/project.asp?lang=e&ProjectID=2655.

28. Christine Kay and Tara Kearsey, "Royals Start Tour in Iqaluit," *Northern News Services*, October 7, 2002.

29. Terry Pedwell, "Princess Anne Begins Two-Day Visit to Ottawa," *Toronto Star*, November 10, 2014.

30. A.H. McLintock, ed., *Encyclopaedia of New Zealand* (Wellington: R.E. Owen, Government Printer, 1966).

31. Ibid.

32. The new flag was approved by Her Majesty on February 23, 1981. *Public Register of Arms, Flags and Badges of Canada*, 4:459, http://reg. gg.ca/heraldry/pub-reg/project.asp?lang=e&ProjectID=464.

33. Luke Richmond, "ADFA Farewells Governor-General at CDF Parade," *Navy Daily,* March 4, 2014, http://news.navy.gov.au/en/Mar2014/Events/ 888/ADFA-farewells-Governor-General-at-CDF-Parade.htm#.WQg ZatKGOUk.

34. See, for example, the lion's face at *Government Communications, Papua New Guinea*, web.archive.org/web/20161101115751/http://commu- nication.gov.pg/index.php/navigation/Cuba_relations_news.

35. See Gregor Macaulay, "A Constitutional Anomaly and a Legal Vacuum," *New Zealand Law Journal*, July 2017, 193.

36. "UK Coins," *The Royal Mint,* www.royalmint.com/discover/uk-coins.

37. "The Royal Portraits," *The Royal Mint,* www.royalmint.com/discover/ royalty/the-royal-portraits.

38. W.K. Cross, *Canadian Coins, A Charlton Standard Catalogue,* 60th ed. (Toronto: Charlton Press, 2006), 750.

39. Ibid.

40. *Public Register of Arms, Flags and Badges of Canada*, 5:466, http://reg. gg.ca/heraldry/pub-reg/project.asp?lang=e&ProjectID=1978.

41. Senate of Canada, "The Diamond Jubilee Window," www.parl.gc.ca/ About/Senate/jubilee/window-e.htm.

42. For a thorough analysis of the development of the Canadian honours system, see Christopher McCreery, *The Canadian Honours System,* 2nd ed. (Toronto: Dundurn, 2015).

43. Karen Fox, "A Pernicious System of Caste and Privilege: Egalitarianism and Official Honours in Australia, New Zealand and Canada," *History Australia* 10, no. 2 (2013): 202–26; Christopher McCreery, *The Canadian Honours System*; Brian Clifford Anderton, "Honour Bound: A Study of Royal Honours Systems in New Zealand and the Other Commonwealth Realms," (M.A. thesis, Victoria University, 2015).

44. New Zealand Post, "'Then & Now' Images of Queen Make for Memorable Stamp Issue," media release, March 1, 2012, www.scoop. co.nz/stories/CU1203/S00014/then-now-images-of-queen-make-for-memorable-stamp-issue.htm.

45. Royal Collection Trust, "Maple leaf brooch," www.royalcollection.org. uk/microsites/queenandcommonwealth/MicroObject.asp?row=93& themeid=944&item=93; "Fern brooch," www.royalcollection.org.uk/ microsites/queenandcommonwealth/MicroObject.asp?row=94& themeid=944&item=94; "Wattle brooch," www.royalcollection.org.uk/ microsites/queenandcommonwealth/MicroObject.asp?row=96& themeid=944&item=96.

46. Patricia Treble, "The Crown Is Everywhere. So Why Don't We Understand It?" *Maclean's*, January 14, 2016.

11 |

A Tale of Two Sovereigns; or, How the Queen of Canada Helps the Queen of the United Kingdom

John Fraser

This essay formed part of an address by John Fraser, founding president of the Institute for the Study of the Crown in Canada, delivered at the historic Charterhouse in London on August 18, 2016. The Charterhouse is the last building standing in London that was used as a court for Queen Elizabeth I. The talk launched an exhibition, also in the Charterhouse, of the paintings of Charles Pachter, including the iconic painting of the Queen riding sidesaddle on a moose. Ironically, what was once intended as whimsical satire on the idea of the Canadian Crown became a beloved symbol of the Crown's appeal.

In normal circumstances I would have come very humbly to the Charterhouse. That is because humility is something Canadians tend to do, rather well actually, especially when visiting the Mother Country or the mighty republic to the south of Canada. I have to say, though, after taking in the results of the Brexit vote or contemplating the current state of American politics, our traditional humble routine is getting to be a hard act to maintain. Alarmingly, smugness is now creeping into our Identikit, and a smug Canadian is not only an oxymoron, he is also someone you really don't want at your dinner table.

The aim of this essay is to parallel, thematically at least, the nature of the paintings on display. In other words, leaven a serious subject — the constitutional monarchy in both our countries — with a touch of whimsy and a perspective not ordinarily pondered when issues affecting the Crown arise. So let me start, then, at the beginning, or at least a sort of beginning.

And in that sort of beginning, in Canada there was only the Indigenous population. Then the French came at the start of the seventeenth century and in the name of the King of France set up trading relations with the Indigenous Peoples, who, soon enough, turned into three main groups: the ones we now call First Nations, the Inuit in the high north, and the Métis — or mixed race — all along the trading routes. That produced a colony and a variety of informal treaties, or trading understandings, with the Indigenous population. Then the British came in the name of their king and defeated the French in 1759. That produced some revamped loyalties with the First Nations, as well as a whole new set of trading treaties. This time, however, there were royal proclamations, endorsed and passed by the British parliament, many of which still stand as law in Canada.

Then, then, then…. Then the American colonists got "attitude," as we say about teenagers, and by 1776 a sizeable faction rejected life under the British Crown and created a republic under an elected head of state or presidency. Well, sort of elected. Some Canadians, like me, think that the College of Electors, the body that actually votes for the head of state in the United States, keeps re-electing George III every four years. That's because the makers of the American Constitution modelled the powers given to their head of state on those of the Hanoverian monarchy.

What is of interest here is that a large group of American colonists elected to remain under the Crown and moved north to Canada, along with several First Nations that were allied to the British, the Mohawk First Nation being chief among them. The Mohawk chiefs, many of whom had become Christian, brought with them a communion service given to them by Queen Anne in 1704, when their predecessors had made an official visit to the Court of St. James and were accepted by the Crown as leaders of their nations. Among other things, the Mohawks had negotiated a military alliance with the British government against the French, an alliance that held sway right through all the continental turmoil the Americans still like to call a "revolution." That's also why, when the war ended with a Declaration of Independence, the allied First Nations joined the other British Loyalists and also moved north to Canada. Moved rather smartly, as it turned out: the alternatives being tarring and feathering at best, or, at worst — particularly for First Nations people — something appallingly close to total annihilation.

The Canada of today is rooted in all this complex history that begins with an initial accommodation by the Crown with the First Nations, a promise of language and denominational rights to the French colonists abandoned by their mother country in 1763, increasing wariness of the new republic to the south after independence, intense loyalty to the British Crown, and — as always for all of Canada's peoples — the eternal struggle to survive the gruesome winters. A lot of that heritage continues, in one form or another, although it has to be admitted that added to the Canadian Identikit now are hockey, socialized medicine, Tim Hortons doughnuts, and an obsession to get as far away south of the country as possible between November and April.

In 1867, after a series of civil and perfectly un-revolutionary debates, the contemporary Canadian confederation was born peacefully, under the Crown and in a federation that now encompasses ten provinces and three territorial mandates, or rather nine provinces, three very northern amorphous entities, one quasi-state called Quebec, and in excess of 634 First Nations (and that's not counting the Inuit or Métis, who each now constitute a kind of nation). Don't ask me to explain how the whole thing hangs together and works, but somehow it does, and at the head of it all is the Queen of Canada. Indeed, presiding over this mishmash of a state may be the central reason both Crown and Country have survived and even thrived for 150 years. You wouldn't find too many contemporary Canadians to agree on that point, but then many contemporary Canadians haven't a real clue about their history. This is not a uniquely Canadian flaw, but it's pertinent to this essay.

In the ensuing century and a half since Confederation, Canada has been through two world wars, taken on a huge immigration population, and become one of the most envied countries in the world. Some of its abiding challenges remain, including the ups and downs of co-existence between French-speaking and English-speaking Canadians, regional economic disparities between east and west, and — finally emerging into glaring light — a terrible history of cumulative degradation and failed forced integration of the many First Nation and Inuit populations across the country.

The role of the Crown in Canada has followed the evolution of the country, but it has done so almost covertly — so covertly, in fact, that many if not most Canadians do not fully comprehend or appreciate what has been going on. There is a Queen of Canada and her name is Elizabeth. Although she looks remarkably like the Queen of the United Kingdom and has reigned in Canada exactly as long as the other Elizabeth has reigned in Britain, the two are not — constitutionally or even spiritually or evolutionarily — the same person. This is something the average citizen of the United Kingdom simply doesn't get. My goodness, a lot of the marginal figures in the royal family don't even get it. I once had the "opportunity" of trying to explain it to Princess Michael of Kent and that might diplomatically be called a challenge.

During the two periods I studied or worked in England — first as a graduate student in Norwich and Oxford in the late 1960s, and second as a newspaper correspondent in London during the 1980s — I rarely encountered anyone who didn't think it was absurd for Canadians to be clinging to "our Queen." I never quite found the occasion to try and explain how useful it was to have a sovereign — and the symbolism of a sovereign — who could tide you past the threat of a separatist province, or a corrupt upper legislative chamber, or indeed a very fractious nation threatening to come apart at the seams. But I feel that somehow it is easier to make these points in Britain today. That's because the United Kingdom may yet become a pair of federated kingdoms, if not a trio. Canada offers a valid and working precedent of holding a country together through the symbolism of the Crown. However creaky such symbolism may seem to sober, sensible analysts of *realpolitik*, it is something that simply should not be discounted.

Don't think that I am over-egging my tale. Canada is a constitutional monarchy not exactly seething with royalist fervour. I think the truth of the matter is that 10 to 15 percent of the country is made up with people a lot like me: romantic constitutional monarchists. Perhaps an equivalent percentage are republicans and occasionally go ballistic at the thought that we are still unable to elect our own head of state. The majority of the population, I believe, hold views similar to what a former prime minister, Stephen Harper, claimed that he held: they are passive supporters of the status quo who understand how the Crown represents a certain stability but, equally importantly — if not more importantly — is infinitely less scary than all the posited alternatives.

Ironically, it took the Queen of Australia to make this point in a big way when our constitutional cousins way, way, way Down Under held their own famous referendum on the issue of the Crown. This was in 1999 and the result was a surprise, because Australians had been depicted as clear republicans, especially in the Murdoch press. Defying Murdochism and alleged popular opinion, the Australians voted to retain the Crown and the known constitutional system. The point of the Australian referendum on the Crown, then, was that in federal countries like Canada and Australia, with their own distinctive fissures, internal rivalries, and regional dispari-ties, an unknown constitutional change seems far riskier than the known settlement, which has the merit, not always appreciated for sure, but never-theless the known merit, of actually working quite well.

Part of the reason for this is an evolutionary development in the role of the Crown that Canada shares with Australia and New Zealand, and that is the appointment of a kind of regency to represent the Crown. In all three countries, as in the other realms, the sovereign notionally rules as head of state, and local worthies are appointed by the government of the day to the post of governor general. In federal nations, like Australia and Canada, with provinces or regional states governed by regional legislatures, there are also appointed governors or lieutenant governors performing the same roles within the powers prescribed by their legislative authority.

All these vice-regal figures carry out the constitutional duties of the sov-ereign in her name. It has been a hugely effective way to localize the Crown and give it a distinctive national or regional face. It has also allowed Canada to elevate and celebrate, by appointment, regional, racial, and gender dif-ferences that electorates generally take longer to recognize. It is actually something the Crown in Canada does better than the Crown in Britain.

It has, in fact, been so successful that some observers see the Crown, in the person of the actual sovereign, disappearing bit by bit like the Cheshire cat so that all that is left will be a wave and a smile. In this sense, the judicial and legislative symbols of the Crown — Crown attorneys or Crown lands, for example, or ceremonial maces or vice-regal figures who get above their station and think that they do more than speak on behalf of the Queen but have become, through some weird civil transubstantiation, the body and blood of the sovereign — make the actual ruling figure redundant.

Let me say why this is not going to happen any time soon in Canada. But first, a relevant anecdote about both our queens. In a book that tweaked major interest among the noble platoon of us fussbudgets who actually worry about the constitutional role of the Crown in Canada, there is a tale of how the Queen of Canada came to the rescue of the Queen of Great Britain when her British first minister became particularly irksome. And it wasn't an irritating anti-monarchist Labour Party prime minister, either, but an irritating Tory prime minister named Edward Heath.

The year was 1973 and the Commonwealth leaders' conference was scheduled to be held in Ottawa. According to a riveting account in a book by Philip Murphy entitled *Monarchy and the End of Empire*, published in 2013 by Oxford University Press, Mr. Heath was in a petulant mood and it became very clear how much he loathed the whole concept of the Commonwealth when he was trying to get the nation focused on entering the European community. He used the fact that the monster president of Uganda, Idi Amin, was going to come to the conference and sternly "advised" the Queen not to attend. Heath had done this to her once before, in 1971, and she had acceded to his advice, as a constitutional monarch is obliged to do by precedent and common sense; but the second time he tried it, in 1973, she trumped Mr. Heath — if that phrase is still usable — she trumped him with the help of her Canadian first minister, Pierre Trudeau, who not only advised her to come, but insisted that her presence as Head of the Commonwealth was crucial to the success of the talks. In this way she shamed Mr. Heath into coming himself.

This was a decade after "Truncheon Saturday," when anti-monarchist protesters in Quebec were fairly forcefully put to a police rout and when Quebecers lining the roadway to the Quebec legislature turned their backs on the Queen and Prince Philip as their motorcade went past. It resulted in one of the Duke of Edinburgh's riper iconic observations. "If the links to the Crown are to be severed, we can do it in an amical and civil way," he said. "Believe me, we don't come here for our health. We can think of other ways to spend our time." Still to come in Quebec was the violent separatist eruption seven years later, the kidnapping of a British consul-general and then a Quebec provincial Cabinet minister who was strangled with his own crucifix chain. That was when the father of the current prime minister declared a national emergency and invoked the draconian War Measures Act.

This was, as it has turned out, the nadir of Crown relations in Canada, through no fault of the Queen but because the status quo seemed untenable. Since then, the status quo has recovered and been strengthened, and the institutions of the Crown have quietly gone on in their evolutionary way. One innovation that the Harper government took on was to consult widely on the vice-regal appointments with as broad a section of the public as possible. (This process was discontinued by the Trudeau Liberal administration elected in 2015.) I was one of a number of people asked to assist in this process, in this case with the appointment of the current lieutenant governor of Ontario. In my mandate, I went to law schools and elementary schools, to Rotary Clubs and church socials, to aid agencies and loyal societies: you name a place that wanted a free guest speaker and I would be there. I always asked for nominations and probably got over a thousand, one way or another. Three of the publicly nominated names made it to a final short list of five, but not my favourite nomination, proposed by an elementary school class that held its own in-house referendum. They unanimously chose Mr. Tim Horton, the aforementioned dead hockey player whose name is now widely known because of a doughnut franchise. The goal here was free doughnuts — hopefully with a maple syrup glaze — in the name of Her Majesty!

What surprised me was that most people I spoke to had a pretty good understanding of the vice-regal office, passively supported the constitutional status quo, and even gave me some original insights. I discovered that new Canadians, contrary to what one is usually told, are often the most knowledgeable about the role of the Crown and the most supportive, perhaps because they read more about the institutions of governing in Canada than the native-born. They have also, all of them, sworn an oath of allegiance when they took on citizenship. If you want to find the heart of deeply rooted anti-monarchical spirit, it is lodged for the most part in third, fourth, or fifth generation Canadians who do not see the point of it. Much as I love arguing my corner at some point with die hard republicans, you just have to accept that you can't win. It's like trying to persuade a tone-deaf person who hates opera that there's more to the business than the plots.

Yet, in Canada, there is something so fundamental about the role the Crown still plays and should play that seems to me to trump — that verb again! — every argument for severing our links. And it has to do with the historic and continuing relationship between the Crown and the First Nations. It totally bewilders many non-Indigenous Canadians. They just don't get it. Why would such a downtrodden people feel loyal to such a symbol of colonial oppression and allegedly reactionary actions? That, crudely put, is the evidence of many Canadians' ignorance of their own history. In reality, the "colonial" and "reactionary" entity in Canadian history has never been the Crown: it has been the Canadian government representing the non-Indigenous Canadian people. When the Mohawk First Nation and some of the nations under the Algonquin Federation fled to Canada after the American Revolution, it was to seek the protection of the Crown. When the Royal Proclamation guaranteeing their land rights and cultural practices had been promulgated earlier in 1763, it was the Crown that guaranteed protection. It was the Crown that signed treaties with the First Nations, on a nation-to-nation basis, something some Canadians still gag over when — like the dimmest teenager — they figure out this makes the treaties all legal to this day.

As the decades unfolded, and particularly after Canada became a self-governing dominion, the Royal Proclamation became shrouded in myth and then fell into studied disuse. The Government of the Dominion of Canada established reserves (the model for the apartheid South African regime's homelands, which Canadians hate being told) and rode roughshod over past treaty obligations, disregarding a concept that has always been implicit in Canadian colonial and dominion law: the duty to uphold all the original and legislatively passed commitments and laws.

Listen to what Lord Dufferin, an outstanding governor general in the late nineteenth century, said when he addressed a belligerent British Columbia legislature about its dereliction of duty in dealing with the First Nations on the West Coast of Canada: "The Indian Question in British

Columbia is not satisfactory," Lord Dufferin lectured the provincial legislators in 1876, a decade after Confederation.

> The Government of British Columbia has neglected to recognize what is known as the Indian title. In Canada, this has always been done; no Government, whether provincial or central, has failed to acknowledge that the original title to the land existed in the Indian nations and communities that hunted or wandered over it. Before we touch a single acre, we make a proper and legal treaty with the chiefs representing the bands we are dealing with, and having agreed upon and paid the stipulated price, oftentimes arrived at after a great deal of haggling and difficulty, we enter into possession, but not until that moment do we consider that we are entitled to a single acre.

If we fail to do this, Lord Dufferin implied, if we fail to partake in honourable negotiations, we also fail to honour our word, thus breaking faith not just with established practice, but also with an equitable future for Canada. There will be a price to be paid, he warned. And indeed we are paying some of that price now. Instead of heeding advice from the sovereign's representative, we simply took over vast swaths of land. Along the way, in what was alleged at the time as an act of conspicuous enlightenment, we committed our country to eradicating Indigenous customs, languages, and family relationships in the desire to more quickly assimilate the Indigenous population, to make it — in Professor Henry Higgins's memorable phrase — "more like us."

Is the Crown not actually mired in this ugly business? In fact, the only actual instrument of governance in Canada that resonates alike for Indigenous communities and what they call the "settler community" *is* the Crown. There is a collective memory of symbolic and actual mutual respect: respect for territorial rights, for cultural identity, and for mutual forbearance. Many First Nation and Inuit communities are broken in body and soul and the healing will take almost as long to come about as the wounding did; but the country has begun, and when the Queen of Canada or her son and heir sit down in a peace lodge or a teepee in ceremonial recreations of past undertakings, or don a mantle of the Haida First Nation on the West Coast — producing press pictures in the *Daily Mail* that cause some mirth in the Mother Country at "the things the poor woman has to do over there" — be aware that the sovereign and her heir both know very well that they are helping to hold a country together and also helping to heal it. As the Queen memorably said in 1990, "I am not a fair-weather friend."

This is such an interesting juncture to conclude on. That both Crown and First Nations have survived in the manner that they have is due to many factors, but a symbolic as well as practical part of the reason is a kind of unacknowledged mutual support. The First Nations have always looked to the sovereign to uphold what is increasingly understood to be the "honour of the Crown" — the intricate network of treaties, laws, and promises that underscore both the separateness of the First Nations and also our interdependence. And the Crown, in its turn, has cheerfully allowed itself to be usefully co-opted by the First Nations to act as the symbolic conscience of the nation, an emblematic promise that we will try to correct the injustices of the past and build on what we share. In Britain, the Queen of England may yet have to "negotiate" with the Queen of Scotland, and these two great ladies may yet be able to reconcile the seemingly irreconcilable. If so, they can both be grateful to the Queen of Canada for being such a useful pathfinder.

And this, too: when an Indigenous governor general is finally appointed in Canada, the symbolism of that visit in 1710 to Queen Anne by the Mohawk chiefs of the Iroquois confederacy and the Mohican chief of the Algonquin confederacy will have come full circle, and the circle is the single most salient symbol in Indigenous metaphysics. Keep that in mind when you see a depiction of Queen Anne's successor as she symbolically "troops" the colours of Canada astride a moose, an image that, if you know the history and current reality of Canada, is both whimsical and ridiculous, and also deeply moving.

Contributors

Peter Boyce, AO

Peter Boyce, former vice-chancellor of Murdoch University and professor of political science at the Universities of Queensland and Western Australia, is adjunct professor in the politics and international relations program at the University of Tasmania. He is the author of *The Queen's Other Realms* (Federation Press, 2008). He is an Officer of the Order of Australia.

John Fraser, CM

Author and journalist John Fraser is president and CEO of the National NewsMedia Council of Canada. He was Head of Massey College from 1995 to 2014. Previously he was editor of *Saturday Night*. He is the author of *The Secret of the Crown: Canada's Affair with Royalty* (House of Anansi, 2012). A Member of the Order of Canada, he is the founding president of the Institute for the Study of the Crown in Canada.

Carolyn Harris

Author, historian, and royal commentator, Carolyn Harris received her doctorate in European history from Queen's University and teaches at the University of Toronto's School of Continuing Studies. Her third book, *Raising Royalty: 1000 Years of Royal Parenting*, was published by Dundurn in 2017. She is a board member of the Institute for the Study of the Crown in Canada.

Robert E. Hawkins, DCL

Robert E. Hawkins is professor of law in the Johnson Shoyama Graduate School of Public Policy at the University of Regina, where he teaches constitutional and administrative law and government. He has served as president of the University of Regina, vice-president at Nipissing University, dean of arts at St. Francis Xavier University, and associate dean of law at Western University.

Andrew Heard

Andrew Heard is professor of political science at Simon Fraser University, with a wide range of research interests in Canadian and Commonwealth constitutional issues. These include the monarchy, constitutional conventions, the powers of Parliament, and Senate reform. He is the author of *Canadian Constitutional Conventions: The Marriage of Law and Politics* (2nd ed., Oxford University Press, 2014).

D. Michael Jackson, CVO, SOM, CD, editor

Former Saskatchewan chief of protocol Michael Jackson is president of the Institute for the Study of the Crown in Canada, author of *The Crown and Canadian Federalism* (Dundurn, 2013), and co-editor of *The Evolving Canadian Crown* and *Canada and the Crown* (McGill-Queen's University Press, 2012, 2013). He is a Commander of the Royal Victorian Order and a Member of the Saskatchewan Order of Merit.

Honourable Serge Joyal, PC, OC, OQ, FRSC, Ad. E.

Senator Serge Joyal is a jurist and a former federal Cabinet minister, serving as secretary of state from 1982 to 1984. He is the author and editor of several articles and books on parliamentary and constitutional law and the monarchy, including *Protecting Canadian Democracy: The Senate You Never Knew* (Montreal and Kingston: McGill-Queen's University Press, 2003). He is an Officer of the Order of Canada, l'Ordre national du Québec, and la Légion d'honneur in France.

Christopher McCreery, MVO

With a doctorate in Canadian political history, Christopher McCreery is the author of more than a dozen books, including *The Canadian Honours System* (2nd ed., Dundurn, 2015) and *The Order of Canada* (2nd ed., University of Toronto Press, 2017). Private secretary to the lieutenant governor of Nova Scotia, he is a Member of the Royal Victorian Order and a board member of the Institute for the Study of the Crown in Canada.

Barbara J. Messamore

Barbara J. Messamore, associate professor of history at University of the Fraser Valley, is the author of *Canada's Governors General, 1847–1878: Biography and Constitutional Evolution* (University of Toronto Press, 2006), co-author of *Narrating a Nation: Canadian History Pre-Confederation* (McGraw-Hill Ryerson, 2011) and of *Conflict and Compromise: Pre-Confederation Canada* (University of Toronto Press, 2017), and editor-in-chief of the *Journal of Historical Biography.* Her articles have appeared in a number of academic journals.

Sean Palmer

Sean Palmer's Ph.D. thesis, completed in 2010, undertook an extensive examination of the monarchy in all sixteen of the Commonwealth realms. A Canadian living in New Zealand, he has been the chair of Monarchy New Zealand, an educational and advocacy group, since 2012, and in this role has been a regular media consultant. He is a staff member in the New Zealand Parliamentary Service.

The Honourable Steven Point, OBC

Steven Point is a British Columbia Provincial Court judge. From 1975 to 1999 he was chief of the Skowkale First Nation and from 1994 to 1999 tribal chair of the Stó:lō Nation. He was chief commissioner of the British Columbia Treaty Commission from 2005 to 2007 and lieutenant governor of British Columbia from 2007 to 2012. He is a Member of the Order of British Columbia.

Nathan Tidridge

Nathan Tidridge teaches Canadian history, government, and Indigenous studies at Waterdown District High School in Ontario, and is author of *Canada's Constitutional Monarchy* (Dundurn, 2011), *Prince Edward, Duke of Kent* (Dundurn, 2013), and *The Queen at the Council Fire* (Dundurn, 2015). He is a board member of the Institute for the Study of the Crown in Canada and the Ontario Heritage Trust and a member of the national advisory council for the Prince's Charities Canada.

Photo Credits

33   MCpl Cindy Molyneux, Rideau Hall. © Her Majesty The Queen in Right of Canada represented by the Office of the Secretary of the Governor General 2003. Reproduced with the permission of the OSGG, 2017.

40   (*left*) William Notman, Montreal 1862. McCord Museum, I-4437-1.

40   (*right*) University of New Brunswick, Archives and Special Collections Department, Harriet Irving Library.

67   Department of National Defence/Library and Archives Canada, PA-001502.

71   Library and Archives Canada, PAQ-183540.

90   Library and Archives Canada, Acc. No. 1981-55-41 Bushnell Collection.

93   Courtesy of author.

104   Gary Beechey.

117   Library and Archives Canada C-085040.

119   Department of Canadian Heritage.

136   Serge Joyal collection.

140   Serge Joyal collection, Museum of History.

206   "Royal Coat of Arms of the United Kingdom" by Sodacan is licensed under Creative Commons Attribution-Share Alike 3.0 Unported, 2.5 Generic, 2.0 Generic, and 1.0 Generic licence.

207   © Her Majesty The Queen in Right of Canada represented by the Canadian Heraldic Authority, 2005–2011. Reproduced with permission of the Office of the Secretary to the Governor General, 2017.

208   (*top*) © Her Majesty The Queen in Right of Canada represented by

Also by D. Michael Jackson

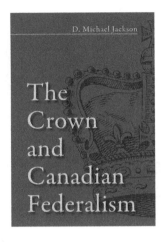

The Crown and Canadian Federalism

D. Michael Jackson

Following Queen Elizabeth II's historic Diamond Jubilee in 2012, there is renewed interest in the institution of the Crown in Canada and the roles of the Queen, governor general, and lieutenant governor. Author D. Michael Jackson traces the story of the monarchy and the Crown and shows how they are integral to Canada's parliamentary democracy. His book underscores the Crown's key contribution to the origins, evolution, and successful functioning of Canadian federalism, while the place of the monarchy in francophone Canada and the First Nations receives special attention.

Complex issues such as the royal prerogative, constitutional conventions, the office of lieutenant governor, and Canada's honours system are made readily accessible to the general reader. Jackson examines the option of republican governance for Canada and concludes that responsible government under a constitutional monarchy is far preferable. He further argues that the Crown should be treasured as a distinct asset for Canada.

Of Related Interest

Battle Royal: Monarchists vs. Republicans and the Crown of Canada
David Johnson

A strong republican movement in Canada stresses that the monarchy is archaic and anti-democratic, an embarrassing vestige of our colonial past. An equally vibrant monarchist movement, however, defends its loyalty to royalty, asserting that the Queen is a living link to a political and constitutional tradition dating back over a thousand years. But is the monarchy worth keeping?

Battle Royal answers this question and many more: What does the Queen really do? What are the powers of the governor general? Has the Crown strengthened or weakened Canadian democracy? If we abolish the monarchy, what do we replace it with? And will we have to re-open the constitution?

Charles will soon become King of Canada, but a Canada highly ambivalent to his reign. This presents the representatives of the Crown with the opportunity to build a better monarchy in both Britain and Canada, one relevant to the twenty-first century.

THE QUEEN AT THE
COUNCIL FIRE
The Treaty of Niagara, Reconciliation,
and the Dignified Crown in Canada

The Queen at the Council Fire:
The Treaty of Niagara, Reconciliation,
and the Dignified Crown in Canada
Nathan Tidridge

In the summer of 1764, Sir William Johnson (Superintendent of Indian Affairs) and over two thousand chiefs representing twenty-four First Nations met on the shores of the Niagara River to negotiate the Treaty of Niagara — an agreement between the British Crown and the Indigenous peoples. This treaty, symbolized by the Covenant Chain Wampum, is seen by many Indigenous peoples as the birth of modern Canada, despite the fact that it has been mostly ignored by successive Canadian governments since. *The Queen at the Council Fire* is the first book to examine the Covenant Chain relationship since its inception. In particular, the book explores the role of what Walter Bagehot calls "the Dignified Crown," which, though constrained by the traditions of responsible government, remains one of the few institutions able to polish the Covenant Chain and help Canada along the path to reconciliation. The book concludes with concrete suggestions for representatives of the Dignified Crown to strengthen their relationships with Indigenous peoples.